COMMUNICATING LEADERSHIP

An Organizational Perspective

Patricia D. Witherspoon
The University of Texas at Austin

Allyn and Bacon
Boston • London • Toronto • Sydney • Tokyo • Singapore

This book is dedicated to those who inspired it,
my students,
and to those who inspire me, day by day:
JMW, TDW, LAW, and KLW.

Series Editor: Carla F. Daves
Editorial Assistant: Andrea Geanacopoulos
Marketing Manager: Karon Bowers
Editorial-Production Administrator: Donna Simons
Editorial-Production Service: Shepherd, Inc.
Composition and Prepress Buyer: Linda Cox
Manufacturing Buyer: Suzanne Lareau
Cover Administrator: Suzanne Harbison
Cover Designer: Jennifer Hart

Library of Congress Cataloging-in-Publication Data

Witherspoon, Patricia Dennis.
  Communicating leadership: an organizational perspective /
Patricia D. Witherspoon.
    p. cm.
  Includes bibliographical references and index.
  ISBN 0-205-15797-1
  1. Communication in organizations. 2. Leadership. I. Title.
HD30.3.W579 1996
658.4'092—dc20   96-20828
                                                           CIP

Printed in the United States of America

10 9 8 7 6 CRS 07060504

CONTENTS

A Personal Note to the Reader   viii
Preface   ix
Acknowledgments   xii

1   Notions of Leadership: Concepts and Theories   1
The Differences between Headship, Leadership,
and Management   2
Concepts of Leadership   3
Concepts of Organizational Leadership   5
    Caveats Concerning Leadership in Organizations   5
    Leadership as the Management of Meaning   6
    A Working Definition of Organizational Leadership   8
Leadership Behaviors   9
Leadership Theories   11
    Great Man Theories   11
    Trait Theories   12
    Situational Theories   14
    Personal/Situational Theories   14
    Humanistic Theories   15
    Behavioral Theories   16
    Exchange Theories   17
Summary   19
Questions to Consider   20
Case Problem   20
Endnotes   21

2   Organizations as "Places" of Leadership   23
Definitions of "Organization"   23
Organizational Theories   26
  Classical Theories of Organization   26
  Humanistic Theories of Organization   27
  Integrative/Systems Theories of Organization   28
Perspectives on Organizational Communication   30
Organizational Changes Affecting Leadership, 1960–2000   31
  Decreased Numbers of Hierarchical Levels
    ("Flatter" Organizations)   31
  Emphasis on the Creation and Use of Work
    Teams/Task Groups   32
  Decentralization of Decision Making   33
  Variable Organizational Rewards   33
  New Communication Technologies   33
  Extensions of Organizational Boundaries   34
Organizational Components Affecting Leadership   35
  Task   35
  Structure   35
  Resources   36
  Culture   37
  Climate   38
Environmental Influences Affecting Leaders   40
  Socioeconomic and Political Influences   40
  Environmental Turbulence/Stability   40
  Outside Reference Groups   41
  Organizational Linkages   41
The Postmodern Organization   42
Characteristics of Twenty-First Century Organizations   44
Integrating Leadership and Organizational Theory   45
Summary   46
Questions to Consider   47
Case Problem   48
Endnotes   48

3   Leaders as Communicators: A Look at "Style"   50
A Change in Research Focus: From Traits to Style   50
The Notion of "Style"   51
Leadership Style: Traditional Perspectives   52
  The Situational Leadership Style   57
  Contemporary Looks at "Traditional"
    Leadership Styles   58
Transformational Leadership   59

Communication Style   64
Summary   69
Questions to Consider   70
Case Problem   71
Endnotes   71

**4   Leaders as Creators and Sustainers
of Organizational Culture   74**
Concepts of Organizational Culture   75
    Sources of Organizational Culture   77
    Functions of Organizational Culture   77
The Notion of Subcultures   82
Communication as a Culture Creating/Re-creating Process   84
Forms of Communication in Organizational Culture   86
    Language   86
    Myths   87
    Rites   87
The Role of Leadership in Culture Creation and Change   89
    Leadership and Culture Creation   89
Leadership in Organizational Cultures of the Future   93
Summary   95
Questions to Consider   96
Case Problem   97
Endnotes   97

5   Leaders as Decision Makers   100
Models of Decision Making   101
    The Rational Model of Decision Making   101
    The Limited Rational Model of Decision Making   102
    The Political Model of Decision Making   103
    The "Garbage Can" Model of Decision Making   104
The Search for and Use of Information in Decision Making   105
    Using Appropriate Styles to Scan for Information   106
    Using Information as a Valuable Organizational
      Resource   107
    Creating Structures That Facilitate Information Flow   107
    Using "Rich" Media   108
Influences Affecting Decision Making   110
    Environmental Influences   110
    Organizational Influences   111
    Individual and Group Influences   112
    Issue Characteristics   113

Processes of Decision Making   *113*
    Accelerating the Process of Decision Making   117
Decision-Making Styles   *118*
Summary   *121*
Questions to Consider   *123*
Case Problem   *123*
Endnotes   *124*

6   Leaders as Change Agents   126
The Nature of Change in Organizations   *127*
The Change Process   *129*
    Reasons for an Organizational Change   130
    Phases of the Change Effort   130
    Change Activities   131
    Conditions Affecting the Leadership of Change   131
Leadership Behaviors in the Process of Change   *133*
    Planning for Change   133
    Implementing Change: The Use of Strategies   134
Communicating Leadership in the Change Process   *136*
"Empowerment" in the Process of Organizational Change   *139*
Being a Change Agent: The Art and Science of Leadership   *141*
Summary   *143*
Questions to Consider   *144*
Case Problem   *145*
Endnotes   *145*

**7   Leaders as Facilitators and as Reflections
of Organizational Diversity   148**
Gender and Leadership   *149*
Race, Ethnicity, and Leadership   *155*
Race, Gender, and Leadership   *156*
Behaviors of Multicultural Leaders   *157*
The Notion of "Organizational Diversity"   *158*
Facilitating Diversity: Leaders' Use of Strategies   *161*
Summary   *164*
Questions to Consider   *166*
Case Problem   *167*
Endnotes   *167*

8 Using New Communication Technologies in Organizations: The Leader as Champion of Communication Innovations   169

Definitions and Types of Information/Communication Technologies   170
Characteristics of New Communication Technologies   172
The Uses and Effects of New Technologies: What Leaders Should Know   173
   Technologies as Tools   174
   Technological Innovation as a Form
      of Organizational Change   175
   Technology as a Component of Organizational
      Culture   178
   Technology's Place in Existing Communicative
      Relationships   180
   Leaders as Users of Communication Technologies   183
   Effects of Communication Technologies on Leaders   184
   The Leader as Technological Champion   185
*Leaders' Use of New Technologies—Implications
for the Future   187*
Summary   188
Questions to Consider   190
Case Problem   190
Endnotes   191

9 Communicating Leadership: Summary Observations and Suggestions for the Future   193

Leadership Communication: Different Perspectives   194
Leaders and Followers: The Notion of Interdependency   196
   Direct Leadership   197
   Indirect Leadership   198
Reconceptualizing the Notion of "Organization"   200
*Reconceptualizing the Notion of Organizational
Leadership   201*
Summary   204
Questions to Consider   205
Case Problem   205
Endnotes   206

Index   207

A PERSONAL NOTE
TO THE READER

This book begins as I think all textbooks should—with a note from the author to the reader. You should know that I began writing this volume in a hotel room in the nation's capital—a room with a view of the monument to the country's first president. Washington, D.C. is a city where leadership is praised more than it is practiced, but that is not unusual. Leadership, as it is discussed within these pages, is not a common phenomenon. Indeed, it is a rare practice in too many institutions, too many organizations.

Reading *Communicating Leadership* cannot make you a leader, but it may teach you something about leadership, and that is its primary purpose. Before you begin reading the first chapter you are assigned, take time to do the following:

1. Read the Contents.
2. Thumb through each chapter and note the headings within it.
3. Recognize that there is a summary, questions for you to consider, and a case problem at the end of each chapter. These "teaching features" will assist you in learning the material. After you have done this, you will have a better sense of what this book is about. In other words, look at the forest, and then begin to study the individual trees.

You should know that for several years I have taught a course entitled "Organizational Leadership," and the topic is therefore near and dear to me. As is the case in many classrooms across the country, this professor learned much from her students, and I am indebted to them for their role in the process of preparing this book.

PREFACE

LEADERSHIP AS COMMUNICATION

For hundreds of years philosophers, historians, and more recently psychologists, political scientists, management theorists, and communication scholars have studied leadership—with its many faces, its many forms. Using numerous laboratory and field studies, researchers have developed a myriad of theories and a plethora of suggestions about the exercise of leadership and the characteristics of those engaged in this process. Yet one of the more well-known researchers on leadership, one who analyzed years of pertinent studies, once wrote that:

> *Four decades of research on leadership have produced a bewildering mass of findings. . . . It is difficult to know what, if anything, has been convincingly demonstrated by replicated research. The endless accumulation of empirical data has not produced an integrated understanding of leadership.[1]*

Put more succinctly, James McGregor Burns, author of one of the better contributions to the study of leadership in the last twenty-five years, has written that leadership is "one of the most observed and least understood phenomena on earth."[2]

For instance, countless studies and numerous observations have resulted in the notion that leaders possess a variety of common traits. They tend to be smart, they are sociable, and sometimes they are good-looking.

---

[1]Ralph M. Stogdill, *Handbook of Leadership* (New York: The Free Press, 1974), vii.
[2]James M. Burns, *Leadership* (New York: Harper & Row, 1978), 2.

However, as discussed in the first chapter, leadership is much more than the possession of traits. Just because someone is elected to an office or appointed to a corporate position does not make him or her a leader. Moreover, you don't have to be the head of an organization to be a leader. Leadership can be exhibited by people at various organizational levels, in various ways.

The purpose of this book is to suggest that leadership is a set of behaviors exhibited in a proactive process—a process dependent on an understanding of, and a facility at, communication. Leaders must have visions of what they want their organizations to be, but these visions must be communicated to those in the organization who will help make visions realities. Leaders make decisions, but they must communicate with others to get information, select the best decision alternative, and implement the decision. Leaders plan, decide, handle conflict, and motivate—to name just a few of their functions. All of these actions require participation in the process of communication and indeed, leadership is to a great extent a communication process. The focus of this book is on the exercise of leadership in organizations, and the critical role communication plays in the process of moving people toward shared organizational goals. As a result, this text considers a number of questions, including the following:

- What are organizational leadership behaviors and what is the role of communication in the exercise of those behaviors?
- How do changing trends and structures in organizations affect leader–follower interaction?
- What is the relationship between leadership and communication styles?
- How do leaders use communication to embed and reinforce an organization's culture?
- How do leaders use communication to acquire and use information in the process of decision making?
- What communication competencies are needed by organizational leaders?
- How do leaders use communication to facilitate the process of organizational change?
- How does an individual's gender, race, and/or ethnicity affect leadership and communication behaviors?
- What effects do new communication technologies used in organizations have on leaders?

These and other questions are discussed in the following pages. As you read these chapters, remember that the study of leadership is complex, in part because although leadership may be a public behavior, it is based on a variety of private experiences, skills, and personal characteristics. Such is also the case when analyzing an individual as a communicator. The purpose of this book is to study the phenomenon of leadership as it is exhibited through one's communication behaviors in an organizational setting. Using this orientation to the study of leadership, it is intended that students will understand the nature of leadership and the importance of communication simultaneously. This book is not designed to teach you to be a leader, but to help you understand the process of leadership as it is accomplished through the process of communication. Such an understanding may assist in exhibiting the leadership behaviors so important to the work and the morale of the organizations in which you will someday participate.

ACKNOWLEDGMENTS

For several years I have taught an undergraduate course at the University of Texas that I developed for the Department of Speech Communication. Students who have enrolled in "Organizational Leadership" have participated in the evolution of this book through their comments during office hours, discussions in class, and their evaluations of the course at the end of the semester.

I am also especially grateful to Marti Dula, one of my former undergraduate students, and doctoral students David Shaw, Kelly Fudge, Dennis Grady, and Pat Parker who provided invaluable research assistance. Kari Kelso served as an editorial assistant with competence and dedication. Manda Rash, my assistant in the dean's office, deserves credit for formatting the final manuscript and, most importantly, for protecting an associate dean's time in order to write. I am indebted to Dr. Mark Knapp, my colleague and department chair, for his encouragement during the months this project was under way and for his ongoing support. Carla Daves, my editor at Allyn & Bacon, was a competent and collegial guide in the process that led to the book's publication. All authors should have someone like Carla with whom to work, and production editors like Kelly Bechen and Lora Kalb, who made the final stages of this process much easier than may be the case for many authors. In addition my appreciation goes to the following reviewers: Margaret Fitch-Hauser, Auburn University; Elaine M. Raybourn, University of New Mexico; Kathleen Watters, University of Dayton; and Theodore E. Zorn, University of North Carolina.

A special thanks is owed Dr. Kathy L. Wohlert, who served as a collaborator on Chapter 8 and a reviewer of several other chapters. Her suggestions as a critic and support as a friend sustain both me and my work.

Finally, I thank my husband, John, and our sons Terry and Andy, for their support during the writing of this text. For many months they received little of my time as I "stole" hours from our days together to research and write.

1

NOTIONS OF LEADERSHIP: CONCEPTS AND THEORIES

The study of leadership is thousands of years old. The ancient Chinese, Egyptians, and Greeks all pondered the qualities of good leaders. Scholars today continue the odyssey of discovery, and they represent a variety of disciplines with unique perspectives on the topic: sociology, psychology, philosophy, history, political science, management, and communication. Just in the twentieth century, numerous theories and studies have focused on the exercise of leadership and the personal characteristics of leaders. Both in laboratory settings and in field studies, social scientists have sought to understand the process of leadership by observing people who were appointed or who emerged as leaders in groups and organizations. The study of leadership, like the study of many complex phenomena, generates volumes of data and comparatively little understanding. In part this is because the exercise of leadership depends on innumerable, interacting variables, forces, and influences—and they are constantly changing.

For many years scholars assumed that leaders possessed a variety of traits or personal characteristics not held by other people. However, in this century some researchers began to discover that many individuals with such traits could not lead anyone anywhere, and that people identified as followers in groups shared some of the same characteristics as the "leaders" in those groups. As we shall discover later in this chapter, leadership is more than the possession of certain traits. Moreover, one does not become a leader solely by sitting in a particular box of an organizational chart. You do not have to be at the top of an organizational hierarchy to be a leader. Leadership behaviors can be exhibited by people at various levels within an organization.

THE DIFFERENCES BETWEEN HEADSHIP, LEADERSHIP, AND MANAGEMENT

Sometimes it is beneficial to describe a phenomenon by determining what it is not. Leadership is not *headship*, or holding a position of authority regardless of abilities. Just because a person is appointed to a job or a position does not make him or her a leader. Additionally, *management* is not necessarily leadership, although some managers may be leaders. John Gardner, former Secretary of Health, Education and Welfare in President Lyndon Johnson's administration, and founder of Common Cause, Inc., a national public interest group, has been both a leader and a student of leadership. He offers six ways that leaders differ from managers.[1]

1. They think longer term—beyond daily crises.
2. They look beyond their own unit and grasp its relationship to larger realities.
3. They reach and influence constituents beyond their immediate jurisdictions.
4. They put heavy emphasis on vision and values and other intangible concepts related to interaction with followers.
5. They have political skills that allow them to work with multiple constituencies.
6. They think in terms of renewal.

If we consider these criteria in an organizational scenario, a university president is a leader if she is not solely concerned with the everyday tasks that flow onto her desk and into her in-box. She must continually assess her institution's needs, considering not only the institution as it currently exists, but maintaining a vision of what she wants it to become. She is always future-focused, while at the same time understanding the need to develop and competently implement communication strategies that accomplish organizational goals one day at a time.

This university president, if she is a leader, must understand that her organization does not operate in a vacuum. Its goals, processes, and products are inextricably linked to a state or local economy for funding purposes; to college-going rates of high school students; to the fluctuations in the job market that may affect alumni financial support; and to a variety of federal and state laws that affect faculty retirement age, money available for student loans, and licensure requirements for professional occupations (e.g., engineers, nurses, pharmacists).

As a leader, this university chief executive will also have some influence over constituents in her community other than faculty, staff, students, and other administrators. She must use communication effectively: in public speaking settings, small-group meetings, and one-on-one conferences to influence potential donors of funds; with local and state officials who pass legislation affecting her organization; and with community leaders whose impression about, and support of, the university must be positive to continue a good relationship with its "neighbors."

When considering her organization as it exists and as the entity she would like it to become, the president must consider the responsibilities of leadership that depend on communicating values and ideals. She must understand the importance of not only *having* a vision, but *communicating* it to her "followers," the internal constituencies within the university.

Our university president also must have political skills, according to Gardner, so she may successfully work with a variety of constituencies (e.g., faculty, students, alumni, parents, state and local officials, and staff). Such political skills include the abilities to mediate, negotiate, and persuade. In organizations where change is continual and a significant factor in their daily operations, as is the case with many organizations in the 1990s, such skills become particularly important when attempting the empowerment of followers to enhance their participation in decision making.

Finally, our university president must always think in terms of renewal. She is not afraid of change; she welcomes it. This is not an insignificant trait in leaders, for many of us are afraid of, or at least uncomfortable with, change in our personal lives and at our places of work. Within organizations change to some individuals may mean changes in duties, or the elimination of a job. Change may cause uncertainty, and therefore anxiety, within organizations. Effective leaders understand this phenomenon and marshal ongoing attempts at renewal with attention to communicating continuously to followers the reasons, strategies, and desired results of renewal.

Outlining the differences between leaders and managers helps, in part, to define leadership by describing qualities of people in leadership positions, but it does not give us a definition of the *process* of leadership, especially from a communication perspective.

CONCEPTS OF LEADERSHIP

One could devote an entire book to the definitions and concepts of leadership in large part because, as is mentioned earlier, for many years numerous scholars from a variety of disciplines have studied the phenomenon. Stogdill and Bass offer a variety of concepts that essentially act as definitions. Such concepts include leadership as: the focus of group processes; the effect of personality; the art of inducing compliance; the exercise of influence; a form of persuasion; and an effect of interaction.[2]

Of particular interest to our perspective are the concepts that recognize, to some degree, the interrelationship between leadership and communication. Consider, for instance, leadership as the *art of inducing compliance*, which implies coercion as well as persuasion. This definition is similar to one given to the author during a seminar for executives. One individual who had served in the Vietnam War had heard the following definition from an officer: "Leadership is being able to pluck a chicken without having it scream." As catchy as this phase is, it describes the process only as one through which a person makes people do what they may not want to do—certainly an understandable perspective in the context of leadership during wartime. Similarly, President Harry Truman once defined a leader as "a man who has the ability to get other people to do what they don't want to do, and like it."[3] (This definition comes from a chief executive whose thoughts about leadership were framed in the context of a particular historical setting. Truman lived during two world wars, was commander-in-chief during the final months of World War II as well as the Korean War, and was a member of a generation of Americans who rarely saw women identified as leaders in politics, the military, or corporate America.) The notion of leadership as the art of gaining compliance only considers the effect of a leader's behavior on followers, and from a rather negative perspective. The mutuality of influence that takes place in the process of leadership is not considered in this conceptualization.

Another concept mentioned by Stogdill and Bass is that of leadership as the *exercise of influence*. This less dictatorial approach to guiding followers is "an interaction process in which an individual, usually through the medium of speech, influences the behavior of others toward a particular end."[4] What is missing in this definition, however, is the mention of influences that *followers* have on leaders through their communications.

Stogdill and Bass also note that leadership may be conceptualized as an *effect of interaction*. Emphasizing leadership as the result of group action, Bass offers this definition for effective leadership: ". . . the interaction among members of a group that initiates and maintains improved expectations and the competence of the group to solve problems or to attain goals."[5] However, the dynamics of an individual's behavior in directing group activity are not part of this concept. Thomas Cronin, a noted political scientist, suggests that leadership is a process of "getting people to work together" toward common goals, and though it involves vision, purpose, and mobilization of people and resources, it is ultimately "a relationship or a chemistry between leaders and their associates."[6]

In considering these various conceptualizations, it is important to note that many studies of leadership have been conducted in small groups and have not focused on individuals with organization-wide responsibilities. While this book intends to do justice to the analysis of leadership wherever it is found, the focus here is on the process of leadership as it is conducted among individuals with significant responsibilities for the accomplishment of tasks and social goals important to an entire organization or relatively large divisions within that organization.

CONCEPTS OF ORGANIZATIONAL LEADERSHIP

Caveats Concerning Leadership in Organizations

Before developing a definition of *organizational* leadership that will foster understanding of the concept as it will be discussed throughout this book, it is important to consider two important notions about leadership that potentially minimize, rather than exalt, its importance in organizations. One such notion is that the influence of leadership on organizational effectiveness may be minimal—for very good reasons.[7] For instance, in organizations leaders tend to be selected (with the exception of those that emerge in work groups). As a result, only certain types of leadership styles, perhaps those nonthreatening to the individuals doing the selecting, may be chosen. Such styles may generate little change and therefore little effect on organizational outcomes. Second, once an individual is in a leadership position, he or she is generally interested in keeping it and may not wish to "rock the boat." Such individuals, therefore, will have little impact on organizational activity. (In general, we will not consider such a person as a leader in this text, but researchers in the past have associated such behavior with leadership and it is important to share their perspectives.) Finally, there are a myriad of environmental and organizational influences that affect the exercise of leadership and many of them are beyond the leader's control, for example, changing markets, fuel shortages, wars in certain parts of the world, federal legislation, and alterations in consumer buying patterns. Further, in this rapidly changing global environment, leaders may have decreasing control over fewer resources and policies.[8]

While this perspective is a cogent argument supporting the view that leadership has little effect on organizational performance, empirical studies supporting it have looked at the effect of executives on profit margins and mayors on budgets, equating administration with leadership. However, an administrator is not necessarily a leader, and these studies may say more about the lack of effectiveness among administrators and managers than they do about leadership. Nevertheless, the effect of leadership on organizational outcomes is an important subject of study and deserves further, and extensive, research. Of course, as Pfeffer suggests, even if leadership behavior does not influence organizational performance or effectiveness, "it is important because people believe it does."[9] In his opinion, leadership "is associated with a set of myths reinforcing a social construction of meaning" that legitimizes those in leadership positions and attributes organizational performance to them.[10] An important question to consider, therefore, is whether leadership may be significant in organizations because it influences morale, task and social relationships, and organizational factors that are difficult to measure as "outcomes."

The suggestion that leadership, as an instrument of organizational effectiveness, is a mythical belief is reinforced by those who have studied the *romanticization of leadership*. Such individuals postulate that some, perhaps many, people who work in organizations have developed "highly romanticized, heroic views of leadership—what leaders do, what they are able to accomplish, and the general effects they have on our lives."[11] Leadership, as romanticized, is viewed as a major organizational process, singularly important to organizational events and activities. There is a faith among followers, a larger-than-life trust, in those who occupy formal positions of authority. Meindl, Ehrlich, and Dukerich suggest that the romanticization of leadership may be due to an overall faith in organizations as places of human activity, sites of values that represent the interests of organizational members, and perhaps even their conceptions of society in general. It is possible "that the romance and the mystery surrounding leadership concepts are critical for sustaining followership and that they contribute significantly to the responsiveness of individuals to the needs and goals of the collective organization."[12]

Romanticizing leadership and attributing organizational outcomes to leader behaviors with seemingly little evidence are two examples of how organizational members may regard leaders as symbols—symbols of organizational success (or failure) and even symbols of the organization itself. Under these circumstances, when a leader communicates he or she is viewed as a representative of the organization to its external audiences (e.g., clients, customers, stockholders). In schools, the military, and in some corporate settings, however, leaders have been shown to make a difference to the success of an organization. We will make that assumption in this book, and we will stress that any success is due, in part, to a leader's facility at communicating with a variety of organizational constituencies, including those *within* the organization. It is therefore critical that we look for a moment at the concept of leadership as the management of meaning.

Leadership as the Management of Meaning

To describe leadership as the management of meaning is to acknowledge it as a process through which leaders frame and shape the context of a situation using actions and utterances.[13] They explain, *in ways they choose*, ideas, decisions, actions, and external forces—virtually any internal or external phenomenon—to organizational members. From this perspective, communication behaviors used by a leader, such as public speaking, small-group discussion, and one-to-one counseling, are integral to the leadership process.

A related notion, offered by management theorist Karl Weick, is that a leader is a *medium* through which meaning is managed using various communication behaviors.[14] In his opinion, the leader helps organizational members make sense out of what is going on in the environment by synthesizing and explaining the myriad of factors, influences, and events affecting their workplace in terms that are understandable to them. Leaders, Weick reasons, must be consummate surveyors of the environment in which their organizations live—people who are adept at obtaining, explaining, and using information. In his words, "followers see through the eyes of their leader" and such an individual "gets the pictures for them and reveals various projections of these impressions to them."[15] A leader acting as a good medium will: (1) exhibit a variety of communication functions; (2) avoid simplifying information; (3) be adaptive when dealing with sources of information that differ; and (4) be able to handle the complexity that is created as one communicates with different followers at different times and on different topics.[16]

Managing meaning obviously is more than disseminating information through some mode or channel of communication. Leaders must share a *common language* with followers in order to create shared meanings.[17] One difference between an idealist and a leader is that the leader can put his or her ideas into understandable language. Having a vision and communicating it to others so that people can work together to make it a reality are very different behaviors. Only the latter is a leadership behavior. Indeed, together leaders and followers enact visions, solve problems, make decisions, and reach goals by talking in a language they both understand. Coaches and players communicate in the language of a particular sport, and other leaders and followers share meanings through understood words and phrases. The "language" in any type of an organization must constantly be renewed through continual communication between superiors and subordinates. Just as organizations are continually changing, so does the language of leading and following, through an interdependent communication process.

Rather than regarding "the management of meaning" as one leadership role, consider at least three communication roles or functions assumed by the leader as he or she engages in this process. A leader is an *interpreter* of organizational situations, events, jargon, and environmental influences—anything that affects the organization and should be explained to followers as stakeholders within it. In this role the leader interprets information on a surface level and gives meaning to that information to make it of use to organizational members. A leader is also an *educator* in the management of meaning—one who, to use the Latin word for the phenomenon we are discussing (educare), leads others "out of" ignorance. So a leader not only interprets but educates followers as to what should be learned from the events, factors, influences, and so on, in the context being framed through a shared language. Finally, the leader is an *advocate* as meaning is shared—he or she supports, defends, literally "calls out" to others persuasively to create, as well as to manage, the meaning in organizational contexts that will facilitate the accomplishment of organizational goals. He or she must therefore understand the need for rhetorical adaptation under varying sets of circumstances, for example, when downsizing of an organization is required; when productivity must be increased; when a subordinate must be reprimanded or rewarded. A leader must understand, and use, in Aristotle's words, the available means of persuasion. He or she must understand audience, situation, and the process of message development to create and manage meanings that will move people toward the accomplishment of organizational and individual goals. In this sense the leader is very much a rhetor—a speaker who uses logical, emotional and ethical appeals and who understands rhetorical situations—during those times that require communication from the leader to meet organizational needs.

Leadership as the management of meaning is a critical conceptualization in this book since its focus is on leadership from a communication perspective. However, there is danger in emphasizing the leader's role in the communication process while excluding a mention of followership since leaders and followers are in related, interdependent roles within organizations. Robert E. Kelley delineates the following roles and characteristics:

Leaders "have the vision to set corporate goals and strategies, the interpersonal skills to achieve consensus, the verbal capacity to communicate enthusiasm to large and diverse groups of individuals, the organizational talent to coordinate disparate efforts, and, above all, the desire to lead."[18]

Followers "have the vision to see both the forest and the trees, the social capacity to work well with others, the strength of character to flourish without heroic status, the moral and psychological balance to pursue personal and corporate goals at no cost to either, and, above all, the desire to participate in a team effort for the accomplishment of some greater common purpose."[19] Note that most of the strengths of followers should also be strengths of leaders! As we shall see throughout the following pages, leadership is an interactive process that depends on effective communication with followers. In organizations, a number of those followers evolve as leaders themselves. Indeed, for those who aspire to positions of leadership, an understanding of, and experience in, followership is critical. The appreciation of followership, therefore, is reflected in the definition of leadership we now consider.

A Working Definition of Organizational Leadership

While there may be over a hundred different definitions of leadership, one that may be suitable states that the process is "the demonstrated ability—to secure coordinated collective action—toward mutually desirable ends—by members of a group—within the context of group activity."[20] However, in organizations leadership may be exhibited by people who were appointed to their positions without the involvement of group members; hence the problem of discussing leadership as operating only within a group setting. Accordingly, an *organizational* leader must have the ability to coordinate, through communication, the work of groups of groups, or interdependent social units, and facilitate "intergroup processes" by negotiating understanding of shared tasks among all of an organization's stakeholders.[21]

Taking these ideas together, consider the following components of a working definition to guide our study of leadership from a communication perspective.

- In an organizational context, leadership is both a proactive and reactive phenomenon.
- It is the result of interaction among individuals engaged in common organizational activity, and concurrently it is the management of meaning within and between organizational groups to facilitate the accomplishment of tasks and the personal and professional development of group members.
- It calls for the creation and dissemination of messages through verbal and nonverbal behaviors.
- It requires that messages be developed in accordance with an understanding of organizational context, or the situation that requires the creation of messages, as well as the potential recipients of messages—that is, the organization's internal and external audiences. Internal audiences are an organization's employees or workers. External audiences may include customers/clients, stockholders, and members of the general public.

This is an ambitious definition for leadership, especially with its dual focus on organizational performance *and* individual development. However, it is a definition suitable for leaders who must guide their organizations into the twenty-first century, as we shall see in Chapter 2.

LEADERSHIP BEHAVIORS

To understand organizational leadership, one must also understand the actions that individuals take to move individuals, groups, and/or organizations toward their goals. Such actions are examples of leadership behaviors and most, if not all, of these behaviors depend on leader–follower interaction if they are to be accomplished. Yukl and his colleagues identified nineteen behavior categories based on several years of observing leaders.[22] A brief listing and description of some of them are provided below to add to the mosaic we are creating that represents a "picture" or "mural" of leadership.

- Consideration—showing support for subordinates
- Praise-recognition—providing praise and showing appreciation for subordinates' contributions to the organization
- Decision participation—consulting with followers in the process of decision making
- Delegation—granting authority and responsibility to subordinates to accomplish the organization's tasks
- Role clarification—specifying duties and responsibilities for followers to avoid confusion and ambiguity about one's organizational roles
- Information dissemination—providing information to workers about their tasks, the organization at large, and policies, procedures, or events affecting the organization and its members
- Problem-solving—proposing solutions to task-related problems
- Work facilitation—obtaining and disseminating the necessary resources for organizational members to accomplish their work
- Representation—developing contacts with an organization's external audiences, or those external to a particular work unit within an organization in order to promote the interests of the unit or the organization
- Interaction facilitation—fostering opportunities for organizational members to communicate with each other in order to accomplish work and develop collegial social relationships
- Conflict management—working with organizational members to constructively deal with intergroup or interorganizational conflict, whether related to task completion or social relationships
- Criticism/discipline—providing constructive criticism or discipline related to one's poor performance, the violation of organizational policies, and so on

These are just a few of the behaviors of leaders; others include planning, coordinating, goal setting, and inspiring. This behavior will be discussed in more detail later in the text as an integral component of transformational leadership.

Note that the exercise of all these behaviors depends on multiple modes of communication and both verbal and nonverbal behaviors. Indeed, through the process of communicating, another major leadership behavior is that of *organizing* in general (e.g., facilitating reporting relationships and creating teams out of individuals).

A look at the many concepts and definitions of leadership, and a few of the behaviors associated with those who exhibit it, present some of the portrait of what organizational leadership "looks like." However, no complete picture is possible without a review and discussion of the major theories that have guided the study of leadership.

LEADERSHIP THEORIES

There are numerous theories, or ways to think, about leadership. This book focuses on those theories that are concerned about the interrelationship of leadership and communication. Such theories have emerged in the twentieth century, in part due to dramatic changes in organizations, or more specifically, changes in the characteristics and expectations of people who work in organizations. The growing interest in this century on workers' rights, the evolution of labor and management relationships, increased expectations not only for safe working environments but also for self-fulfillment at work, the advent of new technologies that have changed the nature of work in organizations and their resultant products (i.e., goods to services to information), are contextual factors that have affected the development of leadership theories. Theories developed since the midpoint of the century have been cognizant of these factors and the importance of leader–follower interaction in the exercise of organizational leadership. Before looking at the theories with this perspective, however, it is beneficial to consider early theories of leadership for purposes of comparison.

Theories are a product of the sociopolitical and historical context in which their creators live. As we review the major theoretical orientations to leadership spanning the late nineteenth and the twentieth centuries, it is important to understand that theoreticians and researchers necessarily take their view of their work, in part, from their view of the world and what its effects are on their personal and professional existence. They also consider the context in which other human beings live and work. The early theories of leadership looked at societal situations and postulated opinions based on observations of countries or nations, not organizations.

Great Man Theories

During the early part of the twentieth century, a few theorists studied European kings and members of royal families who ruled several centuries ago, and suggested that great (i.e., wealthy, high status) men become leaders. Such individuals, they suggested, possess superior traits that foster their emergence into leadership positions. Obviously this finding is not surprising, considering the sample these individuals studied. Those born to privilege, to private tutelage, to great wealth, and in countries espousing the divine rights of kings are going to emerge as "leaders" or at least heads of countries. (It is interesting to note that despite the great influence on nations by women such as Joan of Arc, Queen Elizabeth I, and Catherine the Great, the reigns or influence of women were not studied—there were no "great person" theorists.) However, as we have discussed, headship is not leadership—holding a position and leading people toward mutually desirable goals are two very different activities. These theories, even in the early part of this century, failed to take into account the rise of the educated masses and the movement of nonaristocrats into leadership positions. Such was the case as the effects of the Industrial Revolution were being felt, and upward mobility in organizations, such as factories, was not based on social position but on ability and hard work.

The focus on the great man theories is only on the leader, not on interaction with others; indeed, not on any dimension relating to followers. As scholars pondered the notion of great men as leaders, some began to realize that leadership existed in places other than castles, especially in those democratic societies that were becoming increasingly influential in the socioeconomic/political map of the world. They reasoned that if leaders are superior individuals, even if they are not born into privileged families, they must embody certain traits—traits that can be identified, and perhaps compared with, those possessed by individuals who are not recognized as leaders.

Trait Theories

During the first half of this century, leadership researchers focused on the notion that people who are acknowledged as leaders possess superior qualities or characteristics as compared to traits possessed by followers. Leaders were identified as being more sociable, intelligent, competitive, sometimes even better looking, than followers. Much of the trait research was conducted in the military, and over time researchers discovered that followers possessed many of the same traits as leaders. In 1948 Ralph Stogdill published a major review of trait research.[23] He synthesized and summarized numerous studies, always believing that traits should be studied along with other phenomena affecting leadership. Bass has suggested that the factors associated with leadership in early trait research can be clustered into the following categories.[24]

Capacity—for example, intelligence, judgment
Achievement—for example, scholarship, knowledge
Responsibility—for example, dependability, persistence, self-confidence
Participation—for example, activity, sociability, cooperation
Status—for example, socioeconomic position, popularity

In 1970 Stogdill again reviewed a variety of trait studies. This time he categorized leader characteristics as being either personality traits (e.g., integrity, assertiveness); task-related characteristics (e.g., responsible, having high needs for achievement, task orientation); or social characteristics (e.g., cooperative, active, possessing good interpersonal skills).[25] Despite his attention to trait studies for many years, Stogdill remained until his death a firm believer in the notion that leadership qualities must be exhibited or used, not just possessed, in order for leadership to be manifested among followers. In 1981 Michael Maccoby studied six leaders in very different types of organizations: a foreman, union leader, plant manager, chief executive officer in a foreign car manufacturing company, assistant secretary of commerce, and a congressman.[26] Spending considerable time with each of them, he found they shared basic personality traits: intelligence, ambition, optimism, competitiveness, and a sense of humor. Also, all were persuasive communicators, had caring attitudes toward others, were flexible in their management of people, and they had a willingness to share power. In 1985 Bennis and Nanus published a study of ninety leaders from different walks of life, including an orchestra conductor, and identified four traits held by these individuals.[27] These individuals, they suggested, knew how to accomplish the following:

Manage attention. They possessed a compelling vision that attracted the interest of followers.

Manage meaning. They knew how to effectively communicate that vision.

Manage trust. They were reliable or "constant" in their behavior toward followers.

Manage self. They knew their skills and could utilize them effectively in the exercise of leadership.

Finally, Peters and Waterman observed that leaders in "excellent" companies possess administrative skills, technical skills (i.e., they understand the work of the company and have skills related to the conduct of this work), and communication skills.[28] Such companies value customers and employees and show a dual interest in achieving organizational goals while helping employees develop personally and professionally.

Despite the years of research on the personal characteristics of leaders, trait theories are only viewed in the last decade of the twentieth century as supplemental to other leadership theories. As is the case with the great man theories, trait research does not consider leadership as a process that depends on leader–follower interaction and the sharing of meaning. Moreover, it ignores the importance of situational context in this dynamic relationship. Stogdill eloquently made this point in the later years of his work when he emphasized that leadership is a "working relationship among members of a group" and as a result, "an adequate analysis of leadership involves not only a study of leaders, but also situations."[29]

Situational Theories

The Emperor Napoleon, sometimes used as an illustration of the great man theories of leadership, reportedly once said: "I have conceived of many plans, but I was never free to execute one of them. For all that I held the rudder, and with a strong hand, the waves were always a good deal stronger. I was never in truth my own master; I was always governed by circumstance." Essentially, this general was espousing a situational theory of leadership—that leaders are at the mercy of the context in which they find themselves, and indeed that leadership is the result of being in the right place at the right time. Situational theorists would observe that Franklin Roosevelt was an able leader because he was an American president during an economic depression and a world war, and that across the ocean, Winston Churchill was a great leader because he was prime minister during World War II. In other words, situations make leaders out of people who find themselves in positions of authority, especially in times of crisis. At other times, in other places, such individuals might not exhibit leadership behaviors or might not be recognized for them. These theories have little credibility today, because research in groups, organizations, and societies has shown that leadership should be attributed to more than just a set of circumstances in which an individual finds himself or herself. Such studies suggest that leadership should at the very least be considered as the product of the commingled influence of a person and a situation.

Personal/Situational Theories

Would Herbert Hoover have been as good a leader as Franklin Roosevelt during the 1930s and 1940s in the United States? Would any person other than Sam Walton have been as good an organizational leader for Wal-Mart? Perhaps so; but perhaps not. The point is, Sam Walton possessed several attributes that made him an effective organizational leader *at a time* when a discount outlet store like his was gaining favor throughout the country by American customers. Franklin Roosevelt was a brilliant politician with the personal and professional traits identified as those common to successful leaders, and he found himself in an environment with the opportunity to use his skills, experience, and expertise while manifesting traits of leadership. The personal/situational theorists espouse the belief that leadership is the result of a good match between personal traits and a situation that requires the exercise of those traits. General George Patton's aggressiveness, understanding of military history, and exercise of discipline were suitable characteristics for leading men in wartime; he was not regarded, much to his chagrin, as a viable political leader after World War II. Those subscribing to the personal/situational conceptualization of leadership only consider leader and context—again there is little interest in followers as co-participants in the exercise of leadership. However, these are the theories that, at least implicitly, begin to acknowledge the importance of followership. Why? Because the "situations" in which leaders find themselves are in part created by the presence of followers, the characteristics of those followers, the attitudes of the followers toward the leader(s) and the organization, and the effects of environment and the organization on the interaction among those involved in the process of reaching mutually agreed-upon goals.

It took a variety of societal changes in this country to create an interest in studying leadership through a new frame of reference that would focus on followers as equal partners in the leadership process, particularly in organizations. The development of the modern factory, and resultant changes in laws relating to employee rights and the development of labor unions, helped focus the attention of researchers on a new perspective through which to study leadership, and organizational leadership specifically.

Humanistic Theories

The worth of the individual, in society and in organizations, is the cornerstone concept in the humanistic theories of leadership. In them is the basic belief that leadership exists to allow each individual to fulfill his and her own needs and accomplish organizational goals. One of the landmark contributions to this theoretical orientation is Douglas McGregor's notion that leaders operate under one of two assumptions. Theory X assumes that people show up for work solely to get a paycheck; they are generally passive and unmotivated in the workplace. Those leaders who subscribe to Theory Y, however, believe that people desire to work for the sake of personal satisfaction; they want to be productive, desire responsibility, and wish to contribute to the accomplishment of organizational goals.[30] Under these circumstances, leaders treat workers in positive ways to encourage their contributions and to help them develop personally and professionally in the workplace.

Research conducted by Rensis Likert and his associates supported the theory that treating people like contributing organizational members, as opposed to nameless, faceless workers, could enhance productivity. He found that leaders who allowed organizational members to participate in decision making and problem solving, and were interested in workers as human beings, had more productive work units. Indeed, his research led to the formulation of a general rationale for organizational improvement that relied partly on democratizing leadership.[31]

The role of communication is important in the humanistic theories of leadership, since leaders show interest in followers' needs through verbal and nonverbal behaviors. Moreover, communication between leaders and followers becomes the instrumental process through which they are engaged together, albeit in varying degrees, in problem solving, decision making, and the development of social relationships in addition to necessary task-oriented relationships. The importance of these relationships becomes the basis for theories of leadership focusing on the interdependence between leader and follower behavior.

Behavioral Theories

The underlying assumption of these theories is that leader behavior affects follower behavior, and vice versa. Moreover, borrowing B. F. Skinner's findings in behavioral psychology, there is an emphasis on the use of reinforcement and reward if subordinates behave as desired. However, it is not possible in real-life organizations to treat all subordinates the same all the time. As a result, *contingency* theories of leadership postulate that different sets of leader behaviors (or styles, as will be discussed in Chapter 3) depend on demands imposed by a given organizational situation.[32] When there is a deadline to be met, a leader may be directive and more task oriented than during other times of the work week. When working conditions are less stressful, he or she may be participative, democratic, and concerned generally about positive social relationships with and among followers. The exercise of leadership under a variety of contingencies is accomplished through varying communication behaviors, appropriate under different circumstances, for example, small group meetings, one-on-one consultations, the use of memos and/or formal documents, and so on. Additionally, a leader's cognitive resources (defined as intellectual abilities, technical competence, and knowledge obtained through training or experience in the organization) may make a difference in organizational performance under certain conditions.[33] The assumption for this *cognitive resource* theory is that leaders with significant cognitive resources make more effective decisions and plans than leaders with less cognitive competence, and that leaders communicate these decisions and plans using directive behavior. Again, the importance of leader behavior toward followers and their potential responses is the basic notion upon which this theory is based. As Fiedler and Garcia write: "Unless we believe in telepathy, we must assume that the verbal or gestural behavior of leaders affects the way group members behave and perform their tasks."[34]

Another major leadership theory within this set of theoretical orientations is the "path goal" theory, which focuses on motivation as the leader's key behavior toward subordinates.[35] To motivate followers, the leader must clarify the path to desired organizational goals and provide appropriate rewards. The main function of the leader, therefore, "consists of increasing personal payoffs to subordinates for work-goal attainment, and making the path to these payoffs easier to travel by clarifying it, reducing roadblocks and pitfalls, and increasing the opportunities for personal satisfaction en route."[36] To illustrate this concept, consider a football team. The coach develops a system of rewards for effective play, perhaps stars awarded on helmets, develops successful plays, ensures players train adequately to help reduce on-field injuries, scouts the opposing team whom he will play each week, and, overall, prepares the team mentally and physically for each game so they will successfully find the path to the opponent's end zone a sufficient number of times to win each game.

Exchange Theories

The notion that leader behavior affects follower behavior, and vice versa, was a natural segue into research on leader–follower interactions, the effects of such interactions, and the ways leaders, followers, and organizations are affected by communication behaviors within organizations. Consequently, exchange theories have developed that focus on social interaction between leaders and followers and the nature of these interactions. One such theory, known as the *leader/member exchange* or *vertical-dyad linkage,* suggests that leaders behave differently toward individual followers. They do not behave the same way toward a group or the organization as a whole because they categorize followers as being either members of an in-group or an out-group.[37] Those followers assessed as being part of an in-group get more attention and perhaps more rewards from a leader. Members of out-groups do not reap these benefits. Communication, obviously, is the process through which leaders show attention, give rewards or, conversely, interact negatively with those individuals they perceive as members of an out-group. In a university social organization, for instance, a leader may belong to, or at least prefer interaction with, a clique of individuals who may be more popular than another clique. Under these circumstances, his or her communication with them would show favoritism. Perhaps she would join them frequently on social occasions. Perhaps he would praise more of their members in organizational meetings. The point is, the leader would not communicate as much, or as positively, with members identified as being in one or more out-groups.

As is illustrated in these pages, leadership theory has evolved from a narrow focus on personal traits to a broad look at the exercise of leadership as an interaction process affected by the behaviors of leaders and followers and the constraints or opportunities afforded by the situational contexts in which they find themselves. More recent theories look to *multiple influences* on leadership, such as conditions in the organizational context and influences surrounding an organization in its environment. Jacobs and Jacques, for instance, have developed a theory to suggest that leaders at higher levels in organizations are responsible for understanding the environmental influences around them, and explaining these influences to the hierarchical level below them to reduce uncertainty caused by such influences.[38] The reasoning behind this theory is that by reducing uncertainty, a leader may enhance productivity at the lower level. Here again, albeit stated in different terms, is the notion of the leader as medium, or the leader as the manager of meaning.

Two other "theories" deserve mention in this chapter. We will discuss them in more detail in Chapter 3 as "styles." The conceptions of leadership as "transactional" and "transformational" essentially have revolutionized the study of leadership. These contributions are offspring from the behavioral and exchange theories, and they are grounded in the realization that leadership is an interactive, communicative process, dependent on shared meanings.

Transactional leadership is itself an exchange: I give you a raise for more work done; or, I award you a car if you sell a specified amount of cosmetics. This approach to leadership is fair; followers as well as leaders understand the basis of the leader–follower relationship. However, the goal of this approach is the fulfillment of organizational goals primarily, with fair treatment of followers who assist in meeting those goals.

Since 1978, when political scientist James McGregor Burns discussed *transformational* leadership in a major contribution to the study of the societal phenomenon, a number of organizational theorists and researchers have focused on this approach to leadership. Born in a society concerned about equality of rights in the workplace and the fulfillment of both individual needs and organizational goals, and created in an environment characterized by rapid socioeconomic, political, and technological change, transformational leadership seeks to empower organizational members *and* successfully initiate and manage change so that an organization adapts to environmental influences. As Bernard Bass has stated: "Transformational leadership is closer to the prototype of leadership that people have in mind when they describe their ideal leader."[39]

These are not all the theories of leadership developed over the last several hundred years, not even those espoused over the last fifty years. However, they are major ones that represent the evolution of the study of leadership. We are particularly interested in those that acknowledge leader–follower interaction, and they are provided as a basis on which to build an understanding of organizational leadership from a communication perspective. Keep in mind, as you proceed through the following chapters, that theories based on years of leadership research only equal part of our jigsaw puzzle. While many of the pieces fit and show us understandable elements of this phenomenon, the whole puzzle is yet to be seen in its entirety.

As is mentioned earlier in this chapter, many of the conceptualizations of, and theories about, leadership are based on research conducted in groups existing in laboratory or field settings. Because our focus is on *organizational* leadership, we are particularly concerned about the process as it is affected by characteristics and components of organizations and influences found in the environments surrounding them. It is, therefore, important for us to analyze organizations as "sites" of leadership emergence and practice.

SUMMARY

Leadership is a phenomenon that has been studied for thousands of years by scholars in a variety of disciplines. It is a process that relies on communication. Organizational leadership behaviors emerge during interaction among individuals working toward a common goal or engaged in activity of mutual interest.

Multiple perspectives on, and concepts about, leadership make it virtually impossible to create an all-encompassing definition of the phenomenon. A working definition, from a communication perspective, should include the following components:

- Leadership is both a proactive and reactive phenomenon.
- It calls for the creation and dissemination of messages through verbal and nonverbal communication.
- It requires that messages be developed in accordance with an understanding of organizational context and the potential recipients of messages—the organization's internal and external audiences.
- Leadership is the result of interaction among individuals engaged in organizational activity. Concurrently, it requires the management of meaning within and/or among organizational groups to facilitate task accomplishment and enhance the personal and professional development of organizational members. By what they say and do, leaders create meaning for other individuals, interpreting information from environmental influences and organizational events and activities, and facilitating a shared understanding of that information.

Theories that have guided the study of leadership are the products of the sociopolitical and historical contexts in which their creators lived. Early theories of leadership focused on what leaders were, in terms of background and personal characteristics. Later theories focus on what leaders do and what their behaviors are as they interact with others in situational contexts.

The "roots" of contemporary theories of leadership are embedded in contexts for social change that emerged during the first half of the twentieth century. Concerns about workers' safety and quality of life in large factories and the results of the Industrial Revolution prompted the development of labor unions, laws to protect employee rights, and increased expectations among individuals about how they should be treated by those for whom they labored. Behavioral and exchange theories provide the concepts most applicable to the study of leadership from a communication perspective because they look at leader–follower interaction—the relationships established among and between organizational members as it is constituted through communication.

QUESTIONS TO CONSIDER

1. Is there a difference between leadership and management? Why or why not?

2. Do leaders really affect an organization's performance or its effectiveness? Why or why not?

3. What does "romanticizing" leadership mean?

4. How do leaders "manage" meaning, and what significance does this concept have for the study of organizational leadership?

5. Compare and contrast the following theories of leadership: trait, situational, humanistic, behavioral, and exchange.

CASE PROBLEM

A small public relations firm is going to merge with a large, regional advertising firm within the next two months. The public relations firm no longer can compete with larger firms who offer integrated communication services to clients. The advertising company is interested in becoming an organization that offers such services to clients. Those in charge of the merger, the chief operating officers of both organizations, need to explain the reasons for the merger to their respective organizations to insure a smooth transition.

What leadership theories are applicable to those studying leaders' interactions with followers in this context? What messages should each leader emphasize as he attempts to "manage meaning" for his respective organizational members? What channels of communication, or media, should each individual use to communicate the proposed change to his organization? What channels of communication might be used to develop shared goals among the members of these organizations?

ENDNOTES

1. John W. Gardner, *On Leadership* (New York: The Free Press, 1990), 4.
2. Bernard M. Bass, *Bass and Stogdill's Handbook of Leadership*, 3d ed. (New York: The Free Press, 1990), 11–16.
3. Harry S. Truman, *Memoirs* (New York: Doubleday, 1958), 139.
4. Franklyn S. Haiman, *Group Leadership and Democratic Action* (Boston: Houghton Mifflin, 1951), 13.
5. Bernard M. Bass, *Bass and Stogdill's Handbook of Leadership*, 20.
6. William E. Rosenbach and Robert L. Taylor, eds., *Contemporary Issues in Leadership*, 2d ed. (Boulder: Westview Press, 1989), xiii.
7. Jeffrey Pfeffer, "The Ambiguity of Leadership," *Academy of Management Review* 2 (1977): 106.
8. Ibid., 107.
9. Ibid., 110.
10. Ibid., 111.
11. James R. Meindl, Sanford B. Ehrlich, and Janet M. Dukerich, "The Romance of Leadership," *Administrative Science Quarterly* 30 (1985): 79.
12. Ibid., 100.
13. Linda Smircich and Gareth Morgan, "Leadership: The Management of Meaning," *Journal of Applied Behavioral Science* 18 (1982).
14. Karl Weick, "The Spines of Leaders," in *Leadership, Where Else Can We Go?* eds. Morgan W. McCall, Jr. and Michael M. Lombardo (Durham, NC: Duke University Press, 1978).
15. Ibid., 47.
16. B. Aubrey Fisher, "Leadership: When Does the Difference Make a Difference?" in *Communication and Group-Decisionmaking*, eds. Randy Y. Hirokawa and Marshall Scott Poole (Beverly Hills: Sage Publications, 1986), 207.
17. Louis R. Pondy, "Leadership is a Language Game," in McCall and Lombardo, *Leadership, Where Else Can We Go?*
18. Robert E. Kelley, "In Praise of Followers," in Rosenbach and Taylor, *Contemporary Issues in Leadership,* 131–132.
19. Ibid., 132.
20. Thomas M. Scheidel, "The Study of Leadership," B. Aubrey Fisher Memorial Lecture, Salt Lake City, Utah, April 23, 1987, 6.
21. James Krantz, "Lessons from the Field: An Essay on the Crisis of Leadership in Contemporary Organizations," *Journal of Applied Behavioral Science* 26 (1990): 61.
22. Gary A. Yukl, *Leadership in Organizations* (Englewood Cliffs, NJ: Prentice-Hall, 1981), 121–125.
23. Ralph M. Stogdill, "Personal Factors Associated with Leadership: A Survey of the Literature," *Journal of Psychology* 25 (1948): 35–71.
24. Bernard M. Bass, *Bass and Stogdill's Handbook of Leadership*, 76.
25. Ralph M. Stogdill, *Handbook of Leadership* (New York: The Free Press, 1974).
26. Michael Maccoby, *The Leader* (New York: Simon & Schuster, 1981).
27. Warren Bennis and Burt Nanus, *Leaders* (New York: Harper & Row, 1985).

28. Tom J. Peters and Robert T. Waterman, Jr., *In Search of Excellence* (New York: Harper & Row, 1982), 287–289.
29. Ralph Stogdill, *Handbook of Leadership*, 65.
30. Douglas McGregor, *The Human Side of Enterprise* (New York: McGraw-Hill, 1960).
31. Rensis Likert, *The Human Organization* (New York: McGraw-Hill, 1967).
32. Fred E. Fiedler, *A Theory of Leadership Effectiveness* (New York: McGraw-Hill, 1967).
33. Fred E. Fiedler and J. E. Garcia, *New Approaches to Effective Leadership: Cognitive Resources and Organizational Performance* (New York: Wiley, 1987).
34. Ibid., 7.
35. Robert J. House, "A Path Goal Theory of Leader Effectiveness," *Administrative Science Quarterly* 16 (1971).
36. Ibid., 324.
37. G. Graen, "Rolemaking Processes within Complex Organizations," in *Handbook of Industrial and Organizational Psychology,* ed. M. D. Dunnette (Chicago: Rand McNally, 1976).
38. T. O. Jacobs and E. Jacques, "Leadership in Complex Systems," in *Human Productivity Enhancement,* ed. J. Zeidner (New York: Praeger, 1987).
39. Bernard M. Bass, *Bass and Stogdill's Handbook of Leadership,* 54.

2

ORGANIZATIONS AS "PLACES" OF LEADERSHIP

To better understand organizations as entities in which leadership is exhibited and observed, it is important to consider theoretical perspectives on what an organization is and how people communicate in the process of organizing. This book presents a unique view of organizational leadership by looking at the relationship between leadership and organizational communication theories. Just as we looked at concepts of leadership before reviewing its theories, we will first look at the concept of "organization" before reviewing the major theories that have guided the study of organizations and the ways people communicate within them.

DEFINITIONS OF "ORGANIZATION"

When studying leadership in organizations, it is important to understand what "organization" means. Is it a place, a group of people, a process? At one time or another all of these terms may define "organization".

To many individuals the *place* they work, the building and the people it "contains," comprises an organization. However, within the last fifty years, theorists' notions of an "organization" have increasingly focused on the human dimension of this site of leadership. Various definitions emphasize an organization as "a system of consciously, coordinated activities or forces of two or more persons,"[1] as groups of groups,[2] as coalitions of individuals who set goals through interaction,[3] and as a complex social unit designed to achieve a specific purpose.[4] Note that all of these definitions, which span several decades, emphasize the notion of an organization as an aggregate of people who are interactive beings. As we shall discuss later in this chapter, early theorists conceived of organizations as formal, complex, hierarchical structures; as bureaucracies that possessed the following "traits":

1. A locus of power—a person or group of persons who is the source of decisions and influence. The chief executive officer of a corporation, the president of a university, or the coach of a team may be the locus of power in his or her organization. However, it is also possible, as discussed later in this chapter, that power does not reside in a formal position but in an individual who exhibits leadership behaviors like decision making and problem solving, a person whose power is attributable to the possession of information.
2. Substitutability of personnel—people come and go in organizations; they enter and leave positions. When they do, other individuals take their places in the process of task accomplishment. In other words, "no one is indispensable."
3. A division of labor—the work of the organization is distributed among individuals, each of whom has assigned tasks to do.
4. A history of their pasts—how and by whom the organization was founded, the stories and legends transmitted through generations of employees, and the major successes and failures of its management. All these remembrances are part of an institutional memory.[5]

While these are certainly elements of organizations, there are several characteristics one can identify that better emphasize their uniqueness as social units dependent on the interaction among the people who comprise them.

Karl Weick, a management theorist, has helped foster a dramatic change in the conceptualizations of an "organization" during the last twenty-five years. In *The Social Psychology of Organizing*, he states that the traditional notion of an organization is a myth—if you search for one you cannot find it. Instead he suggests that "organization" is a process and "consists of plans, recipes, rules, instructions, and programs for generating, interpreting, and governing behavior that are jointly managed by two or more people."[6] In short, an organization depends on social construction, not the creation of concrete and glass. Its raw materials are "talk, symbols, promises, lies, interest, attention, threats, agreements, expectations, memories, rumors, . . . appearances, loyalties, and commitments, all of which are more intangible and more influenceable than material goods."[7] The process of organizing involves arranging, categorizing, and patterning; in other words *ordering* ideas, experiences, and interactions through interdependent behaviors that form social processes understood by the people exhibiting those behaviors.

The elements of *organizing as a process,* according to Weick, are as follows:

- Equivocal or ambiguous information creates a perceived need for organizing.
- People make sense of information, experiences, and the other raw materials of organizing by interpreting previous happenings.
- Interdependencies that exist among people are the substance of organizations, yet they are fluid and shifting.
- Networks of self-regulating links among individuals are realized in the form of coordinated behaviors between two or more people.[8]

The underlying concept in support of this notion of organizing is that people share meanings to make sense out of ambiguous information and unpredictable situations. Also important to Weick's concept is the process of *enactment,* a process "by which organizational members create their environments through their chosen actions and patterns of attention."[9]

An example of this notion of organization was publicized extensively by the major television networks on the evening of January 17, 1994. Earlier that morning, a major earthquake struck the San Fernando Valley in southern California, causing numerous deaths and billions of dollars of property damage. Several major highways were severely damaged, virtually cutting off many area communities from Los Angeles. The quake occurred before dawn, and by evening some Californians in the hard-hit areas were seen driving to a few scarce lighted areas, including tennis courts in Van Nuys, California, because much of the electrical power in the area was disrupted. Essentially these individuals began creating ways to assist each other, sharing information, and attempting to make some sense of the tragedy in which they were involved, to varying extents. This was an example of the way organization is created by interdependent behaviors of individuals, who through interaction engage in collective activities to achieve shared goals. Their experiences and feelings on that day, as well as individual stories of stress and escape, guided their interests in coordinating future actions. Here was a situation where community was created out of chaos.

On a day-to-day basis, however, people relate to their places of work as locations that generally are not created out of crisis, where they accomplish tasks and develop social relationships through verbal and nonverbal communication. The notion of organizations as bureaucracies is alive and well, especially among those who work within them. It is important to consider that the bureaucratic model of organizations, which emphasizes hierarchical structures driven by formal policies and procedures, is not problematic in and of itself. However, inflexibility, as manifested by people, is. Leaders are affected by the extent to which organizations are bureaucratic entities; they also are influenced by the sense-making processes of organizational members and the results of those processes. The perspectives that people hold about why people participate in organizations, and how they communicate within them, are perhaps the most critical influences on the exercise of leadership. Therefore, understanding theories of organization, and their influences on communication between leaders and followers, is essential to our study of organizations as "places" of leadership.

ORGANIZATIONAL THEORIES

Historically, theories about the purpose and functions of organizations have focused on the accomplishment of tasks (productivity), the fulfillment of human needs (people), or the concurrent goals of achieving productivity while meeting the personal and professional needs of workers. As is the case with leadership theories, perspectives on organizations developed out of an historical context that influenced their birth and maturation.

Classical Theories of Organization

As is mentioned in Chapter 1, it is natural that theorists' perspectives of organizations are affected by the era of history in which they live and study. As the Industrial Revolution stimulated the growth of factories, owners and managers increasingly paid attention to the interrelationship of task and worker and the importance of that relationship to productivity. Indeed, the focus of the organization's existence was on performance and output, with little if any concern about the needs of workers or the quality of their work environment.

One of the early, or classical, theories of organization was the notion of *scientific management* espoused by Frederick W. Taylor in 1911.[10] An efficiency expert, Taylor studied the process of working. He suggested that management be viewed as a science to facilitate people doing as much work as possible, as efficiently as possible. In his opinion, the focus of an organization should include the following:

- Hiring and training workers for specific positions and tasks
- Prescribing methods for doing specific tasks
- Equally dividing the organizational workload between management and workers
- Overseeing workers to assure their use of prescribed methods of work

Keep in mind that Taylor's opinions came, in large part, from his observations in the field, including coal shoveling in steel mills, and from the nature of most organizations during this era. People often brought their own tools to work and used few, if any, systematic procedures. Additionally, the role of supervisors was not well-defined and workers were often misused. To keep production at a rate acceptable to owners and managers, they worked long hours to compensate for disorganization.

Max Weber, a German sociologist writing in the early part of the twentieth century, suggested the advantage of *bureaucratization in organizations* by emphasizing the need for logic, order, and formality within them.[11] His perspective proposed the following critical components of those "places" where the primary if not sole function is to accomplish work:

A division of labor

Rules and procedures

Job descriptions

Hierarchical authority

Formal communication, typified by memos and reports, to be distributed along the organizational chain of command

Communication in the classical, or traditional, organization is top-down and task-oriented, as well as formal. There is little interest in leader–follower interaction for social purposes; communication's function is to distribute information for the predominant purpose of task completion.

Humanistic Theories of Organization

As worker misuse and abuse became a societal issue during the 1920s and 1930s, labor movements and unions developed and laws were passed to protect workers' rights. After World War II, the workforce became increasingly well-educated; more people went to college. This growing segment of the workforce held greater expectations about how they should be treated as workers and because they were college graduates, companies paid these workers more money. Hiring them was a greater investment in the workforce than had been the case in the past. Most of these workers were hired into white collar, professional positions and were white males. They held more clout in organizations than had immigrants, women, minorities, and uneducated white males who had been the mainstays of factories and manufacturing companies. In this sociocultural environment, professors and researchers became consultants and began to look at the relationship between worker morale and productivity. The general perspective of the humanistic theories is that relationships among people at work have a major impact on the work accomplished in the organization.

One model exemplifying the humanistic perspective of organization is the *human relations* model, which emphasizes that superiors are concerned about the personal and professional needs of subordinates. Concern about employees' social and psychological needs are based on a belief by supervisors that "employees who are treated with tender loving care are more satisfied and therefore more productive."[12]

This model is based on the work of Elton Mayo and his colleagues who found that attention to workers by management increased their cohesiveness as work groups.[13] In organizations where this model is used, communication is supportive, although still originating at the top of the organization.

The evolution of the humanistic perspective of organizations also is represented by the *human resources* model which reflects the work of Douglas McGregor. (See Chapter 1.) In this model, leaders treat people well to increase productivity and because they believe it is the right thing to do for the professional and personal development of subordinates. Communication under these circumstances may indeed be bottom-up as well as top-down, and there is a propensity to encourage lateral communication—that which transpires between and among individuals at the same organizational level. Followers are encouraged to participate in decision making and problem solving. The frequency, as well as the amount, of communication may be increased between leaders and followers and sufficient information is provided subordinates to assist the fulfillment of their tasks and keep them informed about the organization and its environment. Because communication is a valued process, an atmosphere of trust is created among leaders and followers.

Of course, within organizations different perceptions exist among workers as to the degree of trust they should have in their leaders. Levels of trust depend on how workers perceive they are treated in comparison to their colleagues. *Equity theory* focuses on employee perceptions of the rewards they get compared with those received by others for their respective levels of work. This perspective focuses on the discrepancy felt by organizational members under these circumstances.

Integrative/Systems Theories of Organization

Dramatic changes have affected organizations in this and most other societies since the 1960s. These include changes in technologies through which work is accomplished, increasing environmental influences (such as foreign competition) on organizations, and socioeconomic concerns such as equal employment opportunity laws, an economic recession, and effects of organizational activity on the physical environments in which they reside. Through integration of the classical and humanistic theories of organization, scholars have realized the importance of viewing organizations as places that must concurrently emphasize the importance of productivity and people. An example of this organizational perspective is the *sociotechnical model*, which suggests the importance of attending to the efficient use of technology *and* the social needs of work groups. This perspective grew from studies of the British coal industry where scholars attempted to integrate new technologies, and usage of them, into task processes dependent on work groups.

Theorists also have recognized that organizations are sets of interacting parts affected by environmental influences. There is a continuous flow of information among the components of the system and with the environment surrounding the organization. Just as a human body is comprised of sets of subsystems (e.g., respiratory, circulatory, lymph) and is affected by the weather, relationships with other people, and other environmental factors, so is an organization comprised of interdependent parts and subsystems (e.g., design, production, marketing) similarly affected by external influences. The process facilitating interaction among the parts and subsystems is communication. According to the *systems theory* of organizations, communication should be fluid and frequent to maintain an optimal operating level for the system or organization. The integrative theory of organization emphasizes that communication facilitates the fulfillment of human *and* organizational needs and provides for critical organizational interaction with external constituencies.

One of the theoretical perspectives emanating from an awareness that an organization's environment has significant influence on an organization is the *resource dependence* theory.[14] This perspective emphasizes that environments possess resources on which organizations depend for survival. As a result, organizations are constantly in the process of negotiating for resources and competing with other organizations in the search and acquisition of them. Leaders are responsible for managing this dependent relationship, and they are continually affected by the availability of resources and the competing relationships that scarcity or abundance creates. For instance, college football coaches are in constant competition to recruit the best high school players for their teams. They vie with each other for graduating seniors, who are athletic resources, in order to create winning teams.

Another perspective emphasizing environmental influence is the *institutionalization* theory which suggests that "organizations conform to the expectations of the environment by adapting 'appropriate' (rational) structures and behaviors."[15] An organization legitimizes itself to the environment by communicating that it is rational through shared meanings with internal and external stakeholders. The organization creates these meanings by acquiring and using information—and leaders are those primarily responsible for these processes. Charitable organizations, for instance, depend on their "good names" within a community when it comes time to seek donations from citizens. Groups that meet civic expectations are legitimized and they are rewarded with monetary gifts.

These are major theoretical perspectives on what "organization" means. They evolved from scholars' observations of human experience and interaction in a changing socioeconomic and political context. The role of organizational leadership, and leader–follower interaction, changes from one perspective to another depending on the conceptualization of "organization." Perceptions of leadership, its form and functions, also vary depending on the perspectives that exist on the nature of communication within organizations.

PERSPECTIVES ON ORGANIZATIONAL COMMUNICATION

A variety of textbooks are available to analyze communication as a process in organizations. It is not the purpose of this book to discuss organizational communication theories in detail. However, for the purposes of general understanding, four perspectives are summarized below. They suggest different approaches to the study of organizational communication.[16]

- The *mechanistic* perspective focuses on message transmission via channels. Scholars are concerned with message accuracy, the choice of channel, how information flow is facilitated or blocked, and the optimal amount of information in effective messages.
- The *psychological* perspective emphasizes the receiver in the communication process and focuses on individuals as message interpreters considering the contextual factors around them.
- The *interpretive-symbolic* perspective is concerned with the continuous development of shared meanings among individuals. It suggests that communication shapes organizational structure and culture and is formed by them as well, and that organizations both form and respond to their environments.
- The *systems-interactive* perspective focuses on sequences of communication behaviors, suggesting that recurring patterns of interaction predict organizational outcomes.

These perspectives reflect an evolutionary focus from a concentration on the movement of messages to continuous and interdependent communication behaviors among individuals. As such, these orientations to interaction in organizations follow the evolutionary development of theories of leadership and of organizations. Obviously, the conceptualizations researchers have about organizations, and the communication within them, necessarily affect the study of leadership; but remember, just as historical contexts and socioeconomic and political environments change, so do the theories that develop within them. They are only a part of what helps us understand organizations as "places" of leadership.

To add to our understanding of these "places," it is critical to understand: (1) the changes that have affected organizations as loci of interaction in the latter part of this century; (2) the organizational components and environmental factors that affect leadership; and (3) the characteristics of organizations we are beginning to witness and will see in the twenty-first century.

ORGANIZATIONAL CHANGES AFFECTING LEADERSHIP, 1960–2000

Amid social, economic, technological, and political changes, organizations in this country have witnessed dramatic internal changes. Such changes are not seen in all the society's companies, corporations, and associations, or its schools, hospitals, and religious organizations, but they are becoming increasingly evident in many of them. Since the 1960s, the civil rights and women's movements have influenced both laws and behaviors affecting the rights of minorities and women in the workplace. Foreign competition and an economic recession have forced some companies to reconsider how their work can be done to maximize profit as well as the fulfillment of employee needs. We have become a society dependent on the production and dissemination of information. Additionally, the creation of new technologies affects how we work, relax, shop, make decisions about health care, and conduct the myriad of activities important in the lives of Americans in the 1990s. The social, economic, and technological changes we are witnessing all have potential and real impacts on federal, state, and local laws, and on a variety of policy-making bodies including city councils and school boards. Societal changes that have emerged in the last four decades relate in some way to changes in many of our organizations. In turn, these changes affect the interaction between leaders and followers in the conduct of everyday organizational life. The organizational changes most pertinent to a study of leadership from a communication perspective include the following.

Decreased Numbers of Hierarchical Levels ("Flatter" Organizations)

In the last two decades of the twentieth century, organizations have found it financially advantageous, or necessary, to streamline their workforces. Additionally, because of increased usage of computers, top management in many companies access information at their own desks. Middle managers, whose major if not sole purpose was to bring superiors information, slowly have become obsolete. Consequently, as a reaction to financial pressures and the acceptance of new technologies as instruments of information acquisition, analysis, and dissemination, hierarchical layers in organizations have been reduced. The effects of this change on leader–follower interaction deserve increased scholarly inquiry. Some of them are as follows:

- Faster communication, as well as more timely problem solving and decision making, with less distortion of messages since fewer people are involved in the transmission of those messages
- More fluid communication among and between organizational levels
- An increase in the quality and quantity of communication between superiors and subordinates. Hierarchical levels may act as barriers between leaders and followers in organizations. A decrease in layers of management may minimize psychological distance, and sometimes status differentiation between superiors and subordinates, thereby increasing the potential for improved communication between them.

Emphasis on the Creation and Use of Work Teams/Task Groups

As corporate America has become increasingly concerned about competition from the Japanese in the latter part of the twentieth century, some corporations borrowed Japanese management techniques. One technique is an emphasis on work groups or project teams. Using these emergent structures, people come together, interact in a variety of settings, make decisions, and solve problems faster than if they were encumbered by hierarchical reporting relationships. Work is accomplished through free-flowing communication among organizational members who take pride in the work of the group and who enjoy the social relationships that may develop during its attention to tasks. While project teams are often found in newer types of industries, such as the computer industry, work groups increasingly are being used in hospitals for patient care, in schools as teachers integrate learning activities, in automobile factories as workers assemble cars as a team rather than as an assembly line, and in other companies that place a premium on creativity and innovation in product design, assembly, distribution, and marketing. Just as participants in Elton Mayo's studies in the 1930s found that people enjoyed the attention paid to them by supervisors and responded with increased productivity, so we find that people enjoy interaction with each other in the workplace to accomplish organizational goals. By fostering the creation of teams and supporting them by providing human, material, and financial resources, leaders may find opportunities for increased interaction with a variety of organizational members, and these members may find opportunities to exhibit behaviors in groups that will enable them to emerge as organizational leaders.

Decentralization of Decision Making

One characteristic of bureaucratic organizations is that they depend on formal structure and centralized decision making by those at the highest level of the organization. As organizations have seen the benefits of fewer hierarchical levels and the increased use of work teams, their leaders have become more apt to delegate decision making to lower levels in the organization and/or to those levels where the decisions can be made by those most knowledgeable about the issue or problem at hand. The assumption behind this decentralization is that people who work closest to certain issues and problems know best how to address and solve them. Individuals should make decisions about the tasks for which they are directly responsible—as opposed to those individuals at higher levels who may have little knowledge, expertise, or interest in the issue or problem for which a decision is needed. A more fluid flow of communication within the organization, including increased and improved interaction between leaders and decentralized decision makers, may be a by-product of this evolving organizational change.

Variable Organizational Rewards

Members of organizations are motivated by more than extrinsic rewards, such as money. They work to be contributing members of social units, to participate in achieving organizational goals, to be a part of ongoing social relationships, as well as to earn livelihoods. As a result, leaders in organizations understand that intrinsic rewards such as praise, formal recognition, opportunities for advancement, and time off the job are valuable to workers. In recent years, flexible reward systems have been developed so that a variety of rewards can be bestowed on organizational members, as is appropriate to various task accomplishments. A weekend trip at a resort, a Friday afternoon off, a holiday bonus, a free lunch for a successful work team, are all forms of recognition that supplement salaries and help award, and motivate, organizational members. Such a reward system is a form of leader–follower interaction that fosters positive relationships between them.

New Communication Technologies

The introduction of computers into organizations to serve in numerous roles, such as word processor, accountant, statistician, and mail carrier, has created dramatic changes within organizations. Not only have computers assumed a variety of functions, they have become channels for communication among workers. It is possible to make decisions and solve problems in groups without being face-to-face if you are linked with one another via certain networking hardware and software. Audio and teleconferencing now allow members of multinational corporations to hear and/or see each other as they participate in meetings thousands of miles away from each other. All of these technologies allow people to communicate faster, from different distances, and facilitate the work of the organization. The effects of these technologies on leader–follower communication are still being ascertained in ongoing research studies, but the potential exists for leaders to be able to communicate with followers in different parts of the United States, or around the world, so they may work to foster performance and cohesion among various organizational units and subunits that are geographically dispersed.

Extensions of Organizational Boundaries

Through mergers, acquisitions, and the growth of multinational corporations, organizations increasingly have extended their boundaries beyond their own individual locales. Additionally, because many organizations are influenced by federal and state laws, policies of external constituencies, competition, and a plethora of other environmental concerns, their boundaries are "fuzzy"; it is sometimes difficult to determine where an organization "ends" and the environment "begins." The effect of this change on leader–follower interaction is multidimensional; leaders need to spend more time scanning the environment to understand issues of potential importance to the organization, and their communication with organizational members must reflect their acquired knowledge of these issues. Additionally, leaders must work carefully to facilitate the development of communication networks *within* their organizations and to enhance those *between* the organization and its external constituencies. The importance of fluid, ongoing communication between an organization and its environment, or between leaders and an organization's external stakeholders, is magnified when one considers the increasing environmental influence on resources available to an organization and the distribution of those resources within an organization by decision makers.

The organizational changes discussed above are effects of environmental influences and/or reactions to perceived needs and goals among organizational members. As we shall see later in this chapter, several of these "trends" are expected to become characteristics of twenty-first century organizations. On a day-to-day basis, however, a number of organizational components affect leaders and their interactions with internal and external stakeholders. Several of those most salient to the leader–follower relationship are discussed below to better understand the pressures and possibilities placed on that relationship.

ORGANIZATIONAL COMPONENTS AFFECTING LEADERSHIP

While a number of organizational elements affect organizational leaders (e.g., size of organization, work-force demographics, adequacy of resources), those particularly important to the leader–follower relationship include the following.

Task

While this term refers to the general purpose of an organization, for example, building airplanes, preparing and serving fast food, selling insurance, educating elementary school pupils, and so on, it also refers to specific tasks encountered as a workforce endeavors to achieve the organization's general purpose. The need to complete a report by five P.M., serve noon-hour customers at a fast-food restaurant, develop a city's master plan, or create a new generation of computers to combat major competitors, requires different leadership behaviors. As a result, leader–follower interaction is affected differently by these tasks because each imposes different time, psychological, and resource constraints, among others, on the leader and the communicative relationship that will be used to accomplish the task.

Structure

The quality and quantity of leader–follower interaction is greatly affected by the formal and informal structures that are found within organizations. Large, multihierarchical companies that rely on "communication via the organizational chart" do not foster a free flow of communication among hierarchical levels. "Flatter" organizations that emphasize work groups and project teams generally may facilitate more interaction between leaders and followers, and may witness the emergence of leaders in a variety of communication contexts, especially if problems are solved and decisions are made in groups rather than at the top of the organization. The concept of "structure" is complex in the study of organizations and organizational communication. For instance, some complex, hierarchical organizations also utilize work groups. Some organizations built around work teams impose their own brand of formality on intragroup and intergroup interactions. In these cases, and other variations of simple, complex, and integrated structures, reporting relationships, task and social networks, job descriptions, and policies and procedures are all elements of structure that potentially affect the quantity and quality of communication among organizational members, and between organizational leaders and their internal constituencies.

Resources

Leaders have a variety of resources at their disposal in organizations. These include human resources (people); financial resources (capital, operating funds); power; and technologies. By no means is this a complete list, but these resources, the abundance or lack thereof, affect the exhibition of leadership and leader–follower interaction.

Human and Material Resources. A leader is greatly influenced by the degree to which he or she has sufficient people, money, and materials with which to accomplish organizational tasks. Declining revenues affect the range of choices leaders have in implementing visions. The lack of materials such as wood, water, metals, and oil, caused by natural or man-made disasters limits a leader's control over decisions that have to be made on both a long-term and a day-to-day basis. Employee turnover and absenteeism affect the capability of those guiding organizations in executing organizational plans. Moreover, as was discussed in Chapter 1, leaders in our increasingly turbulent global society have diminished control over the resources at their disposal because of ever-changing environmental conditions that affect not only the possession of resources but the distribution of them within an organization. When leaders must work with limited, or declining resources, their abilities to accomplish organizational goals may be impeded. They are increasingly subject to stress, and this stress can affect the quality and quantity of leader–follower interaction.

Power. While authority may be granted to an individual as a right assigned to a given position—power, "the ability to get things done," must be earned.[17] Giving one's power to someone else in an organization does not insure that it will remain with that person. In organizations, power may come to a leader through social alliances, but these connections must be long-term, stable, and include one's superiors, peers, and subordinates.[18] It may also be the result of performance, but that performance must be extraordinary, visible, and relevant; that is, related to a solution of a critical organizational problem.[19] Wielding power, an important resource for a leader that can be saved, spent, and even squandered, is a "given" when one lists leadership behaviors. The extent to which a leader has power, uses it for organizational as well as personal benefit, and delegates it to others, all influence a leader's credibility and his or her communication relationship with others in the organization.

Technologies.   This term refers to the tools used to accomplish work in organizations (e.g., pens, typewriters, computers, telephones, adding machines, assembly line machinery, etc). Leaders in the last fifty years have benefited from dramatic improvements in such technologies, resulting in a decrease in the amount of time it takes to produce goods, make and execute decisions, solve problems, and communicate, in general, to organizational members. Knowledge about and the ability to use these technologies, especially those that are computer based, affect and will continue to affect the task and social relationships between leaders and followers.

The access to and use of resources is a critical organizational component in the lives of leaders. Of equal importance are an organization's beliefs and values—its way of life.

Culture

As is the case in any society, or part of society, the culture of an organization is comprised of its values and beliefs, as affected by its history, heroes, stories and legends, rituals and ceremonies.[20] In Chapter 4 we will analyze a leader as the creator and sustainer of an organizational culture, a critical function for such individuals. It is also important, however, to mention briefly the effect of organizational culture on a leader and on the leader–follower relationship. An understanding and appreciation of organizational culture is particularly pertinent to a leader who is brought into an organization and who is not its founder. Such individuals must understand the importance of culture as the soul of the organization—the philosophies and ethics of its members hold the individuals together as a community. To break traditions, like the annual family picnic, denigrate heroes, like the founder whom one has replaced, and laugh at stories that are sentimentally significant to the workforce, is essentially attacking the people of the organization, not just its practices. So how an incoming leader responds to an organizational culture, even if over time he or she intends to make modifications in it, will affect greatly that person's relationship with followers. Additionally, the culture of an organization affects its leader by serving as the socioemotional environment in which a leader acts. If the culture is rich in traditions, if its values have been shared and sustained among organizational members who are proud of those values, then the continuation of that culture, as an organizational component, must always be considered by the leader as day-to-day decisions and long-term visions are created and implemented. Indeed, an assessment of culture should be a primary consideration as leaders develop visions for the futures of their organizations. On the other hand, if a culture has evolved into an internal environment that is no longer supportive of, or supported by, organizational members, leaders must work to create a new one that is mutually desired by leaders and followers and one that typifies what individuals want the organization to represent. It must be, in a sense, the spiritual embodiment of organizational goals, tasks, visions, day-to-day decisions, problems, and solutions. The quality of organizational culture, and the degree to which the values of that culture are shared and communicated among leaders and followers, affects leaders in virtually all the behaviors they exhibit when communicating with organizational members.

Climate

This component of an organization may be viewed by some students as a rather vague concept. In one scholar's definition it is described as "a relatively enduring quality of the internal environment " that is experienced by organizational members and that influences their behaviors.[21] Another perspective is that climate is a composite set of expectations held by organizational members as to what it is like to work in a specific organization, and in this sense climate is generally referred to as being either supportive or defensive, depending on the positive or negative perceptions held by the people it affects. To better understand this phenomenon that is continuously created and recreated through socialization processes, it is beneficial to look at the dimensions of climate that have been suggested by scholars in their research. For instance, to ascertain perceptions of climate in relationship to leadership, two researchers studied the extent to which employees perceived that:

- Work was well structured
- Job objectives were clear
- They were accountable for their own actions
- Their supervisor encouraged participative decision making
- Their supervisor showed trust, confidence, and respect for them
- A friendly and cooperative work environment existed
- Management was concerned with employee needs
- Information was disseminated sufficiently[22]

One of the findings of this study was that the interactions between leaders and subordinates mediated and structured subordinates' perceptions of climate. Individuals that had a good relationship with their supervisor also had better communication with that individual. Also, their perceptions of the organization's climate were significantly closer to those of the supervisor than those of employees who did not enjoy the same type of superior–subordinate relationship.

One subcomponent of climate is *organizational communication climate,* which consists of one's expectations about communication in the organization, expectations that are "continually interacting and evolving with organizational processes, structured around common organizational practices."[23]

Poole and McPhee suggest that organizational communication climate emerges through the interaction of external influences, organizational influences, and the people in the organization. *External influences* include economic and political trends, technological developments, and sociocultural norms from the organization's environment. *Organizational influences* include those elements already discussed here—task, structure, and technology—that have significant effect on climate. *People* in the organization, however, are those with the greatest effect on the creation and perception of a communication climate through their knowledge, skills, abilities, values, and demographics.[24]

W. Charles Redding once described the ideal communication climate as having the following dimensions: supportiveness, participative decision making, trust, confidence, and credibility; openness and candor and high performance goals.[25] Over twenty years later, this scholar suggested that an important component of organizational climate is the *rhetorical environment* in which individuals work, since many of the "miseries" suffered by American workers "could be alleviated were it possible to modify the rhetorical environments of innumerable organizations."[26] Redding defined these environments as clusters of attributes that characterize persuasive discourse in an organization, including linguistic styles, argumentative tactics, and preferences for certain topics. He emphasized that through rhetoric decisions are made and implemented in organizations. Indeed virtually all leadership behaviors are conducted through the use of rhetoric, and the communication environment created for all organizational members depends in great part on the communicative choices made by their leaders. As we discussed in Chapter 1, an organizational leader manages meaning through what is done and said, and the context created by verbal and nonverbal behaviors is a critical part of an overall organizational climate.

Task, structure, resources, culture, and climate are elements of organizations that have major effects on leader–follower communication. They have been studied from traditional perspectives as important components of modern, bureaucratic organizations. However, newer approaches to the study of organizations use each of these elements, in and of themselves, as ways of looking at organizations. We can use culture as the framework from which to study IBM. We can use climate as the tool to study Disney World. We can evaluate many aspects of a large, complex social service agency by focusing on its structure; and we can analyze a major state university as an organization by concentrating on the adequacy of its resources and environmental effects on the availability of those resources. Most importantly, we can look at the integrated effects of these components to determine their relationship to one another, and the degree to which their "fit" is optimal for meeting organizational and individual goals.

ENVIRONMENTAL INFLUENCES AFFECTING LEADERS

Just as leaders are affected by elements within organizations, they are also influenced by elements in the environments surrounding organizations. Four of the elements particularly important to leaders and to leader–follower communication are briefly discussed below.

Socioeconomic and Political Influences

Organizations exist within environmental contexts that greatly affect a number of organizational activities and relationships. For instance, a fast-food hamburger restaurant is influenced by recessions, consumer attitudes about the relationship of eating meat and high cholesterol, federal regulations governing meat inspection, accessibility to buildings for individuals with disabilities, competition from other fast-food restaurants, and a myriad of other environmental factors affecting the organization's goals, tasks, and customers. The leader of such an organization must understand these environmental influences, incorporate them into decision-making processes, in many cases explain them to employees and customers, and weave a consideration of them into his or her daily work and long-range planning. Such is also the case for leaders in hospitals, where federal and state laws governing medical treatment for indigent patients, the financial health of a community, the presence or absence of adequate numbers of doctors and nurses, and possible epidemics such as AIDS, influenza, and tuberculosis affect both short- and long-term decisions those individuals must make.

Socioeconomic and political influences on leaders' tasks can also affect the leader–follower relationship. When such influences create problems or uncertainties for organizations, stress increases at both a personal and organizational level, and the quality of communication between leader and follower may suffer. At the same time, a surplus of resources may allow leaders to be creative and imaginative in their endeavors, fostering an increasing interest in follower participation in decision making and problem solving.

Environmental Turbulence/Stability

Organizations, as places of leadership, also are affected by the relative turbulence or stability of the environment in which they exist. A computer company, for instance, "lives" in a highly-competitive, ever-changing milieu where communication among organizational members should be free-flowing and fast in order to make decisions quickly. Such interaction is important if, for instance, there is a need to beat a competitor to market with a new type of lap-top computer. Governmental agencies that operate successfully as bureaucratic organizations, and for-profit companies who depend on relatively stable markets, are in comparatively stable environments. Leaders in these organizations may hold their positions for quite some time, as compared to leaders operating in turbulent environments, and may interact with a workforce that has a lower rate of turnover than in other types of industries. As a result, the communicative relationship between leaders and followers in these organizations also may be stable and consistent. That does not mean it is optimal, for stability may breed complacency and an aversion to innovation. In bureaucratic organizations, communication between leaders and followers may be formal and cordial, and predominantly task oriented. It does not necessarily focus on followers and their professional and personal needs.

Outside Reference Groups

Leaders belong to a variety of social collectivities. For instance, the president of a soft drink company may be a member of the Baptist Church, a boy scout leader, and an active member of the Democratic Party. The chief of staff in a hospital may be active in her synagogue, president of a high school PTA, and a member of the community's sailing club. Many of us are participants in several groups because of the interests, beliefs, values, and perspectives we hold as unique individuals. The "memberships" in these groups, because we interact with a variety of different people within them, continually affect our views of the world. Such is the case with individuals who hold or exhibit leadership positions in organizations. Their experiences and interactions in groups outside the organizations become part of their personal outlook on the world, their communities, their relationships, and on themselves. This personal outlook is brought into the organizations they lead each day and affects their interactions with people there.

Organizational Linkages

In our private lives we are members of reference groups because of who and what we are and because of our personal interests and choices. Organizational leaders also find themselves members of social collectivities because of their positions in their own organization; they become links to other groups as a function of their organizational roles or positions. For instance, a dean of graduate studies at a university may be part of the nation's council of graduate deans. She may be on the Chamber of Commerce education committee in the community, selected for participation because of her role on campus. She may also be a member of the board of directors of a city-wide organization that hopes to encourage outstanding high school students to attend college with a view to pursuing graduate education. This type of participation also affects one's work. Through communication with external constituencies, one obtains information, shares opinions, and represents his or her own organization. What the leader learns from these interactions is brought to the organization and affects the conduct of activity and the ongoing evolution of task and social relationships with superiors, peers, and subordinates.

As members of reference groups and as organizational links, leaders manage the boundaries around them at both the organizational and interpersonal levels. There are certainly physical boundaries around organizations—the wooden, brick, or concrete walls that surround them—but other boundaries are socially constructed within organizations. Both leaders and followers pass through boundaries daily, and import ideas and experiences within them.[27] Considering the environmental factors we have reviewed, it is important to consider that the exercise of leadership throughout the 1990s and into the twenty-first century is particularly affected by the increased rate of change occurring in the environment, and an increased interdependence between the organization and its external constituencies related to the acquisition and control of resources. Examples of this growing interdependence are partnerships between corporations and schools to add needed funds to educational budgets, between hospitals and insurance companies to provide high-quality health care, and between universities and high schools to improve the preparation of college-going youth. In the future, leaders must become increasingly adept at understanding and initiating these partnerships and at establishing a variety of networks both in and outside the organization to create communicative relationships that will foster the achievement of individual, organizational, and community goals. One main reason why leaders must possess this ability is that our society, and organizations within it, are involved in a major transformation—a dramatic and irreversible change. Leaders must understand this phenomenon as they interact with organizational members now and in the future.

THE POSTMODERN ORGANIZATION

Within recent years philosophers, sociologists, and others who develop views of the world we live in and how people relate to the world and each other, have suggested that society in the last decades of the twentieth century has become a *postmodern* society. As such, it is a world of turbulence facing irreversible change, as are the smaller social units within it. When discussing the notion of *postmodern organizations*, it is beneficial to compare their characteristics with those of modern organizations—social collectivities in a society that developed during and after the Industrial Revolution, and premodern organizations, which existed before the Industrial Revolution. The following comparisons are summaries of characteristics presented by William Bergquist in his book, *The Postmodern Organization.*[28]

The family farm and "mom and pop" grocery stores are examples of *pre-modern organizations.* Their characteristics include:

- Simple structures
- Unclear missions and boundaries
- Paternal and charismatic leadership
- Oral and face-to-face communication
- The use of manual labor rewarded with food, shelter, and security

Modern organizations are bureaucratic entities, such as a factory or a bank, with multiple hierarchical levels. Characteristics of such organizations include:

- Large and complex structures
- Unclear missions but clear boundaries
- The practice of management instead of leadership
- Formal communication such as the memo and statistical report
- Rewards for labor obtained through wage and salary structures

An example of a postmodern organization in the 1990s is a small, innovative computer software firm, or an independent motion picture production company that seeks to provide programming to cable companies. Principles guiding the establishment and growth of such organizations include the following: decentralization of power, the treatment of employees as renewable resources, flattened hierarchies, cultures built on trust and respect for differences within the workforce, and the use of groups.[29] Note how these principles reflect changes in organizations during the last several decades, as discussed earlier in this chapter. Characteristics of postmodern organizations include the following:

- Flexible structures
- Clear missions
- Diffuse and "fuzzy" boundaries
- Transformational and situational leadership
- Oral communication that may be mediated (e.g., teleconferencing, voice mail)
- Labor rewarded with intrinsic as well as extrinsic rewards

An understanding of postmodern society rests on the awareness that the organizations within it operate continually between order and chaos in a continually turbulent environment.[30] They are always in transition, organized and reorganized in accordance with Weick's concept of organization. They require flexibility in leadership style and a commitment to fostering a learning organization that learns from its mistakes.[31]

A postmodern leader understands the nature of the environment in which her organization exists; she is not afraid of uncertainty and/or ambiguity. While the manager of a modern organization attempts to make sense out of chaos through structures, procedures, and rules, the postmodern leader sees chaos as natural and expected—the reality within which the organization exists. Whereas pre-modern organizations depended on the "great man" as their leader, and modern organizations needed the rational, well-organized manager, the postmodern leader understands and anticipates unpredictable events.[32] He or she is the continually adaptive, follower-focused individual who is the source of integration among random organizational and environmental events. Such leaders focus on partnering, collaborating, and creating community.[33] Whereas management is a form of social control, postmodern leadership is a form of social support in organizations, provided through oral and sometimes mediated communication. For instance, organizational stories and interactions formulate institutional visions, day-to-day plans, and solutions to problems because such communication creates community out of independent individuals. As William Bergquist states: "Conversations tend to bind people together; talk is the glue in most organizations."[34]

Knowledge of and the ability to quickly adapt to a turbulent environment, a focus on followers as members of an organizational community, and an appreciation of communication as the form and substance of the connective tissue supporting organizational life, are requisite characteristics for leaders of postmodern organizations. However, it is important to recognize that not all organizations in the next decade and beyond will be postmodern organizations; some will continue to operate as modern organizations or as composites of both. Indeed, many of us will continue to work in places of leadership that possess the characteristics of modern organizations but are trying to adapt to twenty-first century influences.

CHARACTERISTICS OF TWENTY-FIRST CENTURY ORGANIZATIONS

Any contemporary study of organizational leadership must also consider "places" of leadership as they may appear in the twenty-first century. Characteristics of such organizations are similar to those ascribed to postmodern entities.[35] What can we expect organizations of the twenty-first century to "look" like? Burt Nanus, in his book, *Visionary Leadership,* suggests the following:

1. The labor force will be comprised mostly of highly skilled knowledge workers.
2. Products and services will be mostly packages of information.
3. Organizations will be global in scope. New technologies will facilitate communication among individuals working for the same organization but in different locales. An appreciation of diversity in races, ethnicities, and cultures should be a natural outgrowth of the globalization of the world of work.
4. Organizations will be technologically driven or at least technologically sensitive.
5. Organizations will face, and be characterized by, rapid change and complexity.
6. Organizational activities will be distributed over space and time. Operating in a global environment and depending on a myriad of technologies, an organization will see its work conducted in different places and at different times.
7. Organizations will be multipurpose and serve the needs of many constituencies. Just as Sears sells insurance as well as clothes, Coca-Cola sells clothes as well as soft drinks, and Warner Brothers produces films and souvenirs sold in malls and major theme parks, so will a growing number of organizations find stakeholders in a variety of places both in and outside their extended boundaries.
8. Organizations will have "fuzzy" boundaries. Internal and external stakeholders will transverse organizational boundaries routinely as networks between and among them develop, exist for specific purposes, and then change. Attention to an organization's external constituencies will become increasingly important as the resources they control and disburse are needed by that organization.

These are characteristics of organizations in the future—a future that begins tomorrow. Leaders must understand these characteristics and their implications if they are to succeed in striking a balance between achieving organizational goals and those of individuals in an environment of turbulent change.

INTEGRATING LEADERSHIP AND ORGANIZATIONAL THEORY

As is mentioned in Chapter 1, the content of theories is greatly influenced by the period of history in which the creators of those theories live. Perspectives on leadership have evolved from those that focused solely on a few "great men" and their traits, to those that emphasized the importance of followers' needs and realized the critical relationship between leaders' and followers' behaviors. Theories of organization and organizational communication, because they were developed during similar periods of history as leadership theories, first focused on the importance of the organization as a formal structure (represented by the people at its highest level), then as a "place" where workers deserved attention and information, and finally as a process created through social interaction among those engaged in a common purpose. As societal changes forced the development of a new perspective on organizations and organizing, it also forced changes in the ways scholars and executives began to look at the exercise of leadership. An emphasis on leadership as paternalistic protection gave way to an interest in leadership behavior as a phenomenon that depends on fluid communication among levels, networks, groups, and variously constructed social collectivities within organizations. Moreover, both theories of leadership and of organizational communication began to reflect the importance of external, or environmental, constraints or influences on the processes of organizing and of leadership. As we move into the remainder of the book, having built the theoretical foundations on which its key components are based, it is important to understand the interrelationship between leadership and organizational theories—their concepts and their histories.

As we have seen, there are various conceptions of what a "place" of leadership is. Throughout the remainder of the book, we will look at organizations from both the modern and postmodern perspectives. While we must prepare to be leaders in postmodern organizations, and organizations of the twenty-first century, most of us still work and interact in organizations we have defined as "modern." This notion acknowledges that leaders must understand the evolution of organizations as "places" of leadership; in the mid-1990s they are dealing with organizations undergoing rapid technological and social change. As a result, leaders must understand that there is no one best pattern of behavior that should be exhibited toward followers. Organizational change, as affected by turbulent environments, creates a variety of situational contexts to which they must adapt. Therefore, they must understand the concept of "style" and the importance of its variability as it applies both to leadership and to communication.

SUMMARY

An organization is not a place, a building of concrete and glass. It is an interactive process through which individuals order ideas, experiences, and events, socially constructing shared meanings to facilitate individual, group, and organizational goals. Leaders are influenced by the sense-making processes used by organizational members and the results of those processes.

As is the case with leadership theories, perspectives on organizations developed out of the historical contexts in which their creators lived. The classical theories of organization focus on the interrelationship between task and worker and the importance of that relationship to productivity. Humanistic theories emphasize the personal and professional needs of organizational members and leaders' recognition of how these needs impact the work of the organization. Systems theories consider organizations as open entities, comprised of interacting parts affected by environmental influences.

Social, economic, technological, and political changes in their environments have prompted a variety of changes in organizations. Such changes include the following: (1) "flatter" organizations, that is, a decrease in the number of hierarchical levels; (2) an emphasis on the creation and use of work teams; (3) decentralization of decision making; (4) the use of variable rewards; (5) the use of new communication technologies; and (6) the extension, or blurring, of organizational boundaries.

Both organizational and environmental influences affect the leader–follower relationship. Organizational components affecting this relationship include task, structure, resources, culture, and climate. Environmental influences include socioeconomic and political trends, the degree of turbulence or stability in the environment within which an organization exists, outside reference groups, and linkages with and among organizations.

Theories of organization and organizational communication once focused on the organization as a formal structure characterized by rules and established reporting relationships. More recently, they have regarded "organization" as a process created through social interaction among those engaged in a common purpose and affected by environmental or external influences. These theories and perspectives affect the study of leadership, not as a set of traits possessed by people, but as behaviors exhibited during the continuing evolution of leader–follower relationships.

QUESTIONS TO CONSIDER

1. Explain the following sentence. "An organization is not a place."

2. What is the role of a "leader" in the following theories or models of organization: scientific management, human resources, sociotechnical, resource dependence?

3. Identify and describe five changes in organizations that have been precipitated by social, economic, technological, and political changes in society.

4. In what ways do an organization's task, structure, culture, and/or climate affect leaders or the leader–follower relationship?

5. What competencies should a postmodern leader possess?

CASE PROBLEM

Marilyn Edwards, vice-president of production for a major filmmaking studio, is concerned about the productivity of her unit. She works twelve–fifteen hours per day as the head of an organizational unit that is constantly being pressured to finish major motion pictures on time and under or at budget. She is the center of a structure where twelve different unit heads report to her directly. Much of her time is spent interacting with these individuals. The frenetic pace of shooting and editing film, on time and within a film's budget, takes its toll on Marilyn's employees. They are tired for weeks at a time, with only a two–three week hiatus every six months or so. Consequently, morale is sometimes low—people are touchy and "on-edge" at the end of a production phase. At these times, production values seem to change and quality work sometimes is sacrificed for expediency—finishing a film quickly to save money.

First, identify the organizational components and environmental influences that are affecting Marilyn as an organizational leader.

Should Marilyn decide to hire an organizational consultant to improve morale and suggest cost-containment procedures for the unit? What suggestions might this consultant make to improve the organizational climate of the production unit?

ENDNOTES

1. Chester I. Barnard, *The Functions of the Executive* (Cambridge, MA: Harvard University Press, 1938), 73.
2. Herbert A. Simon, *Administrative Behavior: A Study of Decision-Making Processes in Administrative Organizations*, 2d ed. (New York: Macmillan, 1957).
3. Richard M. Cyert and James G. March, *A Behavioral Theory of the Firm* (Englewood Cliffs, NJ: Prentice-Hall, 1963).
4. Kenneth E. Knight and Reuben R. McDaniel, Jr., *Organizations: An Information Systems Perspective* (Belmont, CA: Wadsworth Publishing Company, 1979), 5.
5. Ibid., 5–6.
6. Karl E. Weick, *The Social Psychology of Organizing*, 2d ed. (Reading, MA: Addison-Wesley Publishing Company, 1979), 235.
7. Karl E. Weick, "Sources of Order in Underorganized Systems: Themes in Recent Organizational Theory," in *Organizational Theory and Inquiry: The Paradigm Revolution*, ed. Y. S. Lincoln (Beverly Hills: Sage, 1985), 128.
8. Karl E. Weick, *The Social Psychology of Organizing*, 13.
9. Eric M. Eisenberg and H. L. Goodall, Jr. *Organizational Communication* (New York: St. Martin's Press, 1993), 108.
10. Frederick W. Taylor, *Principles of Scientific Management* (New York: Harper, 1911).
11. Max Weber, *Essays on Sociology* (New York: Oxford University Press, 1947), 196–198.
12. Cheryl Hamilton, *Communicating for Results*, 4th ed. (Belmont, CA: Wadsworth Publishing Company, 1993), 49.
13. Fritz J. Roethlisberger and William J. Dickson, *Management and the Worker* (Cambridge, MA: Harvard University Press, 1939).

14. Jeffrey Pfeffer and G. B. Salancik, *The External Control of Organizations: A Resource Dependence Perspective* (New York: Harper & Row, 1978).
15. Nancy A. Euske and Karlene H. Roberts, "Evolving Perspectives in Organizational Theory: Communication Implications," in *Handbook of Organizational Communication*, eds. Fredric Jablin, Linda Putnam, Karlene Roberts, and Lyman Porter (Newbury Park, CA: Sage Publications, 1987), 58.
16. Adapted from a table in Dalmer Fisher, *Communication in Organizations*, 2d ed. (Minneapolis/St. Paul: West Publishing Company, 1993), 18.
17. Rosabeth Moss Kanter, *Men and Women of the Corporation* (New York: Basic Books, Inc., 1977), 166.
18. Ibid., 181.
19. Ibid., 177.
20. Terrence E. Deal and Allen A. Kennedy, *Corporate Cultures* (Reading, MA: Addison-Wesley Publishing Company, 1982).
21. R. Tagiuri, "The Concepts of Organizational Climate," in *Organizational Climate: Exploration of a Concept*, eds. R. Tagiuri and G. H. Litwin (Boston: Harvard University Press, 1968), 27.
22. Steve W. J. Kozlowski and Mary L. Doherty, "Integration of Climate and Leadership: Examination of a Neglected Issue," *Journal of Applied Psychology* 74 (1989): 549.
23. Raymond L. Falcione, Lyle Sussman, and Richard P. Herden, "Communication Climate in Organizations," in *Handbook of Organizational Communication* (Newbury, CA: Sage Publications, 1987), 203.
24. Marshall S. Poole and Robert D. McPhee, "A Structurational Analysis of Organizational Climate," in *Organizational Communication: An Interpretive Approach*, eds. Linda Putnam and Michael Pacanowsky (Newbury, CA: Sage Publications, 1983), 218.
25. W. Charles Redding, *Communication within the Organization: An Interpretive Review of Theory and Research* (New York: Industrial Communication Council, 1972).
26. W. Charles Redding, "Communication Research and the 'Rhetorical Environment,'" lecture accepting the Wayne Danielson Award for Distinguished Contributions to Communication Scholarship, Austin, Texas, November 10, 1993, 19.
27. Thomas N. Gilmore, "Leadership and Boundary Management," *Journal of Applied Behavioral Science* 18 (1982).
28. William Bergquist, *The Postmodern Organization* (San Francisco: Jossey-Bass Publishers, 1993), xii–xiii.
29. Eric M. Eisenberg and H. L. Goodall, Jr., Organizational Communication, 186–187.
30. William Bergquist, *The Postmodern Organization*, xiv.
31. Ibid., 101.
32. Ibid., 113.
33. Ibid.
34. Ibid., 136.
35. Burt Nanus, *Visionary Leadership* (San Francisco: Jossey-Bass Publishers, 1992), 173–177.

3

LEADERS AS COMMUNICATORS: A LOOK AT "STYLE"

Influenced by organizational and environmental factors, leaders interact with followers to constitute an organization and to accomplish its tasks. The *way* that a leader behaves toward followers, the set of behaviors he or she exhibits toward them, is an individual's leadership *style*. In this chapter we will look at traditional perspectives of leadership style as well as contemporary views of styles appropriate for organizational leadership. We also will consider the phenomenon of *communication style*, studied initially by scholars in the area of interpersonal communication but certainly applicable to an analysis of how leaders interact with organizational members. Because we are interested in organizational leadership from a communication perspective, the way leadership and communication styles are integrated in the process of leader–follower interaction is an important subject of study in this chapter.

A CHANGE IN RESEARCH FOCUS: FROM TRAITS TO STYLE

In Chapter 1 we reviewed the trait approach to leadership, noting the problems involved in crediting the process of leadership to one's personal characteristics. Beginning in the late 1940s, researchers began to focus more on how leaders behave rather than on what traits they possess. This approach developed for several reasons.

First, as was noted in Chapter 1, research findings relating traits to the exercise of leadership were inconsistent, and indeed unsatisfactory, when traits were studied without regard to situational context. Second, the era in which scholars began focusing on leadership behavior was one character-ized by increasing interest in what leaders *did* as opposed to what they *were* or seemed to be. The world was watching, and listening to, national leaders at the end of a world war attempting to create peaceful coexistence among former enemies. Additionally, corporations in the United States were increasing in size and economic stature. The leaders of many of these com-panies increasingly were voices of influence, not only to employees but also to external constituencies, like stockholders and customers, and indeed members of the public affected by the work and welfare of these organiza-tions. Such individuals included Thomas Watson of IBM, Henry Ford, and Conrad Hilton, to name just a few. Third, leadership research shifted its focus to leadership behavior, rather than traits, as the human relations approach to the study of organizations developed. Elton Mayo and his col-leagues (See Chapter 1) found that leader behavior could have an effect on performance and did have an effect on morale. Moreover, researchers real-ized that leadership behavior could be observed, and findings based on such observations were more valid in the creation and testing of theory. For all these reasons, scholars changed their research focal point from traits to "style," which is the set of behaviors exhibited by leaders toward followers.

THE NOTION OF "STYLE"

The way an author writes, the way an artist paints, the way a vocalist sings, is that person's "style." A country western singer and a rock star may sing the same song, but they will do so very differently. Figure skaters, golfers, even teachers, all have different styles of doing what they do. As individu-als we learn differently, parent differently, and we conduct our business dif-ferently. Moreover, the *perception* of how one writes, sings, or teaches becomes part of that individual's style.

Human beings both perceive *and* exhibit style—a concept difficult to measure or concretely describe. The perception and exhibition of style "are matters of intuition, and the training of intuitive judgment is impossible. Taste is cultivated, not trained; intuition is nurtured, not learned."[1] Our indi-vidual concepts of style are developed out of experiences. We have expecta-tions of what kind of style is appealing, successful, good and bad, or appro-priate, based on the information and perceptions that come from those experiences. The context within which experiences occur is the "environ-ment of language," either verbal or nonverbal.[2]

Exercising leadership depends on the use of verbal and nonverbal lan-guage on words and actions. The different ways that individuals combine actions and language into interactive patterns with followers evolve into an individual's leadership style or styles, as those patterns are perceived by followers. Leadership style is affected by the expectations followers have of how a leader should act, by the leader's perceptions of what behaviors are appropriate in the various roles he or she must assume, and what behaviors will have desired outcomes. A leader's perspective of role requirements depends on the expectations of followers, the task, his or her own needs, interests and values—in short, on the interrelationship of situational and personal characteristics. There is no one best style of leadership, as Fiedler reminds us in his contingency theory of leadership (see Chapter 1). Indeed, leaders may, and do, exhibit several styles in the process of working with organizational members to achieve organizational and followers' personal goals. The varying styles adopted by leaders depend on several factors:

1. The leader's personal characteristics
2. The characteristics of followers
3. The characteristics of the organization
4. Task goals
5. External constraints affecting the organization and therefore the leader

To illustrate the influence of these factors, let us consider a high-achieving leader focused on renewing a failing savings and loan institution that is comprised of loyal workers. This individual may exhibit behaviors that are both task *and* employee centered to achieve his organizational goal and to show his interest in protecting and fulfilling workers' personal goals. A leader building a new real estate company, with new employees, plenty of resources, and a promising niche in the company's business environment, may exhibit a different set of behaviors on a day-to-day basis because she is working in a different organizational and environmental context than the leader of an organization in trouble. In the next section we will review leadership styles identified by scholars in studies conducted since the late 1940s. While we will look at several sets of styles, note that they all differ, to varying degrees, in accordance with their emphasis either on accomplishing tasks or on meeting the personal and professional needs of followers. Good leaders must understand the importance of balancing an attention to task and a commitment to followers so that their styles can concurrently support the attainment of organizational *and* individual goals.

LEADERSHIP STYLE: TRADITIONAL PERSPECTIVES

In a landmark study of leadership in the late 1930s, Kurt Lewin and his associates conducted a study of how boys in groups at summer camp reacted to three different styles of leadership.[3] Some of the groups were assigned *autocratic* leaders—individuals who were trained to give instructions, wield power, be controlling, and make decisions with little or no participation from members of the group. Other groups were assigned *democratic* leaders—people who showed an interest in their group members and allowed participation in decision making. Finally, some groups were given *laissez-faire* leaders. These individuals were told to take no real part in group activities or to establish social relationships with the boys in their groups. The results of this study were as follows: There was more satisfaction among the boys in groups headed by democratic leaders, that is, they enjoyed their group work more than the other campers; and the most dissatisfied boys were in groups headed by autocratic leaders. However, there was no difference in the groups' productivity, regardless of the leadership style used within them.

Numerous studies have been conducted since Kurt Lewin's research to determine the differences between autocratic/directive and democratic/participative styles of leadership. A listing of the characteristics of each style is presented below.

Autocratic Leaders:
- Use one-way communication
- Give directions
- Use persuasion, if not coercion, to get tasks accomplished
- Are task focused (production oriented)

Democratic Leaders:
- Are considerate of the needs and feelings of followers
- Foster follower participation in decision making
- Consult with organizational members in the process of problem solving
- Are concerned with positive social relationships among followers

Since Kurt Lewin's pioneering study of autocratic and democratic leadership styles, numerous analyses have attempted to discover the advantages and disadvantages of each style. In general, such studies have concluded that democratic leadership may be more satisfying to followers, but autocratic leadership fosters productivity in the short term. In the long term, "the positive effects of democratic leadership are evident, especially if the employees' development, commitment, loyalty, and involvement are important to productivity."[4] According to Barge, democratic leadership is preferable to autocratic leadership for the following reasons:

1. Followers have the opportunity to express themselves.
2. The increased participation of followers in decision making equals improved quality of decision making.

3. The implementation of a solution is helped by involving those affected by that solution.[5]

Another significant set of leadership studies was conducted at Ohio State University by Stogdill and his associates beginning in the late 1940s. An interdisciplinary team of researchers focused on various activities conducted by leaders and identified two different behaviors: consideration and initiation of structure. *Consideration* was defined by the scholars as the extent to which a leader shows interest in the welfare of individuals and groups. A leader evidences consideration when he or she congratulates subordinates on work well done, treats them with respect and courtesy, and encourages follower suggestions and contributions in problem solving and decision making. *Initiating structure* was described as the extent to which a leader organizes and implements tasks. A leader exhibits this behavior by focusing communication on policies and procedures, meeting deadlines, and generally attending to task initiation and completion. In more recent research, when comparing leaders who exhibit consideration significantly more than initiation of structure, one of the more consistent findings is that those individuals have more satisfied subordinates, which is indicated by fewer absences and grievances, and lower turnover rates.[6]

Closely related to the democratic/autocratic and consideration/initiation of structure dichotomous styles are sets of behaviors that have been identified as relations-oriented versus task-oriented. A *relations-oriented* leader is primarily concerned with the development of supportive relationships among followers and between leaders and followers. A *task-oriented* leader's primary concern is obviously to complete "work" and fulfill organizational goals. In 1964 Robert Blake and Jane Mouton published a "managerial grid" that is a visual depiction of the integration of task- and relations-oriented behavior among leaders.[7] The grid is comprised of a vertical axis along which leaders are rated one to nine according to their interest in people and a horizontal axis along which leaders are rated one to nine for their interest in production (task completion). By plotting a leader's numerical ratings concerning attention to productivity and to people on this grid, five leadership styles emerge. The names of these styles, and the distinguishing characteristics of each one, are listed below.

Authority-obedience—maximum concern for production and a minimum concern for people

Country-club—minimum concern for production and maximum concern for people

Impoverished—minimum concern for both production and people

"Organization man"—a style that conforms with the status quo

Team management—maximum concern for both people and production

It is the team management style that Blake and Mouton recommend because it strikes a balance between a leader's concern for people and the fulfillment of organizational goals. As we shall see throughout this text, leaders must continually balance an attention to task and an attention to the needs of the people responsible for task completion.

Another "set" of styles studied by leadership researchers relates particularly to the process of decision making. Leaders exhibit behaviors along a behavioral continuum that reflects varying degrees of accepting, and even encouraging, follower participation in problem solving and decision making. At one end of the continuum, *directive* leaders make decisions with little or no input from followers and utilize one-way communication. *Participative* leaders, to varying degrees, invite opinions and information from followers. The following "options" for involving follower participation in decision making are available to leaders; they comprise an adapted version of a directive/participative leadership continuum offered by Vroom and Yetton, that begins with the most directive option.[8]

- A directive leader, without any consultation of followers, will solve a problem or make a decision.
- A leader may obtain information from subordinates and then make a decision.
- A leader may discuss a problem with subordinates individually, get ideas and suggestions, and then make a decision.
- A leader may discuss a problem with subordinates as a group, then make a decision after receiving suggestions collectively.
- A leader may create and evaluate alternatives for problem solving with followers individually and make the decision jointly with them.
- The leader may create and evaluate alternatives for problem solving with followers as a group, and jointly make the decision.

A final option is when a leader delegates a problem to a subordinate, gives him or her the relevant information needed for decision making, and that individual then makes the decision.[9]

Compared to directive leadership, participative leadership may be time consuming in its attempts to involve multiple opinions in the process of decision making and problem solving. Additionally, it may not be appropriate in crisis or deadline situations when a decision needs to be made quickly, or in organizations where directive leadership is the expected norm, such as the armed forces and sports teams. Indeed, while subordinates may prefer participative leadership because of the enhanced role it provides them in decision making, in crisis circumstances they may even support the use of directive leadership. In general, however, there are several advantages of participative leadership, including those identified by W. P. Anthony.

1. It stimulates more peaceful superior–subordinate relations.
2. It increases employee commitment to the organization.
3. It creates greater trust in management.
4. It provides for greater ease in managing subordinates.
5. It improves the quality of decisions.
6. It improves upward communication in the form of feedback from subordinates.
7. It improves teamwork within the organization.[10]

Nevertheless, it is important to remember that most leaders must exhibit directive *and* participative behaviors, but with varying frequency and in differing degrees.

The behaviors that participative leaders exhibit depend on several situational factors, including task characteristics, follower personality characteristics, follower desire to participate, and the position of the leader in the organization, that is, the relative power of that individual.[11] As Bernard Bass has written: "Participation is indicated when the subordinates' acceptance, satisfaction, and commitment are important and when subordinates have the required information. But direction can also be effective when structure is needed or when the leader has the necessary information and the quality of the decision is more important than is the commitment of the subordinates."[12]

Democratic, relations-oriented, and participative leadership styles are *follower-focused* styles. Autocratic, task-oriented, and directive leadership styles are *task-focused* styles. While we may associate task-focused styles with increased performance, and follower-focused styles with increased morale and satisfaction among subordinates, it is important to remember that leaders behave in different ways, at different times, because they encounter daily different situational contexts. Indeed, consider the following propositions offered by Bass that guide a "situational" approach to the notion of "style."[13]

1. Leadership styles vary considerably among individuals.
2. Some leaders are primarily interested in task accomplishment; others in development and maintenance of good social relationships; others do both.
3. The most effective style is one that varies with a given situation.
4. The best attitudinal style is high-task and high-relations oriented.

As is previously stated in this book, leadership is a process dependent on the interrelated behaviors of leaders and followers. This focus on behaviors, as opposed to traits, emphasizes the importance of modifying styles to fit varying situations, including the changing behaviors exhibited by followers. Therefore, it is appropriate that we review a leadership style that depends on the relationship between task and relational behaviors and the situational context in which a leader finds himself or herself.

The Situational Leadership Style

Hersey and Blanchard have analyzed both task- and follower-focused styles of leadership. They consider *task behavior* "the extent to which the leader engages in spelling out the duties and responsibilities of an individual or group," and *relational behavior* "the extent to which the leader engages in two-way or multi-way communication" for the purposes of listening, encouraging, facilitating, and giving socioemotional support to followers. Thus, they have identified four styles of leadership.[14] Style 1 is exhibited by a leader who is high-task oriented and low-relationship oriented. Style 2 is characteristic of a leader who is both high-task oriented and high-relationship oriented. Style 3 is found among leaders in situations where they are high-relationship oriented and low-task oriented, and Style 4 is seen under circumstances when leaders are low-relationship oriented and low-task oriented.

According to Hersey, there are several factors that affect leadership effectiveness in certain situations and therefore the impact of a given style. These factors include:

- Leader attitudes and behaviors
- Follower attitudes and behaviors, and the interaction of them with those of the leader
- Associates of the leader who are needed to help attain organizational goals
- Organizational values, history, and traditions
- Job demands, or the followers' perceptions of their work
- Time constraints
- The interaction of all the above[15]

Hersey also emphasizes that leadership style is based on the leader–follower relationship, which depends in part on the followers' readiness to accomplish a specific task. To him, situational leadership involves the interplay among how much task behavior a leader provides, how much relationship behavior he or she exhibits, and followers' readiness levels. The "situational leadership model" relates different levels of readiness to the four leadership styles. The interaction of Style 1 with low levels of readiness may result in leaders exhibiting a style identified as "telling"—providing instructions and closely supervising followers. Style 2, under circumstances of low to moderate levels of readiness, results in leaders "selling"—explaining decisions and providing opportunities for followers to "buy into" the leader's idea or goal. When Style 3 interacts with moderate to high levels of readiness, "participating" behavior emerges—leaders and followers share ideas and facilitate decision making. Finally, Style 4, in combination with high levels of readiness, may result in "delegating" where the responsibility for decision making and implementation is given to followers.

While these combinations may seem complicated, the important contribution of the situational leadership model is the notion of follower readiness as a component of the leadership process. The more followers are ready and willing to participate in task accomplishment, the more responsibility they are given. More importantly, however, the notion of situational leadership styles focuses on flexible, adaptable leader behavior, where stress is placed on the need to treat individuals *as* individuals, not as a nameless, faceless group of workers. This notion also emphasizes that leaders can do more than adapt to a situation; they can change it by enhancing the skills, motivation, and organizational commitment of followers. Additionally, *leadership behavior* can be exhibited in varying degrees of skillfulness. "Even though a particular style of leadership is appropriate in a given situation, it will not be effective unless the leader has sufficient skill in using that style of leadership."[16]

Contemporary Looks at "Traditional" Leadership Styles

While many leadership theorists and researchers have studied leadership styles as being either task or follower focused, or possessing varying degrees of each, a few scholars in recent years have adopted new approaches to the study of leadership styles.

Fram and DuBrin, for instance, have analyzed whether certain leaders have short-range or long-range time span orientation (TSO). That is, they study whether leadership behaviors focus on short-term or long-range goal setting and achievement.[17]

A leader with short-range TSO exhibits the following characteristics in his or her leadership behaviors:

- Demands frequent information and feedback from followers
- Believes in short-range planning
- Maintains tight control over employees
- Expects quick results from subordinates
- Focuses more on details than concepts

- Spends considerable time in contact with subordinates
- Prefers oral communication

A leader with long-range TSO exhibits the following characteristics:

- Is content with infrequent information and feedback
- Prefers long-range planning
- Exercises loose control over subordinates
- Is content to wait a long time for results
- Focuses more on concepts than details
- Spends a modest amount of time in contact with employees
- Prefers decisions in writing

Thus, time span orientation is another way of looking at leadership style, and is another way of analyzing sets of leadership behaviors.

Living in a global society, it is always important to remember that research on leadership style also has been conducted in countries other than the United States. In Japan, for instance, Jyuji Misumi named and studied two leadership styles he identifies as the following: *Performance*, characterized by problem-solving and goal-achievement behaviors, and *Maintenance*, characterized by promoting resolution of conflict, giving encouragement and support, and promoting the fulfillment of subordinate needs.[18] As one can readily see, these styles are variations of task-oriented and relations-oriented behaviors. Misumi suggests that the "best" leadership style is performance/maintenance—a balance between the two in which task performance is expedited and the leader concurrently pays attention to subordinate feelings. He also acknowledges that some "leaders" exhibit behaviors with low emphasis on both performance and maintenance; a style to be avoided because it illustrates the absence of leadership.

Time span orientation and the performance/maintenance comparison represent contemporary versions of the leadership styles that most theorists and researchers have studied for over fifty years. They represent an emphasis on task or on organizational/group members and their needs, and vary in the degree to which a leader focuses on one or the other. However, in the latter part of the twentieth century a different conceptualization of leadership and leadership style has emerged. It is rooted in the need for leaders to adapt to and master rapid and continuous change.

TRANSFORMATIONAL LEADERSHIP

Rather than "framing" the notion of leadership from the viewpoint of who predominantly makes decisions or wields power in the leader–follower relationship, or to what degree a leader focuses on task as opposed to relational concerns within a group or organization, the study of leadership in the last fifteen years has concentrated on a different conceptualization of the process and its participants.

In 1978, political scientist James MacGregor Burns suggested the term "transforming" or "transformational" leadership:

> *Leaders can . . . shape and alter and elevate the motives and values and goals of followers through the vital* teaching *role of leadership. This is* transforming *leadership. The premise of this leadership is that, whatever the separate interests persons might hold, they are presently or potentially united in the pursuit of "higher" goals, the realization of which is tested by the achievement of significant change that represents the collective or pooled interests of leaders and followers.*[19]

Such leadership, Burns suggested, is elevating and moral, and through it "both leaders and followers are raised to more principled levels of judgment."[20] Transforming leadership, he contended, lifts people into their better selves.

Organizational and managerial theorists have applied the concept of transformational leadership to studies in organizational settings. As we shall see, this leadership is more than a style. While it may also be observed as a set of behaviors, it is much more. It is a *view of the world* that affects leader relationships with followers in the pursuit of organizational goals. Inherent in this relationship are the following assumptions:

- The leader is a change agent.
- The leader emphasizes self-fulfillment among followers.
- The leader seeks to accomplish organizational goals through motivation and intellectual stimulation of followers.

Any discussion of transformational leadership is best begun by comparing it to *transactional* leadership in which the relationship between leaders and followers is based on a series of exchanges. A transactional leader, for instance, creates the expectation that a subordinate will be paid a fair amount for a fair day's work. For working late two hours, this leader agrees to give an employee two hours off on another day. Rewards are *contingent* upon desired follower behavior, and may consist of praise, pay increases, bonuses, promotions, and so on. The advantage of this approach to leadership is that the relationship between followers and leaders is prescribed and clear. Followers know their rewards are contingent on the completion of work; "punishments" (e.g., docked pay, no salary increase, no promotion) are expected when work is not completed. This relationship fosters efficiency, but does not focus on the self-development of subordinates, and fulfillment of their personal goals. This leadership "style" is most interested in the accomplishment of organizational goals. Nevertheless, there are positive elements in the contingent reward process. When superiors use explicit instructions, behave consistently toward followers, and communicate frequently about job-related matters; and when subordinates are involved in setting performance standards and engaging in frequent performance reviews, successful performance and commensurate rewards may occur.[21] However, while some organizations and some activities in organizations may benefit from transactional leadership, it is not the process needed by organizations aspiring to change and thrive.

Understanding the need for the revitalization of many of this society's organizations and institutions in the last years of the twentieth century, Noel Tichy, a management theorist, has called for a "new brand" of leader to guide major change efforts within organizations.

> We call these new leaders transformational leaders, for they must create something new out of something old: out of an old vision, they must develop and communicate a new vision and get others not only to see the vision but also to commit themselves to it. Where transactional managers make only minor adjustments in the organization's mission, structure, and human resource management, transformational leaders not only make major changes in these three areas but they also evoke fundamental changes in the basic political and cultural systems of the organization.[22]

According to Tichy, transformational leaders must be engaged in three "programs of activity": creating a vision; mobilizing organizational commitment to that vision; and institutionalizing the change effort by insuring that organizational members adopt new patterns of behavior. (In Chapter 6 we shall look specifically at how leaders use communication to initiate and implement the process of organizational change.)

Transformational leaders are change agents, that is, individuals who know how to effect major organizational change or transformations. Concurrently they are also leaders who are committed to changing and developing followers. Avolio and Gibbons have studied how individuals develop into transformational leaders during their lifetimes and offer the following antecedents for such development.[23] Such individuals:

- Have a predisposition to set high standards for achievement, which is a result of parental encouragement and expectations
- Have sufficient resources during childhood, even in a demanding or difficult family situation
- Learn how to deal with their emotions, including conflict and disappointment

- Have opportunities to exhibit leadership in a variety of settings as they grow and develop as individuals
- Possess a strong desire for personal development
- Participate in workshops and other developmental activities and establish and maintain relationships with role models
- View all their experiences as learning experiences

As individuals interested in the self-development of followers, transformational leaders share a defining characteristic: they develop feelings of self-efficacy among followers by "acknowledging previous accomplishments, providing emotional challenges, conveying high expectations, and modeling appropriate strategies for success."[24] More specifically, transformational leaders assist in the development of followers by assigning tasks that result in successful experiences, providing emotional challenges that enhance motivation, and conveying the importance of completed tasks.[25] These leaders are both follower-focused individuals—people who specifically strive to empower followers—and change agents. They are committed to guiding ongoing organizational change.

A major contribution to the study of transformational leadership is Bernard Bass's description of the *emotional* and *intellectual* components of such leadership; both are necessary to guide followers in the process of change while insuring their personal development.[26] According to Bass, the emotional component of transformational leadership is *charisma*. To him, this quality is not just an indescribable magnetism based on good looks and/or an appealing public image. It is an unseen element within leaders that arouses *their* needs to achieve, affiliate with others, and wield power. Their motives are passed on to others through communication. Inspiration, a subcomponent of charisma, is a quality that arouses and heightens motivation among followers.

According to Bass, the intellectual components of transformational leadership are *individualized consideration* and *intellectual stimulation*. The former is the process of giving as much responsibility as possible to individual followers so they may make the most of the talents they possess. It is an extension of the notion of "consideration," the set of leadership behaviors discussed earlier in this chapter as identified by Stogdill. Intellectual stimulation, such as providing information and opportunities for decision making, insures that followers conceptualize and comprehend the nature of the problems they face, and the resulting solutions. Together, these components foster self-fulfillment among followers in an organizational context experiencing continual change.

A discussion of transformational leadership should necessarily focus on leader–follower *behaviors*. However, it is interesting to note that some scholars have listed characteristics of transformational leaders to differentiate them from transactional managers. According to Noel Tichy and Mary Anne Devanna, such leaders:[27]

1. Identify themselves as change agents. They are not afraid of change in organizations; indeed they welcome it and enjoy the challenge of initiating and managing such change. Transformational leaders understand that change is really a constant in organizational life, particularly in innovative, learning organizations who must continually renew themselves in order to survive.

2. Are courageous. Initiating change is not always popular. Human beings are notoriously afraid of change in their daily lives—at home and at work. Transformational leaders risk their own popularity to champion innovation, for the benefit of organizational development and the concurrent development of individual followers.

3. Believe in people. They are follower-focused and believe that individuals work in organizations out of a primordial interest in contributing to the welfare of the group. In short, transformational leaders believe in Douglas McGregor's notion of Theory Y. (See Chapter 1.)

4. Are value driven. They possess internal moral standards that guide the "soul" as well as the activities of the organization. Ray Kroc, founder of McDonald's, emphasized the importance of quality, cleanliness, service, and value in the operation of his fast-food restaurants. These values remain part of that organization's culture today.

5. Are life-long learners. Transformational leaders, who guide changing organizations, by definition guide learning organizations. These individuals are always scanning the environment for information, are interested in new ways of doing things, and are continually involved in their own personal development. Such people are apt to be among those trying to learn a second or third language, or are avid readers on airplanes and during vacations.

6. Have the ability to deal with complexity, ambiguity, and uncertainty. These individuals live and flourish in a state of ongoing change. Problems with hard-to-find solutions, complex decisions that must be made, countervailing influences on alternatives, and options from which they must choose to move their organizations forward, are all components of an uncertain environment in which they function and excel.

7. Are visionaries. Transformational leaders look at not only what is, but what they want an organization to be. They are not only follower focused; they are future focused.

Finally, the author adds a final characteristic to Tichy's list.

8. A transformational leader is a good communicator and/or understands the importance of communication within an organization. He or she may not be a good public speaker, but such a person will appreciate the ability to interact effectively in small groups and in one-to-one conversations. These individuals are good listeners, and understand the importance of two-way communication, feedback, and follower input. They know when to use different modes of communication, for example, the memo versus face-to-face communication.

Through actions or speech, individuals exhibit different "styles" of leadership within organizations, and they do so in their own unique ways of interacting with other human beings. Few researchers who study leadership have applied the concept of "communication style" to their work; it is a notion that comes from interpersonal communication theory. However, leaders like other individuals communicate the content of messages in varying ways, and those ways affect the interactive relationship between leaders and followers. Because this text focuses on the exercise of leadership from a communication perspective, it is important to consider the notion of "communication style" and how ultimately communication and leadership styles interrelate in the conduct of organizational life.

COMMUNICATION STYLE

In Chapter 1 we discussed the notion that leadership is the management of meaning, the framing of a context using actions and utterances. The content of a message consists of *what* is communicated. However, the verbal and nonverbal behavior that frames a message—the *way* that content is communicated—comprises one's communication style or "the signals that are provided to help process, interpret, filter, or understand literal meaning."[28] Style gives form to content. In the same way that two oral interpretations of the same poem may communicate that poem differently, different communication styles affect the perception of a message or set of messages.

Everyone, whether a leader or not, has a communication style, or even exhibits several styles, just like leaders may exhibit a variety of leadership styles depending on the situational and organizational context. Communication style is observable; we can determine an individual's style or styles by observing his or her interactions with others.

In his seminal book describing the concept of communication style, Robert Norton emphasizes:

> The way a person communicates to a large extent determines self-identity and affects others' perceptions of the individual. The person's communicator style contributes to and reflects whether the person likes the self. It influences both the amount and kinds of rewards and punishments the person perceives from others.[29]

Just as leadership styles are comprised of leadership behaviors, communication styles consist of sets of communication behaviors, such as gestures, facial expressions, tone and volume of voice, posture, frequency and duration of eye contact, and one's use of pauses. The conscious and/or unconscious use of these behaviors frame the content of a message, and over time, one develops a set of generally consistent behaviors that become one's communication style or styles. As is the case with leadership styles, communication styles are variable but sufficiently patterned. If one was to wear a small recording device for a few weeks or months, transcriptions of its tapes would probably allow a researcher to identify the communication style(s) used predominantly by that individual. Norton has identified the following types of styles:[30]

- Dominant—evidenced by physical manifestations such as direct and sustained eye contact; voice loudness; voice modulation. This person responds longer and louder in a conversation with other individuals.
- Dramatic—uses exaggeration, stories, and metaphors to highlight or understate content
- Contentious—typified by negative dominant characteristics, for example sustained eye contact accompanied with a frown or an angry tone of voice
- Animated—characterized by frequent and sustained eye contact, and the use of many facial expressions and gestures
- Relaxed—identified by lack of tension in the voice and in nonverbal behaviors; a relaxed style may reflect calmness, confidence or both
- Attentive—typified by behaviors such as leaning forward to listen, and responding verbally and nonverbally to other persons in a conversation; an emphasis on active, empathetic listening
- Open—characterized by behaviors that reflect a conversational, affable, gregarious individual who is self-disclosive in conversations with others
- Friendly—identified as manifesting a range of behaviors from a simple lack of hostility to deep intimacy
- Impression-leaving—manifested through a memorable style of communicating. This style is rarely observed. Most of us do not communicate in ways that are impression-leaving, that is, in ways that are so unique we are known for the way we communicate interpersonally. Exceptions might include a favorite pastor or rabbi, a well-respected psychotherapist, a successful mediator, or your closest friend. Such individuals possess verbal and nonverbal characteristics that are memorable to those with whom they interact.

One can look to American presidents as organizational leaders *inside* the White House to see examples of the communication styles described above.

According to several of his former staff members, Ronald Reagan often told jokes or stories at the beginning of meetings to relieve tension among participants.[31] In these settings he was exhibiting a dramatic communication style. During policy deliberations affecting the conduct of the Vietnam War, Lyndon Johnson was identified as contentious in some meetings with his aides. Gerald Ford exhibited an attentive style, not only because he was characterized by staff as a careful listener during his interactions with them, but because he reflected this style in his approach to receiving guests, including foreign ambassadors. On the day that foreign emissaries were invited to meet the president during the Nixon administration, each ambassador was put in a different ceremonial room in the White House so that Nixon could move from room to room and exchange only one or two minutes of pleasantries with the dignitaries. Gerald Ford, however, invited each ambassador into the Oval Office where a ceremonial function became a substantive discussion.[32] Jimmy Carter, who preferred sending memos to staff rather than participating in meetings with them, was perceived as a dominant communicator when he did interact interpersonally. He has been described as cold, direct, business-like, and detached.[33] Additionally, Zbigniew Brzezinski, Carter's national security advisor, has written that Carter sometimes sent conflicting cues to staff and other administration officials in face-to-face encounters. According to Brzezinski, the president used several phrases in his interactions that meant the opposite of what he actually said. "I understand" meant "I don't want to argue with you any more, but I don't agree with you"—an attempt by Carter to pacify the person. "I will stand firm" meant he might change his position. "This doesn't bother me at all" meant he might indeed be deeply troubled.[34] Obviously it was important for staff to understand the intended meanings behind the president's words, and Brzezinski indicates that misunderstandings often were created among staff when the president used these phrases. A nonverbal component of Carter's communication style(s) was his smile, and his former advisor for national security perceived that he used different smiles in different settings.

> *There was first of all the genial smile for public consumption. I was initially deceived by it because it seemed so warm and so forthcoming, and yet once you got to know him you knew that this was an outward smile, one with little individual affection in it. . . . Then there was the smile which he used to mask anger. More often than not, when angry, he would smile even while expressing displeasure, but only if one knew him well did one sense that behind the mask was unadulterated fury. Then there was a shy, relaxed smile, the expression of the individual at ease, which Carter revealed only occasionally to his intimates.[35]*

The communication styles of presidents and other organizational leaders are shaped by their pasts, personal characteristics, and the communicative experiences encountered during a lifetime. While such styles may be manipulated to a certain degree, just like leadership styles, the behaviors that comprise them are embedded reflections of self-identities.

Communication styles are *observable*; that is, one characteristic common to all of them. They are also *multifaceted*; people possess aspects of several styles and can exhibit them in multiple combinations. For instance, it is possible to communicate in friendly, open, and animated ways. Additionally, styles are multicollear; they overlap.[36] Being a dominant and relaxed communicator reflects one who is confident. Style variables may also be clustered to create a style greater than the sum of its parts. For instance, a talkative individual, and one we might expect to be a transformational leader, exhibits active communication behaviors and may be characterized as dominant, dramatic, animated, contentious, and open. An attentive, friendly and relaxed person may be a more passive communicator—and one who is receiver oriented.[37]

As is mentioned earlier, studies of communication style have come from the area of interpersonal communication. How might one apply this concept to the study of leadership communication? What are the styles of follower-focused versus task-focused leaders? In recent years, some scholars have attempted to answer these questions by analyzing the association of certain communication styles with specific leadership styles.

One study of a midwestern hospital, for instance, evidenced the relationship between managerial and communication styles. Those individuals identified as democratic leaders were perceived as animated, attentive, and friendly. Autocratic leaders were thought to be dominant communicators, and laissez-faire leaders (exhibiting no real leadership behaviors) were perceived as friendly and attentive.[38] In another study of two different organizations, a life insurance company and a hospital, managers rated as outstanding and definitely above average were perceived as being open, animated, and less contentious than other managers.[39] Over twenty years ago, before the notion of communication style was well studied, and certainly before it was applied to research on how leaders communicate, W. Charles Redding suggested that better supervisors are good listeners, are adept at giving instructions, are open, sensitive and persuasive as opposed to coercive, and like to use oral communication to interact within their organizations.[40] In a specific study of leadership communication style in an organization in the mid-1980s, two researchers found that

. . . perceptions of a leader being a warm, open, relaxed, and attentive communicator were strongly correlated with subordinate satisfaction with

*supervision; and subordinates were less satisfied with leaders who were
perceived as being dominant in social situations, who were very expressive
nonverbally, who dramatized extensively, and who regularly told jokes, stories, and anecdotes.*[41]

Based on their research, these scholars, Douglas Baker and Daniel
Ganster, suggest that certain communication styles are more appropriate for
leaders to use than others, depending on the content of the message they
wish to communicate. For instance, the dominant style may be better used
to communicate a goal-setting message. A friendly style is appropriate when
offering rewards and recognition for work well done. An attentive style is
useful when listening to employee concerns. In other words, when communicating in organizations, or in any setting for that matter, "style" is the
"dress" for content.

Communication styles exhibited by organizational leaders may vary for
a variety of reasons. A leader may, for instance, change his or her communication style depending on the organizational context. An open and friendly
communication style may be expected in a social service agency. A dominant
and contentious style may be anticipated in a military organization. Specific
communicative settings also influence the use of a particular style. An
impending deadline may cause a leader to adopt a dominant, if not contentious, communication style. A relaxed and attentive style may be used to
mediate conflict between two subordinates. A dramatic style may be used to
motivate individuals in an organizational change effort.

Another reason communication style among leaders may vary relates to
the perceptions of style among one's superiors, subordinates, and peers. The
amount of time one spends interacting with a leader affects his or her perception of that individual's communication style. If one sees a vice-president
only once or twice a month at a meeting, and he is contentious both times,
that person may perceive him to be contentious all the time. However,
another individual may interact with the vice-president on a weekly or daily
basis, and find him dominant but rarely contentious.

Additionally, it is important to note that leaders may manipulate their
style of communication not only to meet varied situational demands, but to
relate to each individual in the group or organization as a separate "audience." For instance, Richard Nixon apparently used profanity with some
members of his White House staff because he knew that language served to
motivate them to action more quickly. He never cursed at other individuals
because he knew they would not be motivated by, and indeed would resent
any perceived verbal abuse.[42]

Organizational leaders, therefore, may change their communication
styles to accommodate organizational context, specific situational demands,
or to adapt to individual listeners. As a result, "adaptive and flexible

communication behavior, based upon accurate situational diagnosis, may . . . be a necessary condition for effective managerial performance" and certainly for the performance of leadership.[43]

The "marriage" possibilities between notions of leadership and communication styles require much more research, particularly in field settings. It is relatively easy to suggest that a dominant communication style should be expected from a task-oriented leader. However, that same style also serves a transformational leader well as change efforts are initiated and maintained and as he or she seeks to involve followers in organizational problem solving and decision making. On a daily basis, organizational leaders face complex situations that require adaptations in their communication behaviors with a variety of constituencies, and individuals within constituencies. A colleague of the author's has remarked that "we are what we say—more than what we eat."[44] That is an important observation for leaders to take to heart. As they manage meaning, that is, interpret information and events so that followers may make sense out of the "organization" around them, they must understand the power of verbal and nonverbal communication. In the next three chapters we will look at this power as it is unleashed by leaders in the process of creating and sustaining organizational culture, making decisions, and facilitating organizational change.

SUMMARY

The *way* that an individual exhibits leadership behaviors through interaction with others is his or her leadership style. Additionally, the *perception* of how that individual enacts the role of leadership becomes part of that style. Concepts of style are developed out of experiences, and the perceptions that come from those experiences. Leadership style is affected by the expectations followers have of how a leader should act, by the leader's perceptions of what behaviors are appropriate in the various roles he or she must assume, and what behaviors will have desired outcomes. There is no one best style of leadership—leaders may exhibit several styles in their interactions with organizational members. The styles adopted by leaders depend on several factors, including: (1) the leader's personal characteristics; (2) the characteristics of followers; (3) the characteristics of the organization; (4) task goals; and (5) external constraints affecting the organization and therefore the leader.

Styles of leadership that are follower-focused—that are interested in the fulfillment of organizational members' goals as well as organizational goals—include democratic/participative/relations-oriented styles. Styles that are task-focused, that show primary concern for the accomplishment of task and the fulfillment of organizational goals, are autocratic/directive/

task-oriented styles. Rather than look at leadership style from the viewpoint of who predominantly makes decisions or wields power in the leader–follower relationship, or to what degree a leader focuses on task as opposed to relational concerns, the prevalent opinion among many who study leadership is that styles vary in accordance with the situational context in which a leader finds himself or herself.

Within the last fifteen years, a conceptualization of leadership has evolved that concurrently looks at a style of leadership that is change-oriented as well as focused on the self-fulfillment of organizational members. *Transformational* leadership is more than a style, it is also a reflection of a leader's basic philosophy about relating to other individuals through motivation and intellectual stimulation. This notion is in contrast to transactional leadership, in which the relationship between leaders and followers is based on a series of exchanges. Rewards are contingent upon followers exhibiting desired behaviors.

Through verbal and nonverbal communication, individuals exhibit different styles of leadership in organizations. The way that an individual communicates, that is, the way content is communicated, is his or her *communication* style, a concept from interpersonal communication theory. In the same way that two movie versions of the same book communicate that text differently, different communication styles affect the perception of a message or set of messages. Communication styles consist of sets of behaviors comprised of gestures, facial expressions, tone and volume of voice, posture, frequency and duration of eye contact, and one's use of pauses. These behaviors frame the content of a message, and over time, they develop as one's communication style or styles. Indeed, one may exhibit more than one communication style; they are variable but sufficiently patterned. Leaders exhibit a variety of communication styles, including dominant, dramatic, attentive, and animated styles. They may change their styles to accommodate organizational context, specific situational demands, or to adapt to individual listeners.

The interrelationship between leadership and communication styles requires more research, especially in field settings. Organizational leaders face situations on a daily basis that require adaptations in their leadership behaviors. Studying leaders in the environments in which they interact with organizational members to create and sustain "organization" greatly enhances our knowledge of the interrelationship between leadership and communication.

QUESTIONS TO CONSIDER

1. What are some of the communication behaviors that are characteristic of follower-focused leadership styles? Task-focused styles?

2. Define "situational leadership."

3. Describe the leadership behaviors of those who have short-range time span orientation (TSO). What are the leadership behaviors of those who have long-range TSO?

4. Define and compare the components of transactional and transformational leadership.

5. What communication styles might be exhibited by follower-focused leaders? By task-focused leaders?

CASE PROBLEM

At the turn of the century a famous film actor/director dreamed of reinvigorating a year-round institute for promising young directors and screenwriters. The institute was then located in Burbank, California. However, she developed a ten-year plan, bought land in the Rocky Mountains near Denver, and sought funding from major Hollywood studios to move the institute to Colorado.

Although most of her colleagues in Hollywood refused to "sink" their money into an educational, rather than a commercial, venture, she initiated the construction of a five-building complex using her own money. She hired Hollywood professionals and faculty from prestigious film schools to run the institute and teach classes, and she delegated all operational responsibilities to them, confident in their abilities and commitment to the task of "growing" new talent.

She instilled her beliefs in the pursuit of excellence, emphasizing that courses would focus on the importance of artistic creativity, technological innovation, and the necessity of hard work. She spoke with small groups of students and faculty on a regular basis, to share her knowledge of filmic techniques. To practice what she preached, she regularly visited film studios in the United States and abroad to view the latest cinematic technologies used in the motion picture industry. By the year 2025 she had created the best organization of its kind in the world.

What leadership style(s) has this individual exhibited? Identify the characteristics and behaviors that justify your answer.

ENDNOTES

1. Leland H. Roloff, *The Perception and Evocation of Literature* (Glenview, IL: Scott, Foresman & Company, 1973), 266.
2. Ibid., 267.
3. Kurt Lewin, R. Lippitt, and R. K. White, "Patterns of Aggressive Behavior in Experimentally Created 'Social Climates,'" *Journal of Social Psychology* 10 (1939).
4. Bernard M. Bass, *Bass and Stogdill's Handbook of Leadership*, 3d ed. (New York: The Free Press, 1990), 435.
5. J. Kevin Barge, *Leadership, Communication Skills for Organizations and Groups* (New York: St. Martin's Press, 1994), 38 and 40.

6. Mahfooz A. Ansari, *Managing People at Work* (New Delhi: Sage Publications, 1990), adapted from p. 23.
7. Robert Blake and Jane Mouton, *The Managerial Grid* (Houston: Gulf, 1964).
8. V. Vroom and P. Yetton, *Leadership and Decision Making* (Pittsburgh: University of Pittsburgh Press, 1973), 13.
9. V. Vroom and A. Jago, "Decisionmaking as a Social Process: Normative and Descriptive Models of Leader Behavior," *Decision Science* 5 (1974): 745.
10. W. P. Anthony, *Participative Management* (Reading, MA: Addison-Wesley Publishing Company, 1978), 27–29.
11. Alan Bryman, *Leadership and Organizations* (London: Routledge and Kegan Paul, 1986), 101–104.
12. Bernard M. Bass, *Bass and Stogdill's Handbook of Leadership*, 471.
13. Ibid., 488.
14. Paul Hersey, *The Situational Leader* (New York: Warner Books, 1984), 31–32.
15. Ibid., 43–47.
16. Gary A. Yukl, *Leadership in Organizations* (Englewood Cliffs, NJ: Prentice-Hall, 1981), 144.
17. Eugene H. Fram and Andrew J. DuBrin, "Time-Span Orientation: A Key Factor of Contingency Management," in *Leadership*, ed. A. Dale Timpe (New York: Facts on File Publications, 1987).
18. Jyuji Misumi, *The Behavioral Science of Leadership* (Ann Arbor: University of Michigan Press, 1985).
19. James MacGregor Burns, *Leadership* (New York: Harper & Row, 1978), 425–426.
20. Ibid., 455.
21. R. J. Klimoski and N. J. Hayes, "Leader Behavior and Subordinate Motivation," *Personnel Psychology* 33 (1980).
22. Noel Tichy, "SMR Forum: The Leadership Challenge—A Call for the Transformational Leader," *Sloan Management Review* (Fall 1984): 59.
23. Bruce J. Avolio and Tracy C. Gibbons, "Developing Transformational Leaders: A Life Span Approach," in *Charismatic Leadership*, eds. J. A. Conger and R. N. Kanungo (San Francisco: Jossey-Bass Publishers, 1988), 289–290.
24. Ibid., 298.
25. Ibid.
26. Bernard M. Bass, *Leadership and Performance Beyond Expectations* (New York: The Free Press, 1985).
27. Noel Tichy and Mary Anne Devanna, *The Transformational Leader* (New York: John Wiley & Sons, 1986), 271–280.
28. Robert Norton, *Communicator Style* (Beverly Hills, CA: Sage Publications, 1983), 47.
29. Ibid., 14.
30. Ibid.
31. Patricia D. Witherspoon, *Within These Walls, a Study of Communication Between Presidents and Their Senior Staffs* (New York: Praeger, 1991), 14.
32. Ibid., 203.
33. Ibid., 204–207.
34. Zbigniew Brzezinski, *Power and Principle* (New York: Farrar, Straus, Giroux, 1983), 22.

35. Ibid., 21–22.
36. Robert Norton, *Communicator Style*, 48.
37. Ibid., 72–73.
38. P. H. Bradley and J. E. Baird, "Management and Communicator Style: A Correlational Analysis," *Central States Speech Journal* 28 (1977).
39. David A. Bednar, "Relationships between Communicator Style and Managerial Performance in Complex Organizations: A Field Study," *Journal of Business Communication* 19 (1982): 71.
40. W. Charles Redding, *Communication within the Organization: An Interpretive Review of Theory and Research* (New York: Industrial Communication Council, 1972).
41. Douglas D. Baker and Daniel C. Ganster, "Leader Communication Style: A Test of Average Versus Vertical Dyad Linkage Models," *Group and Organization Studies* 10 (Sept. 1985): 255.
42. Patricia D. Witherspoon, *Within These Walls*, 94.
43. David Bednar, "Relationships between Communicator Style and Managerial Performance in Complex Organizations: A Field Study," 73.
44. The author wishes to acknowledge this comment by Robert W. Hopper during a panel presentation on the development of multicultural courses for communication departments, College of Communication, The University of Texas at Austin, Austin, Texas, March 26, 1994.

4

LEADERS AS CREATORS AND SUSTAINERS OF ORGANIZATIONAL CULTURE

Since their first attempts to live and work together in groups, human beings have developed shared beliefs, goals, and activities through their interactions with each other. In turn, these communally created values and actions guided their continuing communication, and the endeavors that depended on group interactions, such as hunting, farming, or trading. Over time, people developed ways to identify with each other, such as language, symbols, and rituals, that communicated their uniqueness to themselves and to people outside their respective collectivities. Anthropologists study cultures as *ways of life* among groups, societies, and nations—ways of believing and behaving that create a group identity. One conceptualization of culture, from the viewpoint of cultural anthropology, is that it is a holistic set of patterned physical, psychological, and social products, as well as a shared body of meaning, views about world realities, perceptions, and values. It is created by societal members in their interactions, determines patterns of behaviors and feelings, and is transmitted from one generation to another through traditions.[1] These observations, as we shall see, aptly describe cultures within organizations.

An organizational culture is a way of life in a particular organization. In this chapter we begin with the premise that not only do organizations *have* their own cultures, organizations *are* cultures—systems of values, beliefs, artifacts—that are constituted through the process of communication. We will consider the roles that leaders assume in the development, continuation, and change of organizational cultures. Indeed, one approach to the study of leadership is a *cultural approach* which emphasizes that leadership is the management of meaning. Using language, actions, and symbols, leaders create and continually re-create a shared perception of reality among organizational members that helps them identify with, understand, and behave appropriately in the organization. Before analyzing the relationship between leadership and organizational culture, it is important to understand what organizational culture is, what its functions are, and the role communication plays in its creation and continuation.

CONCEPTS OF ORGANIZATIONAL CULTURE

A general definition of culture as applied to groups, societies, and/or nations states that it is "an historically transmitted pattern of meanings embodied in symbols, a system of inherited conceptions expressed in symbolic forms by means of which men communicate, perpetuate, and develop their knowledge about and attitudes toward life."[2] This is an appropriate definition for organizational culture as well. However, to understand what a culture is one must look at its parts, even though any culture is greater than the sum of its parts. For instance, the culture of a family includes: (1) the informal ways members have of communicating with each other, for example, using "inside" jokes; (2) how they feel about all the other persons in the family; (3) the home they live in; (4) their relationships to other family members outside their physical domain, such as grandparents and in-laws, and the behaviors they exhibit toward each other that illustrate those relationships; (5) the memories they hold, individually and collectively; and (6) the stories they tell to reflect those memories. These are just a few components of a family's culture, and yet a "family" is more than a collection of all these "parts." As these components suggest, the family culture is based on *shared* memories, feelings, and actions. Indeed, among the multitude of definitions that attempt to describe organizational culture, most emphasize that it is based on, or comprised of, shared meanings. As we look at some of these definitions, keep in mind that members of an organization are the communicating components of the process that continually constitutes culture; and they are simultaneously its products.

One of the more renowned contributors to the study of organizational culture and leadership is Edgar Schein, who has suggested that cultures in organizations are comprised of underlying assumptions, values, and artifacts shared by their members. To Schein, assumptions are unconsciously held beliefs; values are strategies, goals, and philosophies; and artifacts are visible organizational structures and processes.[3] According to Schein, an organizational culture is "a pattern of shared basic assumptions that have been invented, discovered, and/or developed by a group as it learns to cope with problems of external adaptation and internal integration. . . ."[4] Again, note not only the explicit reference to shared meanings, but also the implicit reference to communication and group interaction in the process of culture development.

To look more specifically at the "parts" of culture that help define it, consider Schein's "categories of phenomena" that he associates with organizational culture:

1. Observed behavioral regularities when people interact, including language, customs, and rituals
2. Group norms (standards of behavior and performance that evolve as people work together)
3. Stated values
4. Formal philosophy
5. Rules for getting along in the organization
6. Climate
7. Embedded skills—special competencies of group members in accomplishing tasks
8. Shared cognitive frames that guide members' perceptions and language
9. Shared meanings that emerge among organizational members as they interact
10. Root metaphors—images developed to characterize an organization like "family" or "team"[5]

The critical components of organizational culture that appear in most definitions include language, symbols, heroes, rituals, myths, values, beliefs, group norms, and communication practices and patterns. For instance, Disneyland has its own language: employees are "cast members" and tourists who come to the park are "guests"; the language is one characteristic of a "show." Its major symbol is Mickey Mouse, and its major hero is Walt Disney. One of its rituals is the evening fireworks display, which is the last performance of the day.

These components comprise culture, but many of the definitions of organizational culture continually emphasize that culture is a phenomenon created out of shared meanings constituted through communication. Such definitions emphasize that culture is comprised of patterns of interactions, stories that develop among organizational members, and systems of values and symbols that are given meaning through organizational processes and practices.

In short, organizational culture consists of both observable and unseen elements that are created through social interaction. Together these elements help organizational members identify with each other. For example, the beliefs, practices, and language of a Native American tribe create its identity;

these same components create a feeling of unity and guidelines for behavior among members of a sorority, a football team, a for-profit corporation, or a university.

What are the sources of culture? Where do these elements originate? Answers to these questions are important as we pursue an understanding of what organizational culture is and how it develops.

Sources of Organizational Culture

As we have emphasized, culture is created through the interactions of organizational members. This process is a dynamic one; it continually occurs as new members bring values and beliefs with them into the organization from the external environment. As a result, the *environment* within which an organization exists helps give birth to its culture. Hence, Chinese culture affects Chinese organizations. More specifically, the Italian American culture within a section of a city may affect a community center in that area. The economic, political, and social environment in a community affects its public schools.

The *organization's overarching goal and/or task* is another source of organizational culture: what members *do* affects, and is affected by, their values and beliefs and how and why they relate to one another. Additionally, as we will discuss later in this chapter, the beliefs, values, and visions of the founder of an organization and its subsequent leaders, are sources of organizational culture.

There are other factors that help shape a culture in addition to an organization's environment, its task, and its leadership. These factors include the organizational elements discussed in Chapter 2 that affect organizational leaders: structure (including the system of reporting relationships, policies, and procedures); resources (e.g., human, fiscal, technological); and climate (members' expectations of what it is like to work in the organization). Other factors that affect the formulation of culture might include influences from outside constituencies, such as competition, and perceptions of external audiences and constituencies of the organization.

No discussion of the sources, conceptualizations, and definitions of organizational culture would be complete without considering its functions. Indeed, phenomena often derive their definitions from their purposes.

Functions of Organizational Culture

Later in this section we will look specifically at the ways culture is used by those who comprise it—organizational members who are both the communicating components of the process that continually constitutes culture and who simultaneously become the products of the culture they create. In this dual relationship, culture serves a critical purpose: to help organizational members make sense of the information they receive in the form of organizational events, symbols, and relationships. Before analyzing a few of the ways it is used in organizations, it is beneficial to consider several general functions of organizational culture.[6]

1. It provides shared cognitions or knowledge about the organization so that members know how they are expected to act or behave. Formal rules and procedures, and information obtained informally through the grapevine or rumor mill, give people information about the dress code, the ways superiors should be addressed, and whether eight to five is strictly or loosely enforced as prescribed working hours.

2. It provides a shared sense of emotional involvement in, and commitment to, organizational values so members know the values they are expected to adopt, espouse, and reflect. Administrators at a small liberal arts college may emphasize the importance they place on teaching when new faculty are hired and promoted. This value then permeates the campus through faculty attitudes and behaviors toward students.

3. It defines the organization's visible and invisible boundaries to help distinguish members from nonmembers. IBM, 3M, and other large companies not only have physical boundaries around their buildings, employees also wear identification badges at work, and visitors wear badges identifying themselves as nonmembers of the organization. In part these badges are for security reasons, preventing company secrets from being stolen by representatives of competitor companies. However, they also give employees a sense of identification with the organization.

4. Organizational culture functions as a system of control, prescribing and prohibiting certain behaviors. The culture of a classroom or a school may be enacted by teachers, administrators, and counselors to create an environment conducive to learning. That is, rules may be adopted to punish disruptive behaviors, such as bringing weapons to school or talking disrespectfully to teachers. Another set of rules may reward constructive behaviors, such as regular attendance.

By establishing a system of control, culture may serve as a source of stability for the organization.[7] In the case of a school, control may mean fewer incidents of violence or cheating. Of course control also may mean diminished rights, privileges, or freedoms for organizational members, depending on the type of organization and on the leadership exhibited within it. The construction of a culture that values both control and freedom illustrates the need for leaders to understand the notion of "balance" in the creation and maintenance of organizational beliefs, values, and behavioral norms.

An organization's culture is essentially the outward manifestation of its inner "self." It reflects itself in the communication among organizational members, and in their interactions with individuals external to the organization. In this sense, culture is a reflection of a "society" that shares a common purpose; it is people who are continually involved in pursuing shared goals. While the major purposes of an organization's culture may be to help members make sense out of their immediate environment, and reflect what an organization is "about" to its external audiences, stakeholders, and constituencies, there are specific ways that culture is used in organizations that are particularly critical to the exercise of leadership. These ways are presented below.

The Use of Culture for Identification and Affiliation.   As creators of organizations, and those responsible for the subsequent development of those organizations, founders understand that culture helps individuals identify with an organization. Using shared values, stories, heroes, rituals, and ceremonies, leaders help establish a "common ground" among organizational members on which they feel comfortable treading together. If one identifies with not only a building, but the people and what they represent in that building, one tends to want to continue an affiliation with that organization. One identifies emotionally, and affiliates behaviorally, with the organization and the goals, values, and symbolic manifestations of that organization.

The Use of Culture to Process Information.   As organizational members interact with one another, they "gather" information about organizational values, beliefs, and expectations of behavior. In short, members collect a whole host of important organizational dimensions that help them understand how to feel like, and be, an accepted person in the organizational culture. As information is gathered, stored, and used over time, individuals develop "schemas" or knowledge structures that in turn are used to process subsequent information. For instance, during the first months a person works in a McDonald's restaurant, she may hear stories about the hamburger chain's founder, Ray Kroc. She will read and hear directions for frying meat and French fries and operating the soft drink machine. She will hear stories about other employees. She will become familiar with the symbols of McDonald's, such as the golden arches, the "language" of fast-food ordering (Big Mac, McRib, McDLT, etc.) As all this information is processed and stored, it becomes a schema, or knowledge structure. Subsequent information about McDonald's will be processed using this schema to form perceptions about people and events, guide social interactions with employees and customers, and solve problems. In other words, after a schema has developed, information is filtered through it "to be interpreted, generally in ways that are shared by organizational members."[8]

An organizational culture itself affects how information is collected, disseminated, and used, because the values, attitudes, and behaviors that comprise it affect these processes. Indeed, the process of organizing necessarily puts constraints on information acquisition and use because organizational members cannot assimilate all the information available in an organization—and none of them wants to. People have physiological and technological limits that constrain how much information they can, or are willing to, assimilate before making a decision. However, cultural limits usually affect of information processing before organizational members reach their physiological and technological limits. That is because "information gathering and information processing are . . . social skills and . . . far from pushing these skills to the limit, they deliberately stop way short of that limit. Often enough, far from seeking information, they deliberately shed it. They rely on rules of thumb, on proverbs, on sixth senses, and on other similar socially induced shortcuts."[9] These shortcuts are learned in an organizational culture and may reflect how certain cultures value information and hold as well as exercise a bias in its acquisition, analysis, and use. As we shall discuss in Chapter 4, organizational leaders must be sure that information bias does not adversely affect the process of decision making. We will consider the notion of an organizational culture's relationship to individual and group information processing later in this chapter when we consider communication as a culture creation and maintenance process. Clearly the use of culture to process information illustrates one of its primary functions, which is helping organizational members make sense of organizational events, activities, and relationships.

The Use of Culture to Solve Problems.   As decisions in an organization need to be made and as problems occur that must be solved, the shared meanings that develop among organizational members help them devise solutions to those problems. Just as individuals in organizations use schemas to process information for their use, members and groups of members use shared schemas to arrive at decisions and solutions. Therefore, culture is "a living, historical product of group problem solving" and through its use strategies are created and used "that are remembered and passed on to new members" of the organization.[10]

The Use of Culture as a Means of Control.   Theoretically, those exhibiting leadership in an organization may use its culture to control the behaviors, if not the beliefs and attitudes, of organizational members by espousing the beliefs and behaviors that will be rewarded. As one researcher has written: "Properly implemented, the use of culture as a managerial strategy is seen to be potentially very effective in promoting loyalty, enthusiasm, diligence, and even devotion to the enterprise."[11] However, by definition it is difficult to use culture as a means of control since, as we have discussed, culture is created and sustained through formal and informal interactions among organizational members. Leadership, as we have defined it, does not seek to control the behaviors of individuals to solely achieve organizational goals, and all the interactions that create shared meanings are virtually impossible to control. There is no significant empirical evidence that corporations in the United States have used their cultures for the purpose of controlling the behaviors of organizational members. However, we often observe individuals in managerial positions in a variety of organizations manipulating components of a culture for the purpose of controlling behavior. For instance, principals of certain high schools in the southern part of the United States have changed school symbols, such as the Confederate flag, if they have become objectionable to some members of the student body, because the flag represents to some of today's African Americans the South's past use of slavery. Some university campuses have created "free speech" areas, thus attempting to control the size and location of student demonstrations. Some organizations may acknowledge "Women's History" month or "Black History" month by sponsoring a ceremony honoring certain women or African Americans, yet do little to change policies affecting the promotion opportunities for women and African American employees within the organization. In these cases, the ceremony is an attempt to placate organizational members concerned about the lack of such opportunities throughout the organization.

The Use of Culture to Enhance Organizational Performance.   Just as there is much debate over whether leadership can improve organizational productivity and/or performance (See Chapter 1), there is also disagreement as to whether organizational culture can enhance the performance of an organization. One conceptualization that relates culture to performance suggests that a *strong* organizational culture may enhance performance. A strong culture is characterized by a continuity in leadership, stable group membership, numerous commonly held values and shared behavior patterns among organizational levels, and organization-wide success.[12] Kotter and Heskett, two researchers who have studied the relationship between corporate culture and long-term economic performance, report the following:

1. Corporate culture can have a significant impact on a firm's long-term economic performance.
2. Corporate cultures that inhibit strong, long-term financial performance are not rare; they develop easily, even in firms that are comprised of reasonable and intelligent people.
3. While changing culture is difficult, corporate cultures can be made more performance enhancing.[13]

These authors suggest that such a culture can be created if one or two individuals at the top of an organizational hierarchy provide effective leadership "by convincing people a crisis is at hand, by communicating in words and deeds a new vision and a new set of strategies for the firm, and then by motivating many others to provide the leadership needed to implement the vision and strategies."[14] The implementation of a shared vision, values, and strategies leads to improved organizational performance and success; and this success, coupled with ongoing leadership exhibited throughout the organization, creates a new culture that continues to improve performance.

Another look at culture and performance has focused on the relationship between values, beliefs and meanings, and organizational effectiveness. Daniel Denison suggests that effectiveness depends on the degree to which values and beliefs are shared by organizational members and translated into policies and practices consistently. He also emphasizes that organizational effectiveness depends on the extent to which core values and beliefs, as well as policies and practices, are interrelated with the environment surrounding the organization.[15] Denison posits four hypotheses that suggest the relationship between organizational culture and effectiveness:

1. Organizational effectiveness is a function of the level of involvement and participation of organizational members.
2. A shared system of beliefs and values, if widely understood throughout the organization, has a positive influence on members' ability to reach consensus and implement coordinated actions.
3. Organizational effectiveness depends on the capacity of an organization to translate information from its environment into behavioral changes that increase the organization's chances for growth and development.
4. Organizational effectiveness depends on the degree to which organizational members share an understanding of the organization's mission—its function and purpose.[16]

It may be every leader's dream to use organizational culture as a way of enhancing organizational performance and effectiveness; but ultimately culture is "used" by those who comprise it—those who create and re-create it continually, day by day, as they interact. Leaders may be guides in the territory identified as an organization's culture, but they do not unilaterally create or use that territory. Indeed, leaders must understand that an organization rarely, if ever, has a monolithic culture. If organizations are groups of groups as we discussed in Chapter 1, then organizations are comprised of subcultures, or cultures created by groups in organizations.

THE NOTION OF SUBCULTURES

There are numerous ways that subcultures are created in organizations. People who communicate frequently because they are working on the same task, are geographically proximate to one another, share similar personal characteristics such as age, educational level, class, ethnicity, or gender, may develop into groups with shared values and beliefs, and ultimately shared meanings. Individuals who work as an ongoing project team in the development of a software package may create their own subculture. Women managers in a predominantly male organization may communicate regularly to share interests and concerns and create a subculture—their own organization within an organization. Senior citizens in a church may meet socially on a regular basis, develop their own activities, and create projects to assist the pastor; thus creating their own subculture within the church's culture.

Subcultures may develop in formal groups such as work teams, departments within a multihierarchical organization, or as a group of individuals with the same occupation, such as lawyers within a corporation or speech professors within a university. They may also be created out of informal groups, such as friendship circles, power cliques, and employees with similar extracurricular interests who band together to enjoy those interests in organization-sponsored activities, such as bowling teams, cooking classes, and so on.

All of these groups develop as a result of shared experiences that create a common sense of identity, a cohesiveness. When a group encounters other groups with different experiences, norms, and values, conflict between subcultures can occur. In a large, complex organization, for instance, conflict may arise between accountants and attorneys because they have different beliefs about how to attain certain organizational goals. In a university, faculty members in engineering may have differences of opinion with faculty in liberal arts if each group must vie for scarce resources from the president's office.

Conflict between or among groups or subcultures in organizations is not necessarily harmful to the organization, unless it becomes destructive. For instance, subculture conflict, such as fighting within corporations that affects customer service or stockholder trust, may be deleterious if the organizational culture becomes fragmented to the point of weakening the organization and adversely affecting the pursuit and attainment of its goals. On the other hand, subcultures may serve a valuable purpose by engendering and supporting diversity of opinion and facilitating flexibility and adaptation within the organization to avoid institutional rigidity. Such rigidity may be characteristic of the "dominant culture" that is comprised of a majority of organizational members who share the same values, beliefs, and respect for group norms. If the dominant culture of an organization attempts to squelch the development of subcultures, and tries to silence a group "voice" expressing opinions contrary to those of the dominant culture, a counterculture may emerge in the organization. Mergers involving employees of two very different organizational cultures, discontented workers, and individuals who have not received equal treatment by organizational decision makers are all potential members of countercultures within organizations. The purpose of these group cultures is to challenge, undermine, or even destroy the dominant organizational culture. Some dominant cultures may deserve to be destroyed if they are perpetuating values and behaviors that are undermining the organization's goals, or if they are failing to support the professional and personal goals of all organizational members. However, the demise of a dominant culture is serious and may signal the decline, and even death, of the organization. As a result, organizational members, especially those exhibiting leadership behaviors, must understand the importance of communication as a process that creates, maintains, and sometimes saves, organizational cultures.

COMMUNICATION AS A CULTURE CREATING/RE-CREATING PROCESS

In the organization known as the "classroom," the teacher initiates the organizing process through the use of: (1) a syllabus; (2) the instructional methods he or she uses (lecture, discussion, or both); (3) the degree of formality he or she evidences when interacting with students; (4) policies, such as whether attendance is taken; and (5) a host of verbal and nonverbal behaviors. The culture of the classroom is constructed, beginning on the first day of class, through the interactions of those in the course, as well as those who will come in contact with the students and faculty as they conduct their work.

The first part of this chapter was devoted to defining organizational culture and reviewing a few of its functions. However, to understand the role of leadership in creating and maintaining culture it is important to first look at how culture is created through the process of communication. Ernest G. Bormann explains it as follows:

> Culture in the communicative context means the sum total of ways of living, organizing, and communing built up in a group of human beings and transmitted to newcomers by means of verbal and nonverbal communication. Important components of an organization's culture include shared norms, reminiscences, stories, rites, and rituals that provide the members with unique symbolic common ground. Communication is a necessary but not a sufficient condition for organizational culture. Other things are required such as material goods, artifacts, tools, and technology, but without communication these components would not result in a culture.[17]

Bormann's definition of culture is based on the observation that organizational members often create group fantasies as they communicate. Several people talk together and create a story, a dramatic tale that engages them as a group; perhaps they fantasize about what it would be like to have a new boss or a new building. Perhaps they talk about what their section, division, or work group could do with an unlimited amount of financial and human sources.

According to Bormann: "When members of the organization share a fantasy, they have jointly experienced the same emotions; they have developed the same attitudes and emotional responses to the personae of the drama; and they have interpreted some aspect of their experience in the same way. They have thus achieved symbolic convergence about their common experiences."[18] In other words, they have created shared meanings and have reached mutual understandings about themselves through the process of interaction. In turn, *symbolic convergence* fosters a shared rhetorical vision among organizational members; they combine various shared fantasies which results in their obtaining "a broader view of the organization and its relationship to the external environment, of the various subdivisions and units of the organization, and of their place in the scheme of things."[19]

Another conceptualization of culture, indeed a metaphor for it, is that of a "web,"which is a system of strands of connectivity spun by actions and words of organizational members in which they are contained and through which they move.[20] Organizational reality for them is their embedded existence in a set of webs.

Earlier in the chapter we discussed the use of culture to process information. Indeed, culture itself is created through information processing through the use of symbols, schemas, and scripts. A symbol is a sign, a representation that stands for a concept or object. Company logos, slogans, and metaphors are examples of symbols; and they are created by organizational members and in turn serve as unifying reflections of organizational life among those members. As was mentioned earlier in this chapter, schemas are cognitive structures, stored knowledge, that help individuals make sense of new information they receive. For instance, the "background information" one's memory stores on how a supervisor prefers the preparation of reports is helpful when a new report is requested by that supervisor. The employee's response to a request for that report, the verbal and nonverbal behaviors used in the preparation of the document, is the result of his or her use of a "script." A script is a knowledge structure "held in memory that specifies behavior or event sequences that are appropriate for specific situations."[21]

Culture therefore is created through the interaction of symbols, schemas, and scripts as individuals organize, interpret, and use information in the process of developing shared meanings; but what are the forms that this process takes? How would one identify "organizational culture" in a zoo? What would it look and sound like? Leaders must be able to recognize these forms, and understand their importance in organizational life. Therefore, it is important to review the forms of communication that create and reflect an organizational culture.

FORMS OF COMMUNICATION IN ORGANIZATIONAL CULTURE

Organizational culture, as a web of intertwining organizational relationships, is both process and product. As organizational members interact they create and re-create manifestations of the culture that represents them to each other and the outside world. This section of Chapter 4 briefly describes some of the manifestations of culture and some of the forms of communication that simultaneously reflect and re-create an organization's culture.

Stephen Ott suggests that the most effective media for communicating important cultural beliefs, values, and behaviors include "an organization's language, jargon, metaphors, myths, stories, heroes, scripts, sagas, legends, ceremonies, celebrations, rites, and rituals," because they communicate information implicitly and such communication "is heard more clearly and remembered longer than through more explicit mediums."[22] A few of these media are discussed below.

Language

When we enter organizations we adopt and use the language of those organizations—words and phrases that are meaningful to people within them. If we enter a university we understand words like "finals," "semester break," "Comm 301," "GPA," and "scho pro." Language is given to us as members of the culture we join, and we also use it to continue the cultural development process. In a university, students use the "language" they learn when they serve as mentors in freshman orientation; when they work as members of student committees; and when they talk to professors about courses and grades and give evaluations of courses. In a study of the relationship between personal identity and organizational culture, two researchers found that the language used by employees in three different organizations reflected attempts to link themselves to the values and symbols of the organizations using metaphors, echoing language, fantasy dialogue, and personalized examples.[23] A common *metaphor* used by subjects in this study was "family" to describe their relationship to the organizations. *Echoing* was identified as the use of language by one group in the organization that occurs in the language of other organizational groups at different organizational levels. *Fantasy dialogue* was the creation of a story, a dramatized narrative, used for purposes of illustration that created interaction and identification among individuals in the organization. Finally, *personalized examples* were illustrations of how a value or symbol is illustrated in one's own life and work experiences. According to the researchers, organizational members use language "to relate themselves, their personal sense of meaning, and their identity to their organizations of employment."[24]

In his discussion of the use of language in the Navy to create and reflect that organization's culture, Roger Evered observes that the "language used by the members of any organizational group not only characterizes that group but reveals how its members view their organizational world and how their world is construed. In short, *the language they use defines their reality*."[25] In the Navy, as in other organizations, language is a system of symbols that convey meaning, such as words, rules, abbreviations, slang, and so on. Naval terms for different parts of ships, insignia on uniforms, procedures and policies that guide the behaviors of officers and enlisted personnel, are examples of the Navy's language. Each organizational culture and/or subculture has its own language, and that language depicts the culture or subculture "in terms of (a) its similarities to and differences from other organizations, (b) its societal role, and (c) the world view and 'reality' definition of its members."[26]

Myths

These forms of communication are stories that impart meanings. They perpetuate values, create and sustain loyalty, and direct behaviors of organizational members. Stories about the creation of a company by its founder are examples of these narratives. Indeed, organizational leaders may create myths to sustain culture by repeating the key values and goals of the organization in a variety of their communications. Organizational members pass this information along in their own stories as well as those told by other organizational members and leaders. In short, the creation of myths is similar to the art of storytelling in societal cultures where a people's history is carried from one generation to another through the telling and retelling of important events, and the oral promulgation of values and beliefs. Myths are used in organizations to teach, motivate, socialize individuals into an organization, and enhance their loyalty to it.

Rites

Ceremonies and rituals are forms of communication that support and reflect organizational cultures. Together they may be referred to as "rites," or "relatively elaborate, dramatic, planned sets of activities that consolidate various forms of cultural expression into organized events, which are carried out through social interaction, usually for the benefit of the audience."[27] Rites contain several forms of cultural expression including myths, symbols, and language; and they affirm values to organizational members. At Disneyland and Disney World, for instance, a colorful electric light parade comprised of Disney characters precedes a fireworks display that brings an end to each day at the park. Mickey Mouse, the Disney Company's major symbol, heads the processional which features music from Disney movies. Rites such as this one communicate aspects of the organizational culture to people outside that culture—the importance of family entertainment, the need for a "happy place on earth," an attention to beauty and music, and high-quality entertainment for "children of all ages." Other rites, identified by Beyer and Trice, are less dramatic but no less important in organizations. These include:

> Rites of passage—managerial training sessions
> Rites of enhancement—awards for performance
> Rites of integration—company picnics or holiday parties[28]

As these samples illustrate, rites can be regularly scheduled rituals, such as coffee breaks, morning staff meetings, or daily calisthenics before work as are found in some Japanese organizations. Additionally, they may be special ceremonies, such as the awards program sponsored annually by Mary Kay Cosmetics, at which top salespeople receive cars or company-paid vacations. On college campuses commencement is a rite, a ceremony, as are different celebrations of "Homecoming."

All these forms of communication are important to the "richness" of the organizational experience encountered by individuals. All members of an organization create their own "texts," or narratives, about its culture using words and actions.[29] Hierarchical position may affect these texts because one's perceptions are affected by where one is situated in the organization with respect to authority and responsibility. As two researchers who have studied texts found in lower organizational levels of organizations observe: "While managers have greater access to corporate symbols, to the media by which they are dispersed, and to the authority to enforce them, leaders cannot control the symbolizing activity of employees. If a subordinate does not like a directive or an explanation from above, she/he may select and configure a text which acknowledges the original message, but which more satisfactorily meets his/her needs and aspirations . . ."[30]

All organizational members are participants in the forms of communication that simultaneously create and reflect organizational culture; but leaders in organizations, either by virtue of designated position or considerable informal influence, have opportunities to create and alter cultures. Indeed, there is a symbiotic relationship between the two phenomena. Leadership affects culture, and culture affects leadership, by "establishing" the criteria for the selection and success of leaders. Moreover, as Edgar Schein observes:

> *Neither culture nor leadership, when one examines each closely, can really be understood by itself. In fact, one could argue that the only thing of real importance that leaders do is to create and manage culture and that the unique talent of leaders is their ability to understand and work with culture. If one wishes to distinguish leadership from management or administration, one can argue that leaders create and change cultures, while managers and administrators live within them.*[31]

It is to the relationship between leadership and organizational culture that we now turn.

THE ROLE OF LEADERSHIP IN CULTURE CREATION AND CHANGE

The process of culture creation and sustenance is a dynamic one that depends on interlocking behaviors exhibited by a variety of organizational members. Leadership behaviors, those that help move individuals toward mutually agreed upon goals, are particularly important in culture development, maintenance, and change.

Leadership and Culture Creation

The initiating forces behind the creation of a new organizational culture include the beliefs and values of the organization's founders and its original members, and the shared experiences among these individuals. The process of culture formation consists of a founder having an idea for a new activity; the creation of a core group with shared goals; the participation of that group in organizing activities; the entrance of others into the organization, and the development of a history among them.[32] In the process of culture creation, a leader's major responsibilities are to embed values and beliefs, much as one would plant a bulb in winter, anticipating the bloom of a flower in spring. The leader also provides a stable influence, through words and actions, as an organizational culture develops. According to Edgar Schein, the primary mechanisms for embedding a culture are as follows:[33]

1. What leaders pay attention to, measure, and control. If the leader of an AIDS hospice personally observes and reacts, on a day-to-day basis, to how patients are treated by all staff, regardless of their position in the organization, he or she is showing that caring, sensitive treatment of these individuals is a value that must be a visible component of the organization.

2. How leaders react to critical incidents and organizational crises. Richard Nixon essentially panicked after the break-in of the Democratic

National Headquarters in the summer of 1972, when he found out that people paid from his campaign funds were involved in the crime. He supported an attempt to "cover up" what become known as the Watergate scandal, instead of sharing information from the White House with appropriate authorities. The result is that an attempted burglary became a national incident that ultimately resulted in the president's decision to resign from office. His reaction to this critical incident in his administration permeated his staff and a veil of secrecy spread over his close advisers, exacerbating that organization's problems. His reaction to press and public scrutiny became their reaction, damaging White House credibility and ultimately the organization's ability to work toward the accomplishment of its goals.

3. Leaders' criteria to allocate scarce resources. If funds exist in a university to give merit pay to faculty, a president's criterion to give raises only to those faculty identified by students and colleagues as outstanding teachers communicates that effective teaching is a value the organization intends to reward.

4. Leaders' attempts at role modeling, teaching, and coaching. When a high school football coach insists on good sportsmanship, in locker room speeches as well as his own behavior, he is acting as a role model to embed the value of good sportsmanship within his organization.

5. Observed criteria used by leaders to allocate rewards and status. If the president of an automobile manufacturing company rewards employees for excellent customer service through bonuses or other extrinsic rewards like free trips to Hawaii, he is embedding "customer service" as a desired value in the organization.

6. Observed criteria used by leaders to recruit, select, promote, retire, and fire (excommunicate) organizational members. Requiring entry-level workers to have a college degree in a child development center implants the notion among organizational members that a leader intends for her organization to accomplish more than baby-sitting children. Such a criterion may communicate that the organization plans to value the cognitive, emotional, and physical development of the children in its care.

According to Schein, the secondary or reinforcing mechanisms that support these primary ways of embedding a culture include procedures, rituals, the design of physical space, stories and legends, and formal statements or creeds of organizational philosophy.

As an organization matures, its culture is sustained through the forms of communication we have discussed, such as myths, rituals, ceremonies, and the personal narratives of organizational members. Organizational leaders should be continually cognizant of how an organizational culture is affecting the accomplishment of its task(s) and the personal fulfillment of the needs of its members. They must determine if changes are needed, if diversity, or more uniformity, is required in membership, activities, forms of communication, and so on. "In either case the leader needs (1) to be able to analyze the culture in sufficient detail to know which cultural assumptions can aid and which ones will hinder the fulfillment of the organizational mission and (2) to possess the intervention skills to make desired changes happen."[34]

As a culture evolves, leaders may recognize the need to modify beliefs and values, as well as behaviors, through language, rituals, stories, and organizational practices, as well as rules and policies. Recognition, however, is not action, and leaders are sometimes constrained in their attempts to guide cultures. Such constraints include conflicting interests among subcultures, resistance to change among some organizational members, differing degrees of importance attributed to different issues by individuals, and disparities that develop among shared meanings. To overcome such constraints, leaders must become teachers, fostering organizational learning in the process of sustaining culture through the use of words and actions–that is, through the management of meaning. As sustainers of organizational cultures, it is critical that leaders are a part of them so as to understand them, but sufficiently detached to see what changes, if any, are needed to perpetuate cultural strength. According to Schein, "leaders play a critical role at each development stage of an organization, but that role differs as a function of the stage. Much of what leaders do is to perpetually diagnose the particular assumptions of the culture and figure out how to use those assumptions constructively or to change them if they are constraints."[35]

In mature or declining organizations, leaders must be particularly aware of the environment surrounding their organizations and its effects on culture. If change is needed, leaders must be able to initiate it, and not be inhibited by their personal attachment to, or investment in, the culture as it exists in the present. If change is needed and a leader cannot or will not provide it, a new leader may need to be chosen or external consultants may need to be employed. As we shall see in Chapter 6, no organizational change effort can be effective unless organizational members "buy into" the need for the change and have some say in the change process.

There are a number of ways that an organizational culture can be changed by organizational leaders. These include:

- Selecting and hiring new members
- Socializing new members into the organization
- Removing members from the organization who deviate from dominant cultural norms, values, and beliefs
- Reinforcing and changing behaviors
- Altering and reinforcing beliefs and values
- Communicating using words, behaviors, and symbols[36]

Moreover, changing culture may require a change in leadership; often the easiest ways to create change in an organization is to change leaders. Human beings tend to accept changes in beliefs and practices if they are suggested by someone representing a "different" or "fresh" viewpoint in the organization. As a result, it is important to look at the difference between leadership that is effective at sustaining culture, and that which is needed to change it.

Trice and Beyer suggest that there are four types of cultural leadership: *innovative* leadership that either (1) creates a culture or (2) changes a weakened, old one and *maintenance* leadership that either (1) keeps an existing culture vital or (2) reconciles diverse interests among subcultures.[37] According to these authors innovative cultural leadership is characterized by:

- A radical ideology or vision
- Followers' beliefs that the leader has qualities needed to deal with a crisis
- The leader serving as an effective role model
- The ability of the leader to give an impression of being successful and competent
- The leader serving as a motivator
- The communication of high expectations and confidence in followers
- The leader's repeated success in managing crises
- The creation of new structures and strategies or innovative changes in them
- The communication of new values
- The establishment of new traditions

Cultural maintenance leadership is grounded in a conservative ideology that is supportive of the status quo. It is committed to the renewal and/or strengthening of existing structures and strategies or the creation of only incremental changes in the culture; it affirms existing values and continues existing traditions.[38] For these reasons, major changes in organizational cultures are sometimes best made by new leaders, those who have no ties to the old culture and who are not encumbered by the shared meanings that may be contributing to the demise of the organization. Their success depends, in part, on whether organizational members recognize, understand, and are willing to participate in the change effort; on whether the environment surrounding the organization will be conducive to a change effort; and whether the relationship between leadership and followership is mutually supportive.

How do leaders maintain and/or change organizational cultures? They use the forms of communication discussed earlier in this chapter: symbols, language, stories, metaphors, rituals, and ceremonies. Leaders communicate values through their actions and words. They use training, orientation sessions, publications to both internal and external audiences, speeches, the "grapevine," and the process of mentoring potential future leaders. A founder embeds culture, according to Schein, but that planting is also done through the efforts of organizational members who create a shared reality through their interactions with each other. Leaders give a culture continual reinforcement through communication, and they are simultaneously affected by it. They are the voices, rising above others, to both internal and external constituencies. Therein resides one of the critical illustrations of leadership as the management of meaning. Leaders, in comparison to administrators or managers, consider and articulate concerns central to the "social/emotional basis for organizational life," not just the "technical/intellectual aspects of organizational structures."[39]

As creators and sustainers of culture, leaders must be effective communicators who are perceptive and adaptable to continual re-creations of organizational reality as seen through the eyes of organizational members. Such will certainly be the case in the twenty-first century. Leaders will need to welcome new ways of looking at their organizations, because they will face dramatic and continual change.

LEADERSHIP IN ORGANIZATIONAL CULTURES OF THE FUTURE

In Chapter 2 we observed that leadership scholars interested in organizations of the future suggest that such organizations will produce and depend on information to a greater extent than ever before. They also will depend on a highly skilled workforce that will become increasingly "professional" in function . . . and in their expectations of appropriate reward systems to recognize their expertise. These workers will possess increased expectations about their roles in the organization. They will anticipate collaborative and participative involvement in decision making.

Organizations in the next century will be increasingly global in scope, using new technologies to accomplish work and to communicate inter- and intraorganizationally. They will be characterized by rapid and continuous change; indeed, such change will become institutionalized such that, like "death and taxes," it will be taken for granted as a certainty, as opposed to a rarity in organizational life. Global entities, linked via new technologies, will also be multipurpose and serve several constituencies simultaneously, and they may temporarily establish liaisons with other organizations for specific purposes, much like planets moving in and out of each other's orbits.

Global organizations that depend on new technologies will foster organizational structures that are comparatively "flat" as opposed to hierarchical, creating flexibility in form and function. The constant change that will envelop and engage them will require the assimilation of information obtained from the environment as well as from inside the organization.

Understanding the probable characteristics of twenty-first century organizations, how can we characterize their cultures from a general perspective?

- Organizational cultures will become increasingly important to their members because ties to other organizations and/or institutions in the last several decades (e.g., political parties, religious denominations, community groups) have weakened.
- They will continue to be created through communication; but that communication may be mediated by new technologies, such as teleconferencing, voice mail, and interactive computer programs.
- Because organizations will be global in scope, we can expect the development of a myriad of subcultures within them, as a result of the influence of various national cultures on worldwide organizations and the use of different technologies by different groups that will establish common modes of communicating among them.
- Organizational activities will be distributed over space and time, and this distributed work may cause the fragmentation of an organizational culture, and the creation of subcultures.
- Because organizations increasingly will become multipurpose and serve a variety of constituencies, their cultures will be constituted by different, and perhaps disparate, groups within them. Again, a result may be the increasing fragmentation of an organization's culture, and the development of subcultures.
- For all the reasons discussed here and in Chapter 2, cultures will undergo continual change—not just in times of crisis or when the need arises for renewal and/or revitalization.

Considering these potential characteristics of organizational cultures in the future, what forms of communication will organizational members and their leaders use in the creation and maintenance of them?

- Global organizations, and/or those serving a variety of constituencies even in one locale, can be expected to use multiple modes of communication, including new technologies (e.g., voice mail, video and audio-conferencing, computer networking, etc.).
- Cultures will depend on the use of several languages, not necessarily those related to national cultures, but languages related to new technologies, such as those which comprise various computer software packages.
- In the future, changes in organizational structures and technologies will occur to facilitate the rapid flow of information necessary for expeditious decision making in a highly competitive, turbulent environment. Cultures that heretofore depended on the development of shared meanings that

evolve in face-to-face communicative relationships may need to adapt to new modes of information sharing to alleviate uncertainty, anxiety, and perhaps interpersonal and intergroup conflict that is detrimental to the sustenance of an organizational culture.

- Leaders will need to depend on multiple sources of information as they embed, maintain, and initiate changes in cultures through the process of decision making. The quality and quantity of information they receive will be of critical importance as they attempt to guide organizations through uncharted seas of change, toward mutually agreed upon goals.

The global, technological, and ever-changing dimensions of organizational life will require leaders who understand the importance of expeditious and informed decision making. Therefore, it is necessary for us to consider the critical role played by leaders as decision makers, and their use of communication as they exercise decision making responsibilities.

SUMMARY

An organization is a culture, a way of life that is a system of values, beliefs, and artifacts. Organizational culture is an outward manifestation of an organization's "inner self"; a reflection of a "society" that is constituted through the process of communication.

Culture is used in organizations in specific ways that are important to the exercise of leadership:

- For identification and affiliation
- To process information
- To solve problems
- As a means of control
- In some instances, to enhance organizational performance

Organizations as groups of groups are comprised of subcultures. People who work on the same task, share similar demographic characteristics, or who work geographically proximate to each other, may create their own formal or informal subcultures. Such groups develop as a result of shared experiences that create cohesiveness, a common sense of identity. Subcultures may serve a valuable purpose by engendering and supporting diversity of opinion and facilitating flexibility within the organization to avoid institutional rigidity.

Culture is created and re-created through the interaction of symbols, schemas, and scripts as individuals organize and interpret information in the process of developing shared meanings. It is a web of intertwined organizational relationships and is both process and product. The media used to create culture include language, symbols, stories and legends, and rites (rituals and ceremonies).

Leadership behaviors are particularly important in culture development, maintenance, and change. In the process of culture creation, a leader's major tasks are to embed values and beliefs, just as one would plant a flower bulb in winter, anticipating its bloom in spring. As an organization matures its culture is sustained through communication. Leaders monitor how culture affects the work of the organization and the personal and professional needs of its members. They attempt to recognize the need to modify beliefs and values, as well as behaviors, through language, rituals, organizational practices, rules, and policies. In mature or declining organizations, leaders must be able to identify the need for cultural change and initiate that change using training, orientation sessions, publications, speeches, the "grapevine," and mentoring. If a leader cannot or will not facilitate such change, a new leader may need to be appointed or elected.

In the future we can expect work cultures to become increasingly important to some of their members because ties to other institutions, such as political parties, organized religions, and community groups have weakened. Additionally, cultures will continue to be created through communication, but it may be mediated through the use of new technologies. Because of the globalization of many organizations, a variety of subcultures within organizations may develop, becoming multipurposed and serving a variety of constituencies.

QUESTIONS TO CONSIDER

1. Define and give examples of the ways organizational cultures might be used by their leaders.

2. How do organizational subcultures develop and what effects might they have on (1) other subcultures and (2) a dominant culture?

3. What forms of communication create and reflect an organizational culture? In what ways do leaders use these forms as they seek to move individuals and groups toward mutually agreed-upon goals?

4. What are ways used by leaders to create, maintain, and change organizational cultures?

5. What forms of communication might leaders use in organizational cultures of the future, considering the structural, demographic, and technological changes that may occur within them?

CASE PROBLEM

Juan Ruiz recently has been appointed by the Middleville Boy's Club board of directors as the club's new executive director. Known for his innovative changes in a smaller club in another part of the state, the board is interested in Mr. Ruiz making significant changes in the programs of the Middleville Club. This club has had only two executive directors in forty years, and the last one has recently retired. Its programs had been almost totally sports oriented during that time; but because of the growth of the community in which it resides, the clientele of the club has become more diverse in age, educational background, and ethnicity. Most of the staff members have been with the organization for ten or more years, reflecting its long-time interest in sports programs.

Aware of the changes in the community in which the Boy's Club is situated, Ruiz is interested in developing a variety of new programs and in seeking external funding for these programs, including those that focus on job-hunting skills, computer literacy, physical fitness, and public speaking and group meeting skills. He wants to initiate programs that emphasize individual worth as well as the importance of teams, and hopes to provide opportunities for family participation as well as personal development.

What strategies might Ruiz use to change the culture of this organization? What forms of communication might he utilize with the club's different constituencies?

ENDNOTES

1. J. Steven Ott, *The Organizational Culture Perspective* (Pacific Grove, CA: Brooks/Cole Publishing Company, 1989), 181.
2. Clifford Geertz, *The Interpretation of Cultures* (NY: Basic Books, 1973), 89.
3. Edgar A. Schein, *Reframing Organizational Culture*, eds. Peter J. Frost, Larry F. Moore, Meryl Reis Louis, Craig C. Lundberg, and Joanne Martin (Newbury Park: Sage, 1994), 252.
4. Ibid., 247.
5. Edgar A. Schein, *Organizational Culture and Leadership*, 2d ed. (San Francisco: Jossey-Bass Publishers, 1992), 8–10.
6. J. Steven Ott, *The Organizational Culture Perspective*, 68–69.
7. Linda Smircich, "Concepts of Culture and Organizational Analysis," *Administrative Science Quarterly* (September 1983): 346.
8. Robert G. Lord and Karen J. Maher, *Leadership and Information Processing* (Boston: Unwin Hyman, 1991), 148.
9. "A Cultural Theory of Information Bias in Organizations," Michael Thompson and Aaron Wildavsky, *Journal of Management Studies* 23:3 (May 1986): 279.
10. "Cultural Organization" by John Van Maanen and Stephen R. Barley, in *Organizational Culture*, eds. Peter J. Frost, Larry F. Moore, Meryl Reis Louis, Craig C. Lundberg, and Joanne Martin (Beverly Hills: Sage Publications, 1985), 33.

11. Carol Axtell Ray, "Corporate Culture: The Last Frontier of Control," *Journal of Management Studies* 23:3 (1986): 289.
12. John P. Kotter and James L. Heskett, *Corporate Culture and Performance* (NY: The Free Press, 1992), 7–8.
13. Ibid., 11 and 12.
14. Ibid., 106.
15. Daniel R. Denison, *Corporate Culture and Organizational Effectiveness* (NY: John Wiley & Sons, 1990), 5–6.
16. Ibid., 8, 11, and 13.
17. Ernest G. Bormann "Symbolic Convergence," in *Communication and Organizations, an Interpretive Approach,* eds. Linda L. Putnam and Michael E. Pacanowsky (Beverly Hills: Sage Publishers, 1983), 100.
18. Ibid., 104.
19. Ibid., 114.
20. Michael E. Pacanowsky and Nick O'Donnell-Trujillo, "Communication and Organizational Cultures," *Western Journal of Speech Communication* 46 (1982).
21. Dennis A. Gioia and Peter P. Poole, "Scripts in Organizational Behavior," *Academy of Management Review* 9:3 (1984): 449.
22. J. Steven Ott, *The Organizational Culture Perspective*, 97.
23. Bonnie L. Prince and Ray E. Wagner, "Personal Identity and Organizational Culture: Language as Vehicle," paper presented at the Annual Meeting of the International Communication Association, May 1992, Miami, Florida.
24. Ibid., 19.
25. Roger Evered, "The Language of Organizations: The Case of the Navy," in *Organizational Symbolism*, eds. L. R. Pondy, P. J. Frost, T. C. Dandridge (Greenwich, CT: JAI, 1983), 140.
26. Ibid., 141.
27. Janice M. Beyer and Harrison M. Trice, "The Communication of Power Relations in Organizations through Cultural Rites," in *Inside Organizations*, eds Michael Owen Joes, Michael Dane Moore and Richard Christopher Snyder, (Newbury Park, CA: Sage Publications, 1988), 142.
28. Ibid., 143.
29. Mary Helen Brown and Jill J. McMillan, "Culture as Text: The Development of an Organizational Narrative," *The Southern Communication Journal* 56:1 (Fall 1991).
30. Ibid., 57–58.
31. Edgar H. Schein, *Organizational Culture and Leadership*, 2d ed (San Francisco: Jossey-Bass Publishers, 1992), 5.
32. Edgar A. Schein, *Organizational Culture and Leadership*, 2d ed. (San Francisco: Jossey-Bass Publishers, 1992), 212.
33. Ibid., summarized from Exhibit 12.1, 231.
34. Ibid., 378.
35. Ibid., 381.
36. From V. Sathe, *Culture and Related Corporate Realities: Text, Cases, and Readings on Organizational Entry, Establishment, and Change* (Homewood, IL: Irwin, 1985) as listed in J. Steven Ott, *The Organizational Culture Perspective*, 195.

37. Harrison M. Trice and Janice M. Beyer, *The Cultures of Work Organizations* (Englewood Cliffs, NJ: Prentice-Hall, 1993), 264.
38. Harrison M. Trice and Janice M. Beyer, "Cultural Leadership in Organizations," Working Papers, Department of Management, College of Business Administration and Graduate School of Busines, UT Austin, 1989/90, January 31, 1990.
39. Linda Smircich and Charles Stubbart, "Strategic Management in an Enacted World," *Academy of Management Review* 10:4 (1985): 731.

5

LEADERS AS DECISION MAKERS

Leaders depend on communication to create a shared reality, a culture, that identifies and unifies organizational members. In this chapter we shall observe how leaders depend on communication to develop and implement decisions, remembering that the decisions made by those within an organization tell us something about its basic values and beliefs.

A word about the structure and content of this chapter: the research literature on decision making is extensive and fragmented. There are a plethora of topics related to the decision-making process including: (1) the sources from which individuals acquire information; (2) the stages of the decision-making process; (3) the cultural, cognitive, and emotional influences on decision making; and (4) strategies used to invite participation in decision making. Books have been written on leadership and decision making, on information processing and decision making, and on the use of intuition in decision making. This chapter is the result of selecting the major topic areas and research findings that are pertinent to a study of leaders as decision makers, and decision making as a process dependent on communication. Reading this chapter will be a bit like white water rafting—the flow is always there but the ride may be a little circuitous to get us where we need to go.

Herbert Simon, in his landmark treatise on decision making in organizations, states that communication is involved in decision making from two directions.[1] It is responsible for transmitting information to a decisional center (a person or group) and for transmitting a decision to parts of an organization. Communication is integral to the decision-making *process*. In individual, as well as group decision making, it is "the means for creating the social reality in which a decision is shaped and enacted."[2] The form and content of decisions are developed through interaction, and those decisions are also social products of the organizational culture that creates them. Just like leadership, decision making is in itself a communication process, albeit, "a single practice, suspended in a web of other practices" that includes the development of social relationships, task accomplishment, and a host of other organizational activities.[3]

The purpose of this chapter is to look at decision making as a process and examine the interrelationship between leadership and decision making, a critical component of organizational existence. To begin this examination, it is important to consider the different perspectives through which to analyze decision making as a phenomenon.

One way to study decision making is to consider how decisions should be made—a *prescriptive* approach. Another way is to describe how the process actually takes place by studying decision making in action—a *descriptive* approach. A third way is to create models of decision processes and predict decision outcomes based on the use of certain models—an *analytical* approach. Finally, decision making can be studied by focusing on the human aspects of this activity, that is, the behaviors of individuals and/or groups as they engage in the process—a *behavioral* approach.[4] In this chapter we will emphasize the importance of studying decision making as it has been observed in organizations in general, and as it has been exercised as a critical leadership behavior.

In the last forty years the scholars that have theorized about and conducted research on decision making have developed several "models" to describe how the process is initiated, developed, and completed in organizations. To understand leaders as decision makers requires that we look at the various ways that decision making takes place in organizational contexts.

MODELS OF DECISION MAKING

Just as the study of any phenomenon evolves, the study of decision making increasingly has considered the complexity of the decision-making process, the interrelationship of elements that comprise the process, and the influences and constraints on the process. As we shall see, the notion of how decisions are made in organizations evolved from rather simple explanations to an understanding that the process is complex and multifaceted. The "models" of decision making reflect the evolution of thought on how decisions are made.

The Rational Model of Decision Making

In theory, decisions should be made in a logical and thorough fashion based on all available information obtained from all possible sources to make the best decision possible. The classic sequence of steps in such a process is as follows:

1. Definition of the problem
2. Information gathering
3. Development of potential solutions
4. Evaluation of solution alternatives
5. Selection of a decision alternative
6. Implementation of the decision

But we do not live in a theoretical, completely rational world. There are at least three reasons why decision making is not completely rational:

1. Rationality assumes that a decision is based on the best information available. Human beings do not always seek and find the best information before making a decision.
2. Rationality assumes that the consequences of all decision choices are known. Such knowledge is almost always fragmentary.
3. Rationality assumes that a choice has been made among all alternatives. Few of all possible alternatives are ever considered before individuals make a decision choice.[5]

Situational and processing limitations affect human ability to make decisions on a completely rational bases. Examples of this are insufficient use of cognitive abilities because one is tired or bored or in a hurry, as well as the lack of adequate technologies or tools to help gather and evaluate information. We make a limited search for alternatives and consider only some of the alternatives we find. As a result rationality in decision making is limited or bounded because information processors and decision makers and implementers are human.

The Limited Rational Model of Decision Making

To distinguish the rational model of decision making from the limited rational approach, consider the following features of the latter.

- Decisions are responses to problems; the process is targeted to finding solutions to satisfy particular needs rather than generating decisions for all possible situations.
- There are cognitive limits under which humans labor; they do not, and cannot, absorb and use all the information available in the world around them.
- Time pressures force individuals to make decisions with incomplete information, as well as limited analysis of possible alternatives.

- Decision making is a disjointed, rather than a smooth, continual process.
- At times intuition may be the basis for some decisions.
- Humans develop decisions that are satisfactory but not optimal solutions to problems.[6]

An observation related to the notion of satisfactory as opposed to optimal solutions is that much of the time individuals engage in *decision taking* as opposed to decision making.[7] In decision taking, we apply decision behaviors we have learned over time that are based on existing knowledge structures in response to a particular problem. By contrast, when we *make* decisions we use targeted and innovative decision behaviors to develop a decision for a particular problem or issue.

It is easy to identify with the limited rational model of decision making. Most of us use this approach in our daily lives, whether we are choosing a vacation destination, selecting a restaurant for dinner, or purchasing a car. Obviously, the limitations under which we are willing to make a decision vary with its importance to us, but in general individuals in their day-to-day lives, and organizational leaders in the accomplishment of their work, use this approach to decision making quite readily. In organizations, however, there are additional models that decision makers use in the conduct of organizational life.

The Political Model of Decision Making

As is discussed earlier in this text, an organization may be considered a collection of groups with separate functions, values, interests, and allegiances. As a result, decision making in organizations is often conducted for the benefit of coalitions that have formed within the organizations to protect and/or advance the interests of competing groups. For instance, during a campaign to elect a student body president, a student organization may support an individual perceived as being a "friend" of the organization. A decision may be made based largely on the self-interest of that particular student group. Other student groups may argue for student body support of other candidates based on their self interests. Poole and Doelger present the following succinct description of the political model of decision making:

> Members assume that decision making is a process of winning adherents for their own preferred alternative. Their primary criterion is political acceptability, and originality or effectiveness take secondary status . . . The steps implied are (a) get preferred solutions on the table, (b) build cases against other solutions, (c) get the group to converge on the preferred solution by compromising or persuading, and (d) adopt and work out an implementation of the solution.[8]

Obviously this approach to decision making reflects the inherent presence of conflict, negotiation, and compromise in the process. Organizational members become participants in shifting alliances, and coalitions of competing interests, who attempt to dominate or control organizational action. Under these circumstances the information used in the process of decision making, and the process itself, may be manipulated and distorted. That is not to say that the process is inherently bad or sinister; however, it is certainly not completely rational or selfless.

On a day-to-day basis individuals and groups in organizations frequently enact decisions using the political model. Effective organizational leaders, however, must be able to recognize when this approach is creating political conflicts that may become detrimental to the organization. For instance, if one organizational coalition is affecting organizational decision making to the extent that the organization is becoming adversely affected (e.g., causing decreased productivity and/or morale), then the organizational leader must know when to communicate his or her concern about the continued use of the politicized process under those circumstances.

While the political approach to decision making is used on a daily basis in many organizations, it is particularly observable in times of uncertainty. When an airline is suffering financially, decisions among pilots, maintenance crews, and flight attendants about possible strikes due to a perceived lack of adequate pay or benefits are generally made on political bases. When one or more decisions to strike may cripple the airline, from the perspective of organizational leaders, some action to save the airline may be needed so that a coalition's interest does not override that of the organization as a whole. In some instances, an airline's chief executive officer accedes to strikers' demands; in other instances, individuals are fired and other employees are hired in their places.

The "Garbage Can" Model of Decision Making

Another approach to decision making is one that relies on the people and processes in an organization and is completely contrary to the rational approach. Indeed, this approach is best characterized as organized anarchy. That is, decisions are the result of pouring problems, solutions, participants, and opportunities into a mix of possibilities as if one is dumping debris into a trash can.[9] In this decision context, problems, alternatives, and solutions are ill defined; cause and effect relationships are difficult to identify; and participation by organizational members in the process is fluid. This approach to decision making, based on observational research, is commonly used in a myriad of organizations because, as we have seen in earlier chapters, the very notion of "organization" depends on the fluid, dynamic process we call "communication." Through this process individuals and groups create an environment in which tasks are completed and social relationships are created. A few of the consequences of the garbage can "model" are the following:

- Solutions are proposed when problems do not exist.
- Choices are made without solving problems.
- Problems may persist without being solved.
- Some problems, however, are solved.[10]

While the limited rational, political, and garbage can models of decision making are the most notable in the study of how choices are made and implemented in organizations, there have been other models suggested in recent years. Paul C. Nutt, for instance, suggests several models, including the following:[11]

Historical—Concepts are drawn from the practices of others to guide solution development.

Off-the-shelf—Attempts are made to identify the best available ideas and it is assumed that competition among ideas will produce superior decisions.

Search—A decision maker faces a need to make a decision but has no workable idea. This individual mobilizes people she or he trusts, defines the problem for them, and waits for the product of their work.

Nova—New ideas are created to challenge approaches in use within organizations; such ideas may be solicited from internal and/or external consultants.

Each of these models may reflect one of the major approaches to decision making previously discussed in this chapter. What is important is that one understands what leaders must know: decision makers in organizations are not completely rational because of a variety of cognitive, temporal, and other pressures under which they labor; and because they work in dynamic environments where "reality" is continually constituted through the process of communication. The remainder of this chapter looks at components of the process, however it is enacted. We begin by analyzing how information, the raw material used in decision making, is "mined" and processed.

THE SEARCH FOR AND USE OF INFORMATION IN DECISION MAKING

Information, comprised of data, knowledge, opinions, and expertise, is the substance from which decisions are made. Good decisions depend on an individual having information of sufficient quality and quantity so that the selected alternative, the decision maker's choice, is more than a guess. Because important decisions are made at higher organizational levels, leaders require information that is reliable as well as relevant, accurate as well as accessible. In the process of defining problems, generating decision alternatives, and making choices, the information acquired by a decision maker *and* the framing, or interpretation of it, affect decision outcomes.[12] As they begin the decision making process by searching for the information that will be useful in decision development and implementation, leaders must understand that an organization's information-processing capabilities must match its information-processing requirements. Accordingly, they must adopt behaviors that facilitate the search for and use of information. These behaviors include using appropriate "styles" to search for and acquire information; using information as a valuable organizational resource; creating structures that facilitate information flow among all those involved in the decision-making process; and using "rich" sources of information in this process.

Using Appropriate Styles to Scan for Information

As individuals make daily personal and organizational decisions, they scan or search their environments for information—weather forecasts in order to decide what to wear; discussions with friends about movie reviews and what film to see on the weekend; stock market reports to determine in which companies to invest. In the process of organizational decision making, one important leadership behavior is the search for information to make the most appropriate decision possible within a given situational context.

Leaders scan the world both inside and outside the organization for many types of information in order to develop decisions for a variety of purposes. Information is requested to make day-to-day decisions for organizational maintenance; nonroutine information is requested when creating solutions to difficult problems or guiding organizational change; and information is sought from individuals both to develop decision alternatives and to involve organizational members in the processes that will initiate and sustain task and social relationships among them.

In their quest for information, for whatever purpose, leaders may exhibit one or more search or seeking styles.[13] At times an organizational decision maker may exhibit a *delegating* style; assigning the search for information to subordinates to save time and effort. This style depends on the use of competent and trustworthy surrogate searchers.

Sometimes a leader is not a scanner at all but is one who *waits* passively for information to drop like rain on dry soil. Problems and sources of information to develop solutions are identified by others. Ronald Reagan, for instance, depended on his chief of staff and one or two other individuals inside the White House for information in order to make decisions about operational matters as well as critical national problems. Leaders who use a waiting style are at the mercy of other individuals and may abrogate their responsibilities as decision *makers,* finding themselves acting much of the time as decision *takers.*

Finally, a leader may use a *seeking* style, characterized by an active and constant search for information. Such a person has high internal motivation to possess and use information. Lyndon Johnson, for instance, has been characterized as a "sponge" in the White House; he continually read documents and memos, talked often during the day with a variety of staff members and governmental officials, tuned in to three television networks at once, and monitored a news service ticker tape that ran constantly in the White House.

While all scanning styles may be appropriate at certain times in the life of an organizational leader, the use of a seeking style is particularly important. Ultimately a leader is responsible for all decisions he or she makes, as well as the quality of information used to make those decisions. Use of the seeking style is more apt to garner the type of credible information important in leaders' decision-making processes.

Using Information as a Valuable Organizational Resource

It is human nature, as research results confirm, to share information that is positive with one's supervisor while sometimes avoiding the transmittal of "bad news." Organizational members, including leaders, also hoard information and "spend" it like the valuable resource it is to achieve favored status with their superiors, or to create their own power bases. For example, an employee who keeps information from his project team members until a meeting where he can receive public and solitary credit for having that information may undermine the group's work, not to mention its morale. Consequently, organizational leaders must communicate to those from whom they get information that its use is best regarded as a shared organizational activity, because decision making in organizations is often a group process rather than an individual process.

Creating Structures That Facilitate Information Flow

Organizational leaders must understand how various structures facilitate or impede the flow of information to them as well as to other organizational members. In a formal, multihierarchical system, information generally is filtered as it passes through organizational levels. Such systems control the flow of information and therefore access to it. This control prevents information overload on an organizational leader but may deter access to adequate amounts of high-quality information needed to make a decision. Conversely, a fluid structure with few hierarchical levels and open systems of communication encourages the transmission of information, such that an overload of information on decision makers is possible. Organizational leaders would do well to remember the advice of Leonard Hawes in his seminal article on information overload published almost twenty-five years ago: "The dilemma confronting today's organization is which information can be filtered to reduce unnecessary overload without, at the same time, crippling the organization's ability to process new types of information."[14]

Using "Rich" Media

In their search for information, decision makers depend on sources of data and opinions that are accessible and trustworthy. Within the last ten years, considerable research also has focused on the "richness" of information media.

"Richness" refers to a medium's ability to overcome different frames of reference in a timely fashion. Language variety is a characteristic of rich media; such variety allows for the communication of a wide range of ideas. Such media include music, painting, and oral communication. They also provide multiple cues, both verbal and nonverbal, to those engaged in interaction, and the ability to provide instantaneous or rapid feedback.

Face-to-face communication is the richest medium because it depends on the use of natural (conversational) language, multiple cues, and instantaneous feedback. When a leader receives information in a face-to-face meeting, that person sees and hears the depth and breadth of an individual's knowledge about, and perhaps emotional investment in, the subject. Using the telephone gives a person both verbal and some nonverbal cues, as well as rapid feedback and the opportunity to communicate using natural language. Correspondence and reports do not afford the multiple cues of the richer media; they may be prepared using formal as opposed to conversational language. Feedback is comparatively slow, requiring the reader to process the information in the document and then prepare and send a response.

According to Daft and Lengel, who introduced the notion of information richness, rich media are generally used by decision makers at the top of an organizational hierarchy. "For difficult, equivocal topics, managers use face-to-face discussion for interpretation and equivocality reduction. Memos, bulletins, reports, and other media of lower richness are used when the topic is specific and better understood."[15] When problems are ambiguous and unclear. Managers use informal and direct communication, for routine matters they use formal written communication. Effective managers should be able to select among media, depending on their task at hand.

Leaders may also select rich sources of information for symbolic reasons in the process of decision making. They may want to speak directly with individuals to show interest in them and to evidence their commitment to personal forms of communication rather than rely on reports and memos. On the other hand, the use of numerical documents and detailed reports "might be used to signal that extensive study lies behind a supposedly rational decision."[16]

In one study of how owners and managers utilize sources of information, Fann and Smeltzer found that their subjects used rich, informal, and accessible sources of information. They also discovered that these individuals used rich media more often for information processing when the organization was undergoing change and facing uncertainty because "ambiguous situations . . . require the manager to seek out interpretations and come to some mutual understanding with those involved with the decision making."[17] In other words, in organizational contexts characterized by uncertainty, clarity is created if participants in the decision-making process are able to rely on multiple, explanatory cues and instant feedback during their interactions.

These are a few of the behaviors that facilitate leaders' search for and use of information in the process of decision making. The following major points are particularly important to an understanding of the interrelationship of leadership and information acquisition and use.

- Formal information systems may summarize information to the extent that it loses its richness. As a result, leaders must use face-to-face contact to supplement information received from these systems. Face-to-face contact is a faster form of information sharing; and problem solving at top levels of organizations often requires quick decisions that cannot solely rely on information disseminated through formal and slow systems.
- Many important decisions are not the product of single individuals who process information; they emerge as the result of interactions among multiple individuals sharing information.
- Leaders must remember that good news has "upward mobility" in an organization. That is, it tends to travel faster from subordinates to supervisors than bad news, so the sender will not be negatively affected. Information should be reviewed carefully with this in mind if it comes from lower hierarchical levels in the organization.
- Leaders must rely on information that is accessible from sources other than those personally, politically, or hierarchically close to them. They should scan the environment and organization for information from a

variety of sources, remembering that contextual factors such as organizational structure, political coalitions, time pressures, and task constraints affect the acquisition and use of information.

- Decision makers generally seek information that supports their points of view, and they acquire as much of this supportive data as possible. Therefore, the credibility of the decisions based on this information is suspect.[18] Soliciting and using information that agrees only with one's opinions contributes to "information insularity," a situation that restricts a leader's understanding of a problem or a situation because one lacks a variety of opinions, alternative data, or expertise that conflicts with those provided by organizational friends or confidants.
- Information flow and decision making are interdependent processes. Decision making depends on information, and the quality of information one receives depends on the decisions made about where and how to obtain that information.
- The outcome of a decision depends on the quality and quantity of information transmitted to a decision maker *and* that individual's framing of it; that is, how the information is conceptualized and interpreted.

These are just a few of the concepts related to the acquisition and use of information that leaders should understand as they participate in the process of decision making. While that process depends on the quality and quantity of data, opinions, and expertise gathered from others, it is also subject to influences, if not constraints, that affect the evaluation of information, the creation of alternative solutions, and the selection of a preferred solution—in short, the process of decision development.

INFLUENCES AFFECTING DECISION MAKING

As leaders engage in the process of generating decision options based on the information they have acquired, they encounter a number of influences from outside, as well as within, the organization.

Environmental Influences

A decision maker does not live in a vacuum—the outside world, as discussed earlier in this text, affects an organizational leader in the conduct of his or her work, which includes making decisions. Examples of external influences on decision development within organizations include the following:

- Community perceptions of the organization
- Resources controlled by forces outside the organization

- Political issues
- Social issues
- Economic issues
- Technologies affecting the environment in which the organization exists

The following scenario illustrates external influences on the process of decision making undertaken by organizational leaders. The president of a university is seeking land on which to build a badly needed classroom building. However, any decision to purchase land for this purpose is affected by influences that include the following: attitudes shared by community members about the possible encroachment of the university on area neighborhoods; the political clout of the university's "friends" in the community; and the relative strength of the economy in the community surrounding the university which may affect the degree of acceptance of university actions.

Another example: faculty and administrators in a department of communication may routinely make decisions about curriculum revision. To make choices that reflect a sensitivity not only to their own preferences but to student needs, they must consider external factors such as the types of jobs their graduates may hold in the future; the opinions of professionals in the fields of communication about needed courses for majors; and the societal issues that will face communication majors as citizens, about which they should be informed.

Because organizations are open systems and, therefore, are continually and significantly affected by the environments that surround and interact with them, leaders must understand and respond to environmental influences on decision development.

Organizational Influences

There are a host of influences *within* an organization that affect the creation of a decision. Some of those particularly important for an organizational leader to understand include the following:

- The form in which information is transmitted and received and the content of that information (e.g., memo, e-mail, face-to-face discussion)
- The source of information and the credibility of that source
- The relationship between the sender and receiver of information
- The status differences between and/or among senders and receivers of information
- The power relationship between senders and receivers of information
- The proximity of participants in a decision-making process (Are they situated at adjacent desks? On the same floor? In different buildings at the same site? In different parts of the world?)

- Organizational goals (e.g., increased sales; better customer service; improved teaching)
- Tasks, both short-term and long-term (e.g., creation of one car in a day versus monthly automobile production; completion of daily sales reports versus retail clothing sales during a holiday season; getting students through the first day of elementary school versus third grade class preparation for an academic year)
- Resources—Are there sufficient funds to finance a new building, if that is one decision alternative? Are there enough people on the production line to increase output?
- Technologies—What are the available means with which organizational members complete tasks? How is the proposed decision going to be affected by the presence or lack of computers, calculators, or typewriters?
- Structure—How do rules and regulations, reporting relationships, and the ways employees are organized for different tasks affect decision alternatives?
- Values—What organizational beliefs and norms are the guideposts for decisions that leaders must make on short-term and long-term bases?

Environmental and organization-wide influences are not the only ones that affect leaders as decision makers. The characteristics of individuals and groups, and the constituent components of the process of organizing, also affect decision development and implementation.

Individual and Group Influences

As was discussed earlier in this text, organizations are "groups of groups." As a result, characteristics of groups and individual organizational members are important influences on decision making. Such characteristics include the following:

- Individual and group demographics
- Personal and professional goals of organizational members
- Individual and group tasks and functions
- Individual and group values, attitudes, and behaviors

Consider the following examples which illustrate the effects of these characteristics on decision development.

- In selecting members of a team that will be given the responsibility of developing a new ad campaign, an advertising executive will need to consider their diverse accomplishments, experience, interests, and

expertise in working in groups, and their abilities as individuals and as a collective unit.
* In developing a policy to establish flexible working hours for employees, an organizational leader will need to consider several of the demographic characteristics affecting need and acceptance of such a policy (such as employee age range) as well as the norms that have developed among organizational members regarding work habits and expected rewards, and the interrelationship between their personal and professional goals.

Obviously, the *type* of decision a leader must make affects to what extent individual and group characteristics are relevant, and central to the decision. In fact, almost any decision made by a leader should consider, to some extent, the characteristics of organizational members, as individuals or as members of work groups or social collectivities. Similarly, every decision is affected by and derives part of its context from the characteristics of the specific issue under consideration.

Issue Characteristics

Each issue that prompts the need for a decision by an organizational leader is affected by characteristics pertinent to that issue. For instance, some issues contain higher degrees of uncertainty than do others. A decision to fire on a supposed enemy warplane contains more potential uncertainty than a decision to hire an extra summer employee. Additionally, some issues are more complex than others; and some are affected by time pressures whereas others are not affected by temporal constraints. Organizational leaders need to be aware of issue characteristics in order to respond appropriately to decision-making demands. Carefully created decisions reflect an understanding of how uncertainty, complexity, and time pressures may affect their development as well as their implementation.

Having reviewed the considerations involved in searching for information and the influences under which leaders labor as decision makers, it is important to consider the ways decisions are developed to create responses to organizational needs.

PROCESSES OF DECISION MAKING

The decision process is comprised of sets of interactions that identify an issue or problem, collect information, create and evaluate decision alternatives, and implement a chosen action. Understanding how that process evolves and proceeds is critical to an understanding of leaders as decision makers.

In the early 1970s at The University of Bradford in England, a series of studies was conducted on a variety of decisions made in different kinds of organizations. The purpose of these studies was to look at the decision-making process as it was conducted by individuals in top hierarchical levels of organizations. The research used 150 cases in 30 organizations across the country. Data from these studies suggested there are three major ways of making decisions in organizations.

1. *Sporadic processes,* through which decisions are made with considerable interaction; numerous sources of information are utilized and there is significant variability in the information that is obtained. The process is spasmodic and characterized by delays, such that more time is needed than in other processes of decision making.

2. *Fluid processes,* in which decision making is steadily paced and conducted through formal channels. There are fewer delays, but fewer sources of information are used and variability of information is reduced. Less time is taken to reach a decision than is the case with sporadic processes.

3. *Constricted processes,* where decision making is "narrowly channeled"; there is less effort to acquire information and less formal interaction via meetings and committee discussions.[19]

All three ways of decision making, according to this research, are used by top decision makers because the complexity of the problems they face differs, as do their politicality (the degree to which influence is exerted through the process on the decision outcome).[20] Additionally, these ways differ to accommodate varying interests in the process and in the organization.

Most conceptualizations of the decision-making process focus on the need to: (1) identify and articulate why a decision is required; (2) gather information; (3) develop decision alternatives; and (4) select an alternative and implement the decision.

Indeed, Theodore Sorensen, adviser to President John F. Kennedy, once wrote that, theoretically, United States presidents should use a decision-making process that includes:

- Agreement on the facts and the overall policy objective
- A precise definition of the problem
- A canvassing of all possible solutions
- A list of all possible consequences that might flow from each solution
- A recommendation and final choice of one alternative
- The communication of the decision and provision for its execution[21]

This decision process is generally accepted for organizational leaders, including presidents, but none of them lives under theoretical circumstances.

Decision making is a linear process only in theory, not in reality. Understanding this, Bernard Bass, and many researchers who study decision making, have challenged the linear model that sets forth specific, well-defined stages. Bass suggests that the process can begin at any stage and may move backward and forward from one stage or phase to another as decision requirements warrant. The components of Bass's model of decision making, which reflect his conceptualization of the process, are as follows:

- Scanning detects a possible opportunity, threat, or problem.
- Diagnosis calls for more detailed information.
- Discovery and diagnosis determine the direction and location of a search for information.
- Search and innovation lead to a redefinition of the problem.
- Search and innovation provide what is to be evaluated and chosen.
- Search is conducted to validate the proposed solution.
- Evaluation is completed and a choice is authorized.
- A rejected authorization or failed implementation of the decision forces re-evaluation.
- Problem diagnosis determines evaluation and choice.
- Evaluation and a new choice lead to modifications in the diagnosis.
- Implementation experience changes scanning focus for future opportunities, threats, or problems.[22]

The reason for the flexibility in decision development that models such as Bass's provide is that leaders and other organizational members make different kinds of decisions each day. Some decisions respond to organizational exigencies or needs that arise routinely. Other decisions are responses to crises and pressures that must be handled immediately. Still other decisions are made as preventative measures to improve existing situations; they provide opportunities for proactively dealing with environmental or organizational situations that are potentially problematic for an organization or its leadership.

Whatever process or model a decision maker uses to create and implement a decision, there is at least one way to make the process more rigorous and the decision more effective; that is, one that accomplishes the goals of the decision maker and one that has "a better chance than others of attaining the decision maker's objectives and of being adhered to in the long run."[23] That way, according to Irving L. Janis, is *vigilant information processing*, which requires the following:

- Thorough canvassing of a wide range of alternative courses of action
- Surveying the full range of objectives to be fulfilled and the values implicated by the choice

- Carefully weighing whatever the decision maker knows about the costs of negative and positive consequences related to each alternative
- Intensive searching for new information relevant to the further evaluation of alternatives
- Correctly assimilating any new information or expert judgment to which the decision maker is exposed, even when that information does not support the initial course of action
- Re-examining the positive and negative consequences of all known alternatives, including those originally regarded as unacceptable, before making a final choice
- Making detailed provisions for implementing or executing the chosen course of action, with special attention to contingency plans that might be required if various known risks were to materialize[24]

The use of these criteria stimulates a decision maker to adopt a strategy of decision making designed to *optimize* the process; that is, to search for all viable alternatives. By comparison, the strategy of *mixed scanning* classifies decisions as either major or minor, so that one scans intensively only those choices that are deemed most important. *Satisficing* as a strategy relies on basic principles that help a decision maker reduce a complex problem into what will work and what will not.[25]

In a recent treatise on leadership and decision making, Janis discusses his study of *vigilant problem solving* by defining it as the process used by good policy makers who work "to the best of their limited abilities, within the confines of available organizational resources, to exercise all the caution they can to avoid mistakes in the essential tasks of information search, deliberation, and planning."[26] There are, of course, constraints on vigilant problem solving, just as there are constraints on decision making in general, and some are the same. Such constraints faced by an organizational leader and policy maker include: limited time; perceived limitations of resources for information search and evaluation; the complexity of an issue; multiple tasks that need to be accomplished; a perceived lack of dependable knowledge; the need of the leader to maintain power, status, and social support; the need to create a new policy that is acceptable throughout the organization; a decision maker's strong personal motive (e.g., greed); and the creation of emotional stress as a result of conflict over the decision.[27]

Vigilant problem solving, despite these constraints, is one way organizational leaders insure the development of an informed, carefully created, decision. However, in "the real world" the very constraints mentioned above prevent leaders from using vigilant problem solving as a process in the creation of every decision they must make. Indeed, those who observe decision makers have emphasized the role that *intuition* sometimes plays in the decision-making process.

For example, in one study of senior managers in Fortune 100 companies it was observed that these individuals rarely thought in ways identified as "rational." Instead they used "intuition," identified as "the smooth automatic performance of learned behavior sequences" developed through years of experience and practice.[28] While intuition was used in all phases of problem solving, it was specifically used to:

- Sense when a problem existed
- Perform well-learned behavior patterns rapidly
- Synthesize bits of data and information into an integrated picture
- Check the results of rational analysis
- Bypass in-depth analysis and move rapidly to arrive at a decision[29]

Other reviews of the use of intuition by top executives have found that such use takes place primarily in open, rapidly changing organizations for nonroutine tasks that depend on the consideration of broad, as opposed to narrowly focused, issues. According to those executives who use intuition successfully, the settings in which it is most helpful are those where:

- There is a high level of uncertainty
- Little previous precedent for a specific decision exists
- Facts are limited
- Facts do not point to a specific solution
- There is limited time available for decision making and considerable pressure on the decision maker to be right
- Several good alternatives are available[30]

Early in this chapter it was emphasized that individuals generally make decisions with limited rationality because of the day-to-day constraints humans face in the acquisition and use of information. Intuition is a supplementary behavior that many leaders use to facilitate the decision-making process. Further, in an environment where organizations face continual and rapid change, these individuals are adapting their behaviors to increase the speed with which they make decisions.

Accelerating the Process of Decision Making

It is possible that individuals who like to make decisions do so quickly because of incomplete analysis, limited conflict over choices, and a preference for being autocratic in the decision-development process. However, decision makers in turbulent environments who value adaptive organizations accelerate the speed of decision making to remain competitive and guide high-performing entities. In a study of executives in the microcomputer industry, for instance, Kathleen Eisenhardt found that decision makers who purpose-fully and successfully accelerate the speed of decision making exhibit the fol-lowing behaviors:

- Have frequent meetings
- Use real-time information
- Develop multiple alternatives simultaneously
- Seek advice of experienced "counselors," particularly one or two
- Use "consensus with qualification" to resolve conflicts; in other words, they strive for consensus but make a decision if it is apparent consensus will not be reached expeditiously[31]

By comparison, slow decision makers are "bogged down by the fruitless search for information, excessive development of alternatives, and paralysis in the face of conflict and uncertainty."[32]

In the future, in environments and organizations undergoing rapid change, organizational executives would do well to understand the impor-tance of expeditious decision making as a strategic leadership behavior. While the rapidity with which someone makes a decision has not historically been a studied component of one's decision-making style, such may be the case in the future. Just as individuals possess communication and leadership styles, they also exhibit sets of relatively patterned behaviors as they approach the task of decision making.

DECISION-MAKING STYLES

Just as leadership style describes the way in which leaders interact with fol-lowers, *decision style* describes how individuals approach the process of mak-ing and implementing decisions, based on their values, beliefs, experience, and expertise. Much of the research on decision style uses Carl Jung's psy-chological theory on how people process data and how decisions are approached with information in hand.

According to Jung, information acquisition stresses either sensing or intu-ition. A *sensing* person prefers to use hard data or specific information when making a decision whereas an *intuitive* person seeks and accepts qualitative and subjective information and that which describes hypothetical possibilities. Jung also proposed that when making a decision individuals use one of two approaches: thinking or feeling. The *thinking* approach stresses the use of logic and formal reasoning. One who uses the *feeling* approach considers decision development from a personal perspective, based on values and the personal effects a decision will have. Using Jung's theories, some decision-making researchers have identified and studied four decision styles:

ST (sensation/thinking)—an analytical approach
NT (intuition/thinking)—a speculative approach
SF (sensation/feeling)—a consultative approach
NF (intuition/feeling)—a charismatic approach[33]

Depending on the decisional context, however, an organizational leader conceivably may use all four modes or styles. Indeed, summarizing a study of 152 top executives and their decision-making styles, Nutt suggests that those using all four styles achieve a balanced perspective of an organization and its needs. However, he admits, few executives exhibit all four styles within organizations, and "top managers are prone to select key people that they resonate with—that is, people with similar styles. Such an approach is apt to reinforce the *status quo* and to block change."[34] Making decisions in teams, where people can be added who have perspectives different from the executive in charge, creates access for different viewpoints and potentially increases the possibility of more high-quality decisions.

In another study on decision-making style, Pelton, et al., made distinctions between Type 1 and Type 2 decision situations as they observed fifty chief executive officers who had caused significant changes in company direction because of their innovative solutions to organizational problems. Type 1 decision situations were characterized as being simple and analyzable, occurring routinely, with solutions foreseeable and predictable, and perhaps even programmable. Type 2 decision situations were defined as being complex, not routine, with solutions unforeseen and unpredictable. Executives identified as being successful decision makers in Type 2 situations exhibit the following behaviors:

- Recognize a Type 2 situation when it emerges
- Avoid rigid adherence to conventional management principles and formulate effective alternatives
- Develop confidence in using intuition as an aid to effective decision making
- Draw productively on experience but avoid barriers that experience presents
- Change the structure of organizations when appropriate, such as when experiencing unusual growth or unusual demands made on their organizations
- Develop a useful image of the future using planning
- Understand the importance of self-management and teamwork
- Respond to situations with flexibility[35]

Different researchers identify and label decision-making styles in relationship to the specific studies they conduct. What is important to remember for our purposes is that leaders do have different decision-making styles. That is how one can account for different decisions made by people with the same information. Decision-making style, like communication and leadership styles, is personalized to a significant degree, and the relationships among these styles provide a portrait of an organizational leader. What the study of leadership lacks at this time is sufficient research on the interrelationships of these styles and their effects on one another.

Although decision-making style is a reflection of the values, experience, expertise, and characteristics of an organizational leader, its development is also affected by those individuals who work for, or with, that leader. While the focus of this chapter is on decision making as conducted by organizational leaders, one must recognize the importance of participative decision making in an era where the use of teams to accomplish tasks is increasing, or at least is increasingly discussed. Indeed, one aspect of a leader's decision-making style is the degree to which he or she involves others in the decision making process. (See Chapter 3's discussion of participative leadership.) While much research for many years has analyzed group decision making, this chapter has focused on decision creation as the responsibility of an individual, who may certainly involve others in the process for a variety of reasons. An effective organizational leader knows when to make unilateral decisions, when to delegate decision making, and when to participate with others in a group process.

Sometimes group decision making *emerges or evolves* as a process, when an organizational leader informally consults with individuals as a group to consider decision alternatives. The use of groups can also be *purposefully constructed* through the selection of work teams whose major goals include the creation of solutions to problems.

As decision makers, leaders attempt to solve existing problems and create solutions in anticipation of organizational needs. In the latter case, leaders are responding to their interests in *improving* an organization through change, not just maintaining it. As we shall see in the next chapter, such leaders may be interested in dramatic and continual change, that is, in the transformation of their organizations. According to Bass, such leaders are more effective decision makers than others because they are:

- More alert to the beginnings of problems and anticipate the emergence of them
- More flexible and are able to deal with more problems simultaneously
- Quicker to react to emerging problems
- Likely to view problems in a larger context and longer time frame
- Aware that failed decisions are learning experiences
- Interested in both organizational and environmental contexts as they search for information

- More likely to seek information from informal sources rather than conduct a search under prescribed rules
- More likely to change rules and culture as needed
- More likely to practice management by walking around to promote upward flow of information[36]

Whether one is engaged in seeking information, developing decision alternatives, or implementing a preferred solution, the process of decision making depends on communication. In organizations, decision development depends on the construction of shared meanings as information is discussed and alternatives are debated. An organizational leader guides decision development and implementation processes through the use of various communication channels and the creation of multiple messages. As a result, decision making is a form of the management of meaning in organizations. Through the processes of searching for information, identifying alternatives, selecting a decision choice, and implementing that choice, leaders create meaning and interpret it for organizational members. Ideally, these processes enhance both the task and the social relationships among them. Indeed, part of the value of decision making is in the process—not just the product. It is the process that engages organizational members in communal activity to achieve goals at the organizational, group, and individual levels.

At no time is decision making more important than when an organization faces change—and every organization changes continually, in varying degrees. As creators and sustainers of cultures, and as decision makers, leaders also are change agents, especially when organizations must adapt to rapid and dramatic change in the environments that surround them.

SUMMARY

Communication is integral to the decision-making process. Through interaction the form and content of decisions are developed. They are the social products of the organizational culture that creates them. The notion of how decisions are made in organizations has evolved from simple explanations to an understanding that the process is complex and multifaceted.

In theory, decision making is a rational process; but we do not live in a theoretical or completely rational world. We process information under a variety of constraints, including insufficient use of cognitive abilities and inadequate technologies or tools to gather and evaluate information. We make a limited search for alternatives and only consider some of the alternatives we discover. As a result, rationality in decision making is limited because information processors, decision makers, and implementers are human. Leaders as well as other organizational members often engage in decision taking rather than decision making. In decision taking, leaders apply decision behaviors that are learned over time and are based on existing knowledge structures in response to a particular problem. When they make decisions, targeted and innovative decision behaviors are used to develop a decision for a particular problem or issue.

Another approach to decision making reflects the inherent presence of conflict and compromise in the process. Organizational members become participants in shifting alliances, and coalitions of competing interests, who attempt to dominate or control organizational action.

Decisions may also be the result of pouring problems, solutions, participants, and opportunities into a mix of possibilities—the "garbage can" model of decision making. This approach is used in many organizations, and not necessarily consciously, because the very notion of "organization" depends on fluid and flexible communication to complete tasks and create social relationships.

Information is the substance from which decisions are made. Leaders must adopt behaviors that facilitate the search for and use of information. Such behaviors include: using appropriate styles to search for information; using information as a valuable organizational resource; creating structures that facilitate information flow among all those involved in a decision-making process; and using "rich" media in the process.

The following points are important to an understanding of the interrelationship between leadership and decision making:

- Formal information systems may summarize information to the extent that it loses its richness.
- Many important decisions are not the product of single individuals; they are the result of interactions among multiple persons sharing information.
- Leaders must remember that good news travels faster than bad news (information) when it is transmitted from lower levels to higher levels in an organization.
- Leaders must rely on information that is accessible from sources other than those personally, politically, or hierarchically close to them.
- Decision makers seek information that supports their points of view. However, soliciting and using information that agrees only with one's opinions contributes to "information insularity," a situation that restricts a leader's decision-making capabilities because one lacks a variety of opinions and data.
- Information flow and decision making are interdependent processes.
- A decision outcome depends on the quality and quantity of information used by the decision maker and that individual's framing of it.
- Environmental, organizational, individual, and group influences affect the process of decision making, as do issue characteristics.

Most conceptualizations or models of the decision-making process focus, to varying degrees, on the definition of the problem requiring a decision, acquisition of information, development of decision alternatives, the selection of an alternative, and implementation of a decision. Additionally, some decision makers may use vigilant problem-solving, intuition, and accelerated decision making, depending on the situational context in which they are working.

A decision style describes how an individual approaches the process of making and implementing decisions, based on values, experience, and expertise. Decision-making style is personalized to a significant degree, just like leadership and communication styles. That is how one can account for different decisions made by people with the same information.

Decision development depends on the construction of shared meanings as information is communicated and alternatives are debated. Therefore, part of the worth of organizational decision making is in the process as well as its product. It is the process that engages organizational members in communal activity to achieve organizational goals.

QUESTIONS TO CONSIDER

1. Describe the following models of decision making: rational model, limited rational model, political model, and the "garbage can" model.

2. Define "media richness" and identify "rich" and "poor" media by describing their characteristics related to language, verbal and nonverbal cues, and feedback.

3. List and give examples of three environmental and three organizational influences affecting decision making.

4. Describe the processes of decision making identified by: (1) The University of Bradford studies (2) Bernard Bass, and (3) Irving Janis.

5. What is the difference between decision making designed to optimize versus decision making designed to satisfice.

6. Describe the use of intuition in decision making. Under what circumstances is it most helpful?

7. What are ways in which decision making can be accelerated?

CASE PROBLEM

Sam has been elected president of the Corporate Communications Student Interest Group (CCSIG) at his university. This organization is mainly comprised of speech majors, although students in other departments such as management, marketing, advertising, and public relations also take courses in the area of "corporate communication." One of Sam's first responsibilities is to increase the diversity of the organization's membership with respect to race, ethnicity, and university major to facilitate interdisciplinary activities and projects among a variety of university students. This type of campus-wide initiative will require contacting a variety of individuals and groups on campus for ideas and suggestions, and then developing a multiple-strategy plan for membership diversification.

What media should Sam use to acquire information? Why? What decision-making process or processes should he use? What decision-making models are particularly applicable as strategies are developed by Sam and other organizational members? If you were a member of this organization, what strategies might you suggest to Sam?

ENDNOTES

1. Herbert A. Simon, *Administrative Behavior*, 2d ed. (New York: The Macmillan Company, 1957), 155.
2. Marshall Scott Poole and Randy Y. Hirokawa, "Communication and Group Decision-Making," in *Communication and Group Decision-Making*, eds. Marshall Scott Poole and Randy Y. Hirokawa (Beverly Hills: Sage Publications, 1986), 20.
3. Ibid., 25.
4. Mairead Browne, *Organizational Decision Making and Information* (Norwood, NJ: Ablex Publishing Corporation, 1993), 8–9.
5. These and other limits to rationality are discussed by Herbert A. Simon, *Administrative Behavior*, 2d ed. (New York: The Macmillan Company, 1957).
6. Richard Butler, *Designing Organizations, A Decision-Making Perspective* (London: Routledge, 1991), 47–48.
7. Kathy L. Wohlert, "Linguistic Innovators and Organizational Decisions—The Role of Metaphoric Language in Decision-Making," paper presented at the annual meeting of the International Communication Association, Washington, D.C., May 1993.
8. Marshall Scott Poole and Joel A. Doelger, "Developmental Processes in Group Decision-Making," in *Communication and Group Decision-Making*, eds. Marshall Scott Poole and Randy Y. Hirokawa (Beverly Hills: Sage Publications, 1986), 51–52.
9. M. D. Cohen, J. G. March, and P. J. Olsen, "A Garbage Can Model of Organizational Choice," *Administrative Science Quarterly* 17 (1972): 1–25.
10. Richard Butler, *Designing Organizations, A Decision Making Perspective* (London: Routledge, 1991), 55.
11. Paul C. Nutt, "Types of Organizational Decision Processes," *Administrative Science Quarterly* 29 (1984): 414–450.
12. Charles A. O'Reilly, Jennifer A. Chatman, and John C. Anderson, "Message Flow and Decision Making," in *Handbook of Organizational Communication*, ed. Frederic M. Jablin, et al. (New York: Sage Publications, 1987), 618.
13. Vicky Gordon Martin and Donald R. Martin, "The Types and Styles of Managerial Information Scanning," *Management Communication Quarterly* 2 (February 1989): 3.

14. Leonard C. Hawes, "Information Overload and the Organization of 1984," *Western Speech* (Summer 1974): 196.

15. Richard L. Daft and Robert H. Lengel, "Information Richness: A New Approach to Managerial Behavior and Organization Design," in *Research in Organizational Behavior*, Vol. 6, eds. Barry M. Staw and L. L. Cummings (Greenwich, CT: JAI Press, 1984), 223.

16. Ibid., 229

17. Gail L. Fann and Larry R. Smeltzer, "Communication Attributes Used by Small Business Owners/Managers for Operational Decision Making," *Journal of Business Communication* 26 (Fall 1989): 307–308.

18. Charles A. O'Reilly, Jennifer A. Chatman, and John C. Anderson, "Message Flow and Decision Making," in *Handbook of Organizational Communication*, ed. Frederic M. Jablin, et al. (Thousand Oaks, CA: Sage Publications, 1987), 618.

19. David J. Hickson, Richard J. Butler, David Cray, Geoffrey R. Mallory, and David C. Wilson, *Top Decisions, Strategic Decision-Making in Organizations* (San Francisco: Jossey-Bass Publishers, 1986).

20. Ibid., 167.

21. Theodore Sorensen, *Decision-Making in the White House* (New York: Columbia University Presse, 1963), 18–19.

22. Bernard A. Bass, *Organizational Decisionmaking* (Homewood, IL: Irwin, 1983), 175.

23. Irving L. Janis and Leon Mann, *Decision Making* (New York: The Free Press, 1977), 11.

24. Ibid., 11.

25. Ibid., 39.

26. Irving L. Janis, *Crucial Decisions, Leadership in Policymaking and Crisis Management* (New York: The Free Press, 1989), 29.

27. Ibid., 149, adapted from Table 7–1.

28. Daniel J. Isenberg, "How Senior Managers Think," Harvard Business Review (November–December 1984): 85.

29. Ibid., 85–86.

30. Weston H. Agor, *The Logic of Intuitive Decision Making* (New York: Quorum Books, 1986), 18.

31. Kathleen Eisenhardt, "Speed and Strategic Choice: How Managers Accelerate Decision Making," *California Management Review* (Spring 1990): 42, adapted from Table 1.

32. Ibid., 41.

33. Paul C. Nutt, "Flexible Decision Styles and the Choices of Top Executives," *Journal of Management Studies* 30:5 (September 1993): 697.

34. Ibid., 718.

35. Warren J. Pelton, Sonja Sackman, and Robert Boguslaw, *Tough Choices, The Decision-Making Styles of America's Top 50 CEOs* (Homewood, IL: Dow Jones-Irwin, 1990), 148–149.

36. Bernard M. Bass, "Transformational Leadership and Team and Organizational Decision Making," in *Improving Organizational Effectiveness*, eds. Bernard M. Bass and Bruce J. Avolio (Thousand Oaks, CA: Sage Publications, 1994), 118.

6

LEADERS AS CHANGE AGENTS

Heraclitus, a Greek philosopher, once wrote that "nothing endures but change." In organizations, as well as societies, understanding the inevitability of change and the importance of guiding it rather than reacting to it is critical to leaders. Change swirls around our educational, political, economic, and religious institutions, affects our for-profit and nonprofit organizations, and is an integral part of the lives of the people that comprise them. While organizations constantly are changing, even though sometimes imperceptibly to those within them, dramatic, rapid change increasingly is reflected in the strategies and structures, demographics, and technologies of organizations as they move toward becoming postmodern entities (see Chapter 2).

Those responsible for leading organizations must be responsible for leading change—for stimulating rather than stonewalling the process. Such leadership requires seeing the organization not as it is, but as it should be by creating and communicating a "vision" of its future. It requires understanding the nature of change, including the components of the change process, and how environmental and organizational influences affect leaders' attempts to create innovation within organizations. Additionally, it demands knowledge of the multiple strategies available to implement the process and the ways that communication may be used in this endeavor. If change was all that endured in the days of the ancient Greeks, then surely its power speaks eloquently to those of us in multiple and competing societies and organizations around the world. Accordingly, this chapter focuses on the leader as change agent, perhaps the most important role assumed by those responsible for the development of organizations in an era of history when the speed of change around and within many places of human endeavor seems to be accelerating at a frenetic pace.

Before analyzing the role of leadership in a change process, it is important to understand the phenomenon as seen in an organizational context.

THE NATURE OF CHANGE IN ORGANIZATIONS

The notion of change implies motion or movement. In organizations, that motion is "ubiquitous and multidirectional" and change efforts depend on "grabbing hold of some aspect of the motion and steering it in a particular direction . . ."[1] As an organizational leader finds himself or herself assuming the role of change agent, the following conceptualizations of change, taken together, help create a portrait of the process.

- Change is a multicomponent process. While the notion of change as a series of stages is common in research literature, change is first and foremost a process. Any conceptualization of it occurring in phases must assume that there is a great deal of overlapping between and among them.
- Change is both perceptual and behavioral. It is an orientation to a new way of thinking and a set of behaviors to enact that way of thinking.
- Organizational change affects each individual in the multiple roles they assume—as an individual with personal interests and goals; as a member of a work group; and as a member of a family with a stake in organizational decisions. As a result, humans may react negatively to change in organizations because they sense a resultant loss of control over their jobs, their routines, and their lives. Daryl R. Conner suggests that organizational members pass through the following series of stages when adapting to a change they do not want. These stages are similar to those suggested by Elizabeth Kubler-Ross in her research on individuals facing their own deaths.[2]

  1. Stability—the present state, the status quo
  2. Immobilization—initial reaction, and shock related to the change
  3. Denial—rejection; ignoring new information that does not fit into one's old frame of reference
  4. Anger—frustration; lashing out at co-workers, friends, and family
  5. Bargaining—the beginning of acceptance; beginning the process of negotiation to avoid the impact of change
  6. Depression—resignation that a change has taken place
  7. Testing—exploring ways to reenter the organizational process
  8. Acceptance—becoming part of the new organizational context; change may not be liked but is accepted

- Change, like death, is natural. It is the rule not the exception. Ironically, we react fairly well to *sudden* threats to our existence—fires, earthquakes, a perceived imminent mugging, dramatic loss of revenue in a month's time—but we are not particularly good at recognizing threats that appear gradually. The parable of the boiled frog is relevant here: a frog will hop quickly if placed in a pot of boiling water. If placed in cool water that is slowly being heated, however, he will remain and be boiled to death because he does not recognize the danger in that situational context.

- Change may be planned or unplanned. Planned change is deliberately shaped by organizational members. Unplanned change is prompted by forces outside the organization, and the organizational response is reactive rather than proactive.
- Change may be incremental or transformational. Incremental, or first-order change, constitutes minor improvements or adjustments in an organization as it grows and develops. Second-order change is transformational; it is multidimensional, multifunctional, radical, and discontinuous change.

The turbulent environments in which many organizations now exist may necessitate attempts at transformational change to insure adaptation rather than demise among these entities.

- Organizational transformation, or change that dramatically alters the mission, structure, processes, and culture of an organization, involves creating change in an organization's technical, political, and cultural systems. The technical system is comprised of technology, resources, and information—the components of the organization that accomplish tasks. The political system allocates rewards and is the web of interrelationships that influence decisions and decision makers. The cultural system involves those shared values and beliefs that guide the behaviors of organizational members.[3]
- Studying organizational change, and the leader's role in that process, requires a concomitant look at environmental influences on the organization. An organization undergoing change is part of a network of connections to external entities and influences. Competition from other organizations, the changing expectations of organizational stakeholders, and sociopolitical, legal, and technological developments are examples of environmental conditions that may prompt organizational change.
- Change may be introduced through unilateral action, shared approaches, or delegated approaches.[4] Initiating change unilaterally may mean starting the process by decree, replacing key individuals in the organization to assure compliance, and/or changing structures so that change agents occupy significant roles in those structures. Shared approaches to initiating change include the use of groups to begin and oversee the process. Delegated approaches obviously focus on the assignment of the change process to others.

Understanding the nature of change is by no means an exact science. To further understand this process, it is beneficial to consider some of the theoretical approaches that describe how it is initiated and implemented in organizations.

THE CHANGE PROCESS

According to Edgar Schein, the following assumptions underlie his concept of change in organizations:

- The change process involves unlearning as well as learning something new.
- Change only occurs when there is motivation to change.
- Organizational change is mediated through individual changes (in structures, processes, reward systems).
- Because it involves attitudes and values, change is initially painful and threatening.[5]

One of the more famous models of organizational change was described by Kurt Lewin in 1952 and was later adapted by Schein. This model essentially describes three stages in the change process:

Unfreezing—in which motivation is used to help organizational members disconfirm and unlearn existing organizational behaviors and produce sufficient anxiety to motivate their interest in change

Changing—through which new behaviors are developed using new information or a new perspective on old information

Refreezing—in which new behaviors are integrated into organizational routines and change is stabilized[6]

In 1977, Beckhard and Harris suggested that organizational change consists of an organization moving from a present state to a future state by passing through a transition state.[7] This concept is only helpful to the study of change as a process if one understands that the demarcation lines between states are fuzzy indeed. Moreover, one must always be willing to ask the following questions: Do organizations ever really attain the future state, or are they continually in transition? By the time they have reached the future state, has that stage of change become the present state?

Still another perspective through which to study organizational change is offered by Rosabeth Moss Kanter who focuses on the *actors* in the process. She categorizes the "main characters" as being either strategists, implementers, or recipients in a change effort.[8]

Assuming that change does require unlearning behaviors and learning new ones, what are some of the components of the change process? A number of these are discussed below.

Reasons for an Organizational Change

Most leaders undertake a change effort for specific reasons. These may include the need for a change in an organization's mission, or its major purpose, as affected by the environment. A major organizational change would take place, for instance, if owners of a record store decided to sell videos as well. Another major reason for an organizational change might involve the internal structures and activities integral to the operation of an organization. Modifications in an automotive plant from line assembly to team assembly, such as that used by Saturn car makers, would constitute such a change. Achieving organizational control is also an impetus for change. In this instance a realignment of coalitions of decision makers in the organization takes place so that power is dispersed differently than was previously the case. A newspaper that decides to sell its controlling interest to employees and make editorial decisions via a management team illustrates this reason.[9]

Some of the conditions within and external to an organization that may become reasons for, and stimulate, change include the following:

- Rapid growth
- Rapid decline in productivity and/or resources
- Stakeholder pressures on management (e.g., employees, customers, stockholders)
- Organizational or environmental crises that directly impact the organization

Phases of the Change Effort

Studying organizational change requires attention to different theorists' notions of what constitutes its stages or phases. Kimberly and Quinn suggest that the following phases occur in the process of organizational revitalization:

- First a trigger event caused by environmental pressures occurs.
- This event causes a dominant group in the organization to feel the need for change.
- This felt need motivates the creation of a vision of a future state by one or more organizational leaders.
- Using this vision as a guide, commitment for the change is mobilized among organizational members.

- The envisioned change is institutionalized in the culture of the organization through practices, policies, and procedures.[10]

These or other phases and stages in the process depend on several actions initiated by organizational leaders.

Change Activities

To implement a change effort, be it incremental or transformational, a number of change activities must lead the effort. These include the following:

- Identification of tasks
- Creation of structures to manage the change effort
- Development of strategies to establish the need for change among organizational members
- Development of strategies to initiate the change effort among opinion leaders in the organization
- Development of strategies to communicate information, on an ongoing basis, about the change effort
- Creation and/or assignment of human, fiscal, and material resources through which to conduct the change[11]

The goals, phases, and activities driving a change effort are only as good as the commitment and competence of those leading that effort. As a result, we now look at the conditions that affect leaders when they assume the role of change agent.

Conditions Affecting the Leadership of Change

The stress of leadership is compounded when a leader becomes a change agent. Added to one's daily responsibilities is the monumental task of preparing organizational members for a transition, conducting change activities, and continually communicating about the change effort to several organizational constituencies. It takes more energy and time for an organizational leader to simultaneously pursue the accomplishment of ongoing organizational goals *and* the implementation of a change process. Consequently, additional stress is one condition affecting an organizational leader who is implementing a change effort.

Another influence on the leadership of change is the organizational context in which a leader finds himself or herself. Different contexts require different leadership behaviors. An organization facing change requires leaders to provide *instrumental* or substantive leadership, that which provides resources and actions that directly assist the change effort. Organizations that are not in the process of large-scale change may only require *symbolic* leadership for a time, which focuses on maintaining and legitimizing an organization's culture among its members.[12]

The ability to understand the context in which one is operating, as affected by the organizational and environmental influences discussed in Chapter 2, is an important requirement for leaders. The development of appropriate change strategies depends on a leader's understanding of the context in which they will be implemented. Indeed, context both creates and reflects the ways that change is enacted.

Part of the situational context surrounding the leadership of change is affected by resistance to that change among organizational members. Such resistance may be due to perceived threats to the power of certain groups in the organization, perceived disruption of personal and professional security, breaks in comfortable task and social relationships, and a general fear of the unknown. Considering these reasons, resistance will be reduced if a number of principles are followed. These include the following:

- Key organizational members feel that the plan for change is their plan, not one created solely by outsiders.
- Participants see change as reducing, not increasing, current task burdens.
- The change effort depends on values and ideals that are part of the organization's culture.
- Participants feel their autonomy and security is not threatened.
- The change effort is adopted by consensus after discussions among organizational members.[13]

In order to minimize the personal and organizational stress that emerges during change efforts, as well as resistance to those efforts, leaders must understand the relationship of the organization to its environment (including its competitors, relevant sociopolitical issues, economic forces, etc.); the task relationships among functions and structures within the organization; the social and political relationships among groups in the organization; and the unique elements of the organization's culture, including leader–follower relationships. A change effort, particularly a transformational one, is complex and multifaceted. As a result, the initiation and implementation of such an effort depends on the effective performance of multiple leadership behaviors in planning and executing a program of action. Reviewing the range of behaviors used by leaders as champions of change is critical to a study of organizational leadership.

LEADERSHIP BEHAVIORS
IN THE PROCESS OF CHANGE

Guiding a process of organizational change, be it incremental or transformational, requires more than announcing a plan and delegating its execution. It requires that leaders process relevant information and develop ways of thinking about: (1) the organization; (2) the function of leadership in a change endeavor; and (3) the major purposes of the change and its possible effects. It demands a variety of actions to manage the movement of the organization through the process of change. It calls for the creation of multiple messages and the use of multiple channels to communicate the plans for change, and the progress of organizational efforts to effect it among a variety of constituencies. To understand leaders as change agents, it is important to consider in some detail the leadership behaviors involved in planning, implementing, and communicating about, the change process.

Planning for Change

Decisions to initiate organizational change must be based on sufficient and credible information which indicates the need for and the desirability of that change. Information processing requirements are particularly high if an organization plans transformational change because leaders must prepare for the emotional, social, and cognitive adjustments that such change stimulates among organizational members. The search for and use of information to create plans for change depend in great part on leaders' "ways-of-thinking" about themselves, their organizations, the nature of change, and its implications for their organizations. For our purposes, a way-of-thinking "consists of a number of thematic sets of values, assumptions, beliefs, ideas, and thoughts about leadership and strategic development in organizations."[14] Ways-of-thinking are the products of leaders' personalities, experiences, and expertise. How one views his or her organization, the environment, and the need for change are all affected by these "cognitive lenses." Moreover, the elements of a plan for change are a result of, or at least partially attributed to, these lenses—leaders' actions are expressions of ways-of-thinking. Therefore, the organizational change process is very much a reflection of a leader's personal thoughts and actions, based on emotional and relational experiences as well as cognitive ones. Ways-of-thinking guide the planning of change and steer the creation of implementation strategies. While no one strategy or set of strategies is appropriate for all organizations, leaders must work in concert with organizational members, as groups and individuals, to create the strategies most useful in a particular organizational context.

Implementing Change: The Use of Strategies

There is an old but wise saying that in life there are those who make things happen, those who watch things happen, and those who wonder what happened. Change agents obviously make things happen. However, in their selection of strategies, or ways of making change occur, leaders must remember that some organizational members may wish to watch from the sidelines as change is implemented while others may initially feel like victims of rather than participants in the change process. Change strategies should address the need for organization-wide participation in the change effort, as is discussed later in this chapter.

From a general perspective, Rosabeth Moss Kanter has suggested that there are three critical leadership behaviors used by those who know how to master the process of change implementation:

1. Purposing—creating a vision of the future meaningful to organizational members
2. Promoting innovation—encouraging creativity, risk-taking, and experimentation in the change effort
3. Providing a people orientation—using teams, sharing power, and emphasizing open communication[15]

A critical strategy used by leaders in the process of implementing change is that of creating an organizational vision. With feet firmly planted in reality, leaders should strive to see their organizations not as they are but as they ought to be. Consequently, a leader in the role of change agent should ask a number of questions that focus on the future, including the following:

- What major changes can be expected in the needs and wants of those served by the organization?
- What changes can be expected in the major stakeholders (e.g., employees, customers, clients, management) of the organization?
- What major economic, social, political, and technological changes can be expected in the organization's environment?[16]

These questions, as well as others that take stock of the organization's present needs and future aspirations, help craft a picture of a future state to which a leader holds an unseen compass that directs organizational change.

After the process of creating a vision, there are a variety of leadership behaviors needed to foster the implementation of the change effort. These include:

1. Organizing tasks, creating structures to manage the change, and appointing organizational members to various roles in these structures

2. Rewarding behaviors that accomplish tasks in the change effort
3. Communicating with powerful organizational coalitions to enlist their support for change
4. Informing organizational members on an ongoing basis about the progress of the process
5. Serving as a role model for those organizational members working on various change strategies by continually supporting the change in all communications to both internal and external constituencies
6. Motivating organizational members on an ongoing basis to participate in, or support, change-related activities (e.g., small group planning sessions; reassignment of resources; evaluation of tasks, structures, products, and possible subsequent revisions of them)
7. Encouraging teamwork and participation in change-related decisions and the implementation of strategies
8. Providing resources to support the change effort, such as consultants and materials
9. Continually evaluating the progress of the change effort

A critical consideration for leaders engaged in organizational change is that the types of forces mandating change should influence the strategies selected to enact it. For instance, if an internal condition prompting change is ineffective leadership, the selected strategy should focus on rectifying that problem. If there are problems with existing structures in product manufacturing, change strategies should focus on structural change. If disruptive conflict among departments in a company is developing due to competition for scarce resources, strategies for change should emphasize new ways to share resources and/or methods for acquiring more resources. However, it is important for leaders to remember that too few change strategies are one-dimensional—they may focus only on structure, culture, or management. Effective change efforts are those that look at organizational change as a holistic process, and that rely on interrelated strategies to make changes in several critical components of the organization (e.g. structure, culture, and technologies).

Many change programs are also started in organizations with an emphasis on words, not behaviors. Promoting change in training sessions, memos, speeches, and glossy publications is not easily translatable into behavioral changes. Effective change efforts must rely on strategies that demand or enable new behaviors among individuals and groups. Such strategies might include the initiation of new organizational reporting relationships, the adoption of new technologies, or changes in leadership throughout the organization. Successful strategies are those that rely on cooperative interaction among organizational groups, units, teams, and so on, that foster and unite change efforts occurring at top, middle, and bottom levels of the organization.

Another view of the role of leadership in a change effort considers the need for both charismatic and instrumental guidance. Charismatic leadership depends on the motivational strengths of a leader as well as his or her ethos or credibility among organizational members. According to Nadler and Tushman, such leadership focuses on the processes of envisioning (creating and articulating a vision); energizing (demonstrating one's own excitement and confidence in change effort); and enabling (providing personal and material support for the process).[17]

Charisma alone is not sufficient to implement large-scale change. Visioning and cheerleading will not turn a pretty picture into a reality. Instrumental leadership which guides day-to-day behaviors to accomplish specific tasks in the process of organizational change is also necessary. Examples of such behaviors include:

- Setting agendas and timelines to guide the work of groups and individuals participating in the change effort
- Allocating time, money, and personnel for the effort
- Asking questions and monitoring progress
- Reinforcing the need for change in public statements and private conversations
- Creating rewards for behaviors that advance the process

In short, charismatic leadership provides motivation, but instrumental leadership insures action as the process of change unfolds. Throughout the process an important set of leadership behaviors are the communication behaviors used to sustain a supportive organizational climate, reinforce or change the organizational culture, and in general guide the change process.

COMMUNICATING LEADERSHIP IN THE CHANGE PROCESS

Just as communication is integral to the process of leadership, it is also central to the process of organizational change. Through interaction and the sharing of meaning, organizational members identify the need for change, create a communal vision of what their organization should become, decide on ways of achieving change, and implement change strategies. Communication is the process through which change is implemented using language, symbolic action, and selected media.

Leaders, as is discussed in Chapter 1, are interpreters and sensemakers; they are managers of meaning. When initiating change they must use the rhetorical concept of "identification" to bridge differences between them and organizational members, and to create a shared understanding of the need for change and how it should be implemented.

To this end, the notion of "framing" becomes important to the process of organizational change. Framing is fundamentally a communication process—a series of rhetorical strategies through which interpretive schemes or "frames of reference" internal to individuals or organizations are manifested externally. Messages are given meaning by the context or frame in which they are communicated. As a change agent a leader uses words and actions to establish a context for the change effort, to create images and meanings that will focus attention on the need for change, and to encourage participation in the strategies designed to achieve it. In this endeavor he or she must remember that an organization consists of multiple, and often conflicting, frames of reference.

To successfully initiate change, a leader must first get organizational members to realize that there is a need for change. This may be accomplished by "reframing," that is, using techniques that force or enable individuals to go beyond their existing frames of reference and establish new perspectives on a situation. As Bandler and Grinder observe: "The meaning that any event has depends upon the 'frame' in which we perceive it. When we change the frame we change the meaning. When the meaning changes the person's responses and behaviors also change."[18]

An example of reframing is that which takes place in the movie *It's A Wonderful Life.* In the film, George Bailey wants to die. He lives in the same small town in which he was born, and runs the same small savings and loan company his father built. A good citizen all of his life, his dreams of going to college and traveling around the world never come true. As he contemplates suicide, a friendly angel shows George what life in his community, and with his family, would be like if he never existed. Eventually Bailey realizes that although none of his lifelong dreams were fulfilled, all of his day-to-day wishes have been realized—a loving wife, healthy children, a job that helps others, the support of many friends. The angel changes George's frame of reference by giving him a new perspective on his "wonderful life."

There are several communication strategies that are used to frame, or reframe, the context for organizational change. They include the following:

- The creation and dissemination of multiple messages through multiple media, and the redundant use of both
- The use of face-to-face communication among groups involved in conducting the process, as well as seminars to inform, train, and motivate
- The use of mediated communication channels such as videotapes, audio- and/or videoconferencing, newsletters, and brochures to "spread the word" about the change process on an ongoing basis and to motivate interest and participation in that effort

- Delegation of communication responsibilities to opinion leaders, first-line supervisors, and a variety of individuals at different organizational levels who assume roles in the change effort

Leaders bear the responsibility for determining how information should be used to manage meaning in a change effort. Through metaphors, structures, stories, rituals, policies, and symbolic acts, meanings or frames become institutionalized; they become the organization's reality. Framing the context for organizational change, as a communication process, is dependent on leaders' effective use of language and actions.

Of course, even the best attempts at reframing may be difficult within a large and complex organization. Consequently, organizational leaders must be adept at the utilization of a repertoire of sense-making behaviors, including effective information processing. As an organization grows and becomes more complex through the addition of hierarchical levels, an increase in functional units, and/or more personnel, information flow becomes more ineffective as it attempts to accommodate complexity. As complexity increases, so does the time it takes to process information and disseminate it. If the information capabilities of the organization do not meet its processing needs, people do not receive the information they need to accomplish tasks, understand social and political dynamics, and pursue the achievement of organizational goals. When change efforts are initiated, uncertainty increases, and the more uncertainty that exists the greater the need for information to explain, clarify, and reassure.

There are several ways to improve information flow in organizations during change efforts. They include the use of formal information management systems as well as a variety of face-to-face mechanisms (e.g., work groups, project teams, and quality circles). What leaders must understand is that flexible and/or fast means of processing information are necessary in times of change. "Rich" media are particularly useful to leaders in times of change because they overcome different frames of reference rapidly and foster the social construction of a new "reality" to be shared by individuals working toward the achievement of commonly held organizational goals.

The use of framing, and other communication strategies, may help diminish the effects of management characteristics that are known to impede successful organizational change and even foster organizational decline. D. B. Bibeault suggests that these characteristics include:

- Functional blindness—the tendency of management to ignore warning signals in the organization and assert that its problems are only temporary and can be solved with traditional solutions, such as those that have worked before

- Narrow outlook—the inability of managers to look at problems from different perspectives, both across organizational functions and from different hierarchical levels
- Displacement activity—the repeated use of the same behavior because it is familiar instead of risking a change in behaviors to solve a problem[19]

Of course leaders must share the responsibility as well as the power involved in directing change throughout the organization. Indeed, the success of an organizational change process may well depend on the degree to which power is shared.

"EMPOWERMENT" IN THE PROCESS OF ORGANIZATIONAL CHANGE

Leading change is not successfully accomplished through the efforts of one leader. Indeed, as is discussed in Chapter 1, leadership is exhibited by individuals throughout an organization, at different organizational levels. Such is particularly the case during times of organizational change when the success of a change effort depends on the support of many organizational members. Sometimes the most successful change efforts—those that help an organization realize its "vision"—are those where bottom-up and top-down leadership efforts join together in partnership, where organizational members "buy into" the notion that change was necessary to meet both individual and organizational goals. After all, the causes of change in organizations are generally not one or two distinct issues but a spiderweb of problems that are interrelated and need collaboratively created solutions. Organizational leaders, therefore, are well served by actions they take to create leaders among followers in the change effort. They invest power in people who may be functionally and hierarchically closest to the problems that change will alleviate, and, therefore, who are in the best positions to implement change efforts. The heroine of the Hollywood musical, *Hello Dolly*, observed that "money is best used like manure, spread around making young things grow." Power is a similar resource. In times of change it is best used by investing it in others who can help an organization and its members "grow" or develop.

According to Rosabeth Kanter, people who understand the art of leading productive change are "change masters." These individuals bestow tools of empowerment on organizational members to enhance their participation in a change effort. Such tools include:

- Information—data, technical knowledge, political intelligence, and expertise

- Resources—funds, materials, space, and time
- Support—endorsement, backing, approval, and legitimacy[20]

For instance, if employees in a toy store are being asked to participate in a store-wide plan to improve customer service, all employees should be given information, or access to information, about the toys sold in the store and the store's merchandise-return policy. They should also receive training on how to communicate effectively with customers, including dissatisfied ones. Further, if a city recreation center is expected by community leaders to prevent young people from joining gangs, then that center will need funds, space, and other resources to offer programs attractive to adolescents. If an elementary school's Parent–Teacher Association expects teachers to participate in controlling violence in schools by monitoring hallways and lunchrooms, then teachers must receive the support of parents as well as the backing of school administrators.

The use of all these tools is enhanced if leaders encourage: (1) the formation of networks among organizational members (coalitions of supporters), (2) the decentralization of resources to enhance flexibility and mobilization of effort, and (3) open communication systems.[21]

Jaffe and Scott, who have written about empowerment in organizations, suggest that it is built into three "levels."

1. The mind-sets of individuals. Organizational members must believe they are capable of making changes and being sources of creativity and innovation.
2. Personal and intergroup relationships. People must be willing to participate in self-managed agreements, work in teams, and establish linkages among organizational groups.
3. Organizational policies and structures. The formal and official components of the organization, for example, rules, procedures, reporting relationships, and reward systems, must support individual and group empowerment.[22]

These authors also suggest that there are several common characteristics of organizational leaders that may impede the process of empowerment and, therefore, the process of organizational transformation:

1. Incongruence between stated goals and behavior, such as a leader that espouses the worth of empowerment but is autocratic and controlling in leader–follower interactions
2. Emotional illiteracy, such as a leaders' inadequate understanding of the emotional dynamics people face when involved in dramatic change

3. Inability to give up some control to organizational members due to insufficient trust in them as problem solvers
4. Isolation from subordinates
5. Impatience—giving change efforts insufficient time to be successful
6. The entrenchment of middle management who are most threatened during times of change
7. Inadequate understanding of the need for psychological security among organizational members—their need for clarity, for the elimination of ambiguity and uncertainty[23]

While many organizational members may equate empowerment with the giving or sharing of power with *individuals,* recall the notion of an organization as "groups of groups." It is important for leaders to understand that groups may be channels or media of change, targets of change, and/or agents of change. Because groups may assume one or more of these roles, it is critical that leaders provide the tools of emplowerment to organizational groups—those social collectivities whose interactions and activities are crucial to framing the need for change and implementing the strategies to accomplish it.

BEING A CHANGE AGENT: THE ART AND SCIENCE OF LEADERSHIP

As discussed earlier, the process of change depends on both charismatic and instrumental leadership. Initiating change depends on the ability of a leader to create and communicate a vision, a picture of the future. It also depends on his or her ability to develop and implement the strategies that will accomplish change on a day-by-day basis. Therefore, leadership in the change process is both an art and a science.

Within recent years Peter Senge has spent time writing about the importance of the learning organization, one that is continually able to enhance its capabilities and capacities. To build this organization, Senge suggests, its leaders must be committed to five disciplines, or sets of practices:

1. The creation of a shared vision
2. The development of personal mastery or individual visions that development each member's capacity (organizational members, therefore, may live with a creative tension between what is and what they want their futures and that of the organization to be)
3. Constructions of mental models—internal pictures used to interpret the world and make sense of it

4. Team learning, the use of dialogue to share members' internal pictures and create commonly held meanings important to the development of a learning organization
5. Systems thinking, or a world view of connected thoughts, perception, and individual realities[24]

From the perspective of a change agent, becoming a learning organization requires the initiation of change supported by individual commitments that are united into a collective effort through communication.

Leading a successful organizational change effort depends on many factors, as we have seen throughout this chapter:

- The realization among organizational members that a need for change exists
- The creation and communication of a vision that "describes" what the organization should be
- The commitment of resources to develop change strategies, or ways of accomplishing the change effort
- The empowerment of organizational members to participate in the change effort—no process will be successful if left only to top executives, outside consultants, and human resource specialists
- Open systems of communication that foster a free flow of information and the opportunity for rapid feedback about change goals and strategies

The leadership of change, in short, depends on organizational commitment and communication. Commitment is necessary because effective organizational change, which solves identified problems and creates solutions that endure, takes time. Communication is critical because it is the process through which need is identified, strategies are created, and the process is implemented and ultimately evaluated. Communication is crucial to the change process; and the lack of it, the inattention to it, the misuse and abuse of it, negatively affect many attempts at such change.

As is stated at the beginning of this chapter, change is continual and never ending. Organizations may reach goals set as part of a change process, but the state of the organization when these goals are attained may create the need for a new or different change effort. In this way, leading change is a journey and the product is only as good as the process.

Throughout the decade of the 1990s and into the twenty-first century, one of the most significant change efforts in which leaders will be engaged is that of valuing and guiding organizational diversity. In order to do this, they must be aware of the diversity that exists within organizations and resultant implications for pursuing organizational and individual goals. To understand diversity in organizations one should understand diversity as it exists among their leaders, and it is to that subject we now turn.

SUMMARY

The following observations about change give leaders a portrait of the change process.

- Change is a multicomponent process.
- Change is both perceptual and behavioral.
- Change affects organizational members in the multiple roles they assume, as members of work groups, families, and as individuals with personal goals.
- Change is natural.
- Change may be planned or unplanned.
- Change may be incremental or transformational.

"Models" attempting to depict the change process include:

- The notion of stages, where a process of unfreezing takes place (the unlearning of existing behaviors); changing, through which new behaviors are developed; and refreezing, in which new behaviors are integrated into organizational practices
- The concept of states, where an organization moves from a present state to a future state through a transition state

During an organizational change effort, leaders must process relevant information, develop ways-of-thinking about the organization and its purposes, and consider purposes of change and its possible effects. They also must manage the change process through the creation of multiple messages and the use of multiple channels to communicate plans and progress to organizational members. In this effort, individuals exhibit both instrumental and symbolic leadership. The former provides resources that directly assist the change effort while the latter maintains and enhances an organization's culture.

Effective change effort requires the creation and communication of an organizational vision by a leader or leaders. Other leadership behaviors that are then required to implement organizational change include:

- Organizing tasks and creation structures
- Rewarding behaviors that accomplish tasks
- Communicating with coalitions to enlist support
- Continually informing organizational members about the progress of the change process
- Serving as a role model by supporting the change effort on an ongoing basis
- Encouraging teamwork and participation in change-related decisions and strategy implementation

- Providing resources to support the change effort
- Continually evaluating the progress of the change effort

Through the process of reframing, that is, using techniques that prompt individuals to develop new perspectives about an existing situation or problem, organizational leaders establish a context for the change effort. They focus attention on the need for change and encourage participation in the strategies designed to achieve it. Indeed, leaders are well served by actions they take to invest power in organizational members who may be functionally and/or hierarchically in the best positions to implement change efforts.

Leading a successful change effort depends on a variety of factors, including the following:

- The realization among organizational members that a need for change exists
- The creation and communication of a vision that posits what the organization should be
- The commitment of resources to develop change strategies
- The empowerment of organizational members to participate in the change effort
- The use of open systems of communication that foster a free flow of information and the opportunity for rapid feedback about change goals and strategies

The leadership of change requires commitment because such a process takes time. It also requires communication because that is the process through which need is identified and strategies are created, implemented, and evaluated. Leading change is a process that really does not have a destination since change is continual. Organizations may reach a desired future state, only to find that it is a temporary outpost in a never-ending journey.

QUESTIONS TO CONSIDER

1. Explain each of the following conceptualizations of the change process.

   "Change is both perceptual and behavioral."

   "Change is a multicomponent process."

   "Studying organizational change requires a concurrent study of the environment that surrounds the organization."

2. Compare and contrast incremental and transformational change.

3. Identify and describe several leadership behaviors used to foster the implementation of the organizational change process.

4. Describe the role of framing in the change process, and identify three communication strategies used to frame, or reframe, the context for organizational change.

5. Discuss the notion of "empowerment" from the viewpoint of a leader during an organizational change process.

CASE PROBLEM

Ima Leador has been the president of a small liberal arts college for twenty years. Although at age sixty she is not ready to retire from this position, the Board of Trustees of the college has asked her to step down, effective August 31 of this year. It wants to infuse "new blood" into the position and has hired P. D. Smith, a 42-year-old dean of liberal arts at a major state university, as the new president. The Board wants Smith to oversee major changes in the institution's degree programs and fundraising efforts.

The college's three vice-presidents and its six deans have been in their positions about fifteen years and meet at least once a week with the president. All hiring, firing, and promotion decisions are made by the deans and the president. All major decisions about the day-to-day administration of the university are made by the president and her vice-presidents. Working together for the last fifteen years, Leador and the vice-presidents have formed close friendships and frequently socialize during their free time. Leador will become president emeritus and will return to teaching in the English Department on September 1.

1. What communication strategies might Smith use to initiate change in this organization?
2. What strategies should Smith use to involve the deans and vice-presidents in her change plans?
3. As a consultant to President-Designate Smith, you have been asked to conduct a visioning workshop for Smith and her administrative team. Outline the major topics you want Smith and her team to consider at this workshop.

ENDNOTES

1. Rosabeth Moss Kanter, Barry A. Stein, and Todd D. Jick, *The Challenge of Organizational Change* (New York: The Free Press, 1992), 10.
2. Daryl R. Conner, *Managing at the Speed of Change* (New York: Villard Books, 1993), 132–135.
3. Noel Tichy and David Ulrich, "Revitalizing Organizations: The Leadership Role," in *New Futures: The Challenge of Managing Corporate Transitions*, eds. John R. Kimberly and Robert E. Quinn (Homewood, IL: Dow Jones-Irwin, 1984.)

4. Larry Greiner, "Common Approaches to Change," in *Managing Organizational Change* ed. Roy McLennan (Englewood Cliffs, NJ: Prentice-Hall, 1989), 138.

5. Edgar H. Schein, "Planned Change Theory," in *Managing Organizational Change,* ed. Roy McLennan (Englewood Cliffs, NJ: Prentice-Hall, 1989), adapted from 209.

6. Ibid., 209–212.

7. R. Beckhard and H. Harris, *Organizational Transitions: Managing Complex Change* (Reading, MA: Addison-Wesley Publishing Company, 1977).

8. Rosabeth Moss Kanter, Barry A. Stein, and Todd D. Jick, *The Challenge of Organizational Change* (New York: The Free Press, 1992).

9. Ibid., 15. (Kanter et al., discuss similar phenomena as forms of change.)

10. John R. Kimberly and Robert E. Quinn, *New Futures: The Challenge of Managing Corporate Transitions* (Homewood, IL: Dow Jones-Irwin, 1984).

11. This listing is based on a brief outline of change activities adapted from pp. 69–70 in Richard Beckhard and Wendy Pritchard, *Changing the Essence* (San Francisco: Jossey-Bass Publishers, 1992).

12. An example of published research on organizational context and its effect on leadership roles is an article by Kathryn K. Eggleston and Rabi S. Bhagat, "Organizational Contexts and Contingent Leadership Roles: A Theoretical Exploration," *Human Relations* 46:10 (1993).

13. This listing is based on several suggestions offered by Don Bryant, "The Psychology of Resistance to Change," *Managing Organizational Change,* ed. Roy McLennan (Englewood Cliffs, NJ: Prentice-Hall, 1989), 194–195.

14. Bo Hellgren and Leif Melin, "The Role of Strategists: Ways-of-Thinking in Strategic Change Processes," in *Strategic Thinking: Leadership and the Management of Change,* eds. John Hendry, Gerry Johnson, and Julia Newton, (New York: Wiley, 1993), 59–60.

15. Amir Levy and Uri Merry, *Organizational Transformation* (New York: Praeger, 1986), 55.

16. Burt Nanus, *Visionary Leadership* (San Francisco: Jossey-Bass Publishers, 1992), 78–91.

17. David A. Nadler and Michael Tushman, "Leadership for Organizational Change," in *Large-Scale Organizational Change,* eds. Allan M. Mohrman, Jr., Susan A. Mohrman, Gerald E, Ledford, Jr., Thomas G. Cummings, and Edward E. Lawler III & Associates (San Francisco: Jossey-Bass Publishers, 1991), 105–106.

18. R. Bandler and J. Grinder, *Reframing: Neurolinguistic Programming and the Transformation of Meaning* (Moab, UT: Real People Press, 1982), 1.

19. D. B. Bibeault, *Corporate Turnaround: How Managers Turn Losers into Winners* (New York: McGraw-Hill, 1982).

20. Rosabeth Moss Kanter, *The Change Masters* (New York: Simon and Schuster, 1983), 159.

21. Ibid., 160.

22. Dennis T. Jaffe and Cynthia D. Scott, "Building a Committed Workplace: An Empowered Organization as a Competitive Advantage," in *The New Paradigm in*

Business, Emerging Strategies for Leadership and Organizational Change, eds. Michael Ray and Alan Rinzler (New York: Jeremy P. Tarcher/Perigee Books, 1993), 142.

23. Ibid., 144–145.
24. Peter Senge, "The Art & Practice of the Learning Organization," in *The New Paradigm in Business, Emerging Strategies for Leadership and Organizational Change*, eds. Michael Ray and Alan Rinzler (New York: Jeremy P. Tarcher/Perigee Books, 1993).

7

LEADERS AS FACILITATORS
AND AS REFLECTIONS
OF ORGANIZATIONAL DIVERSITY

In this era of human history, characterized by large-scale socioeconomic, political, and technological change, organizational leaders must focus on the development of followers as equal partners in the process of organizational innovation. The last three chapters were devoted to critical roles that leaders must assume—initiators and sustainers of organizational culture, decision makers, and change agents. As the demographics of this society and its workforce dramatically change, perhaps there is no more important task of leadership than that of promoting the personal and professional development of individuals by valuing, and indeed facilitating, organizational diversity.

Diversity has existed in organizations since individuals began forming or joining groups. People have created shared meanings that foster the accomplishment of commonly held goals even though they practice a variety of religions, have different educational backgrounds, and have different life experiences. However, *diversity* is more "visible" in organizations of the 1990s because differences in race, ethnicity, gender, place of birth, and sexual orientation are receiving great attention in the press, the board room, and the company lunch room. Racial, ethnic, and gender differences are more apparent than those related to educational level or marital status.

Consider the following findings from *Workforce 2000*, a report on the American workforce as it is projected to be at the turn of the century.[1]

- The age of the population is increasing; the average age of the workforce by the year 2000 will be thirty-nine, up from thirty-six in 1987.

148

- Between 1987 and the year 2000, two-thirds of the new people coming into the American workforce will be women, and they will rapidly enter higher-paying professional and technical fields than is currently the case. (Given this statistic, we might assume an increase in the number of women who will move into management, executive, and leadership positions.)
- Minorities will comprise a larger share of the new entrants into the workforce than is currently the case. Indeed, they will comprise almost 30 percent of the new entrants into the workforce.
- Immigrants will represent the largest share of the increase in the workforce, and their numbers will be concentrated in the south and west due to the large number of individuals coming to this country from Asia and Latin America.
- Non-whites, women, and immigrants will comprise more than five-sixths of the additions to the workforce until 2000; in 1987 these individuals comprised one-half of the workforce.
- The fasting growing jobs, in terms of numbers, will be in professional, technical, and sales fields, which require higher educational and skill levels than is currently the case.
- By the year 2000 about 47 percent of the workforce will be women.
- In the same year black women will outnumber black men in the workforce; the ratio among whites is three to two, men to women.

These numbers tell us that the faces of organizational members will be increasingly different in the future, as will the face of organizational leadership. Increasing numbers of individuals who are not white males are interested in, and qualified for, positions of greater responsibility.

The purpose of this chapter, therefore, is twofold: (1) to look at diversity *within* organizational leadership, and (2) to consider the role of organizational leaders as facilitators of organizational diversity. It is beneficial to begin with a look at diversity as it currently exists among organizational leaders, and the implications of that diversity for communication within organizations. Accordingly, the first section of this chapter reviews research findings related to men and women as communicators and leaders in organizations. The effects of race and/or ethnicity on leadership emergence and behavior also are discussed. The second section of the chapter considers the notion of "organizational diversity" as a type of transformational change and presents strategies for leaders' use in facilitating such change.

GENDER AND LEADERSHIP

Before discussing the differences, and/or similarities, between men and women as communicators and leaders in organizations, it is important to briefly consider the history of women and work. Since the dawn of civilization, men have been responsible in most societies for solving conflicts and acquiring and managing resources. In other words, men have waged wars, traded goods, and controlled money, and women have served as support persons in these endeavors. As a result of their participation in conflict situations, and in the art and science of bartering, men began to communicate with each other in public places. They grew to understand the use of power. They became adept at, or at least practiced, the processes of persuasion and negotiation. Such skills would become invaluable as the world of work evolved.

In contrast, women's early occupations outside the home were extensions of domestic talents such as sewing, cooking, serving, and eventually teaching. In American society, women began entering other fields of endeavor in the late nineteenth and early twentieth centuries. Female immigrants found work in factories. A few women with formal educations became social workers, nurses, and teachers. There are notable examples of women working as doctors, attorneys, and scientists, but in general the occupations that they entered were still extensions of work learned in the home, and these occupations did not usually put women in leadership roles within organizations. However, as the United States became an urban society, women became partners in "mom and pop" stores evolving into small business owners.

World War II prompted a major change in the status of the American working woman in this century, because women were the mainstay employees in factories when many men joined the armed forces. After the war, some women continued to work outside the home because they valued the type of self-fulfillment such work offered. Additionally, the divorce rate began climbing after World War II, and women became responsible for supporting families as single parents. In the 1950s, as many Americans became more affluent and able to send their children to college, more young women enrolled in and graduated from universities. In the 1960s major social revolutions, especially the women's movement, called for a change in attitudes and behaviors about women's places in society, and demanded changes in laws affecting equal employment opportunity.

As women have entered the workforce in increasing numbers during the last fifty years, men generally have been their supervisors, and the communication between the genders usually has reflected this status differential between them. In her seminal study of men and women in a corporation, Rosabeth Moss Kanter observed that women in an organization typically employed strategies that communicated passivity, nurturance, and open-mindedness. On the other hand, men used strategies that connoted strength, power, assertiveness, and security.[2] Hence, communication strategies were the manifestations of real and perceived relationships between the dominant and the dominated.

Since 1977, when Kanter's research was published, women have entered the workplace and managerial ranks in increasing numbers. As a result, their communication strategies have changed to reflect their status in power relationships. Nevertheless, differences between women and men as organizational communicators still exist and have been analyzed by researchers. The following generalizations have been validated in studies of the effects of gender on communication in the workplace.[3]

- As they communicate, men more often assume task roles, and give more opinions, suggestions, and information than women do. By contrast, women assume socioemotional roles as they react to the contributions of others.
- In mixed-sex interactions, men take more frequent and longer speaking turns than women do, resulting in their talking more in these conversations.
- Men are more likely than women to interrupt others during a conversation in a mixed-sex group, take the floor, change the topic, or criticize the ideas of others. Men interrupt women more than they interrupt other men. Women tend to interrupt each other more in same-sex groups to elaborate on a theme under discussion or ask for clarification—not to disrupt what a speaker is saying. The more powerful the person in an interaction, the more he or she interrupts others.
- Men initiate more topics than women in mixed-sex interactions and have more success with their topics being developed in the group.
- Men are generally not disclosive about personal information in group discussions; women are more self-disclosive and value this characteristic.
- Women sometimes support other speakers by keeping conversations going.
- Men engage in argumentation in public settings with other males. Women, however, use conflict avoidance strategies such as seeking compromises and talking through problems.

These are just a few differences observed by those studying men and women as communicators in organizations. Because of their history in the workplace, most women have not held executive positions that enable them to hone skills in public communication settings. Consequently, around the corporate conference table men often appear to, and often do, "take over" decision-making discussions. However, as an increasing number of women assume leadership roles, they will have more opportunities for engaging in public speech, such as communicating in meetings, giving presentations, and leading discussions where they can practice communicating with constituencies in public. Such practice also helps women avoid tentative and convoluted speech—oral behaviors characterized by a hesitancy to speak out in groups, or the use of too much detail in some decision-making deliberations.

While being detailed is usually equated with being thorough, many great ideas from women are lost because these ideas are buried in a long explanation as opposed to a succinct comment.

A number of research findings have compared the communication behaviors of women and men as organizational leaders. Such findings include the following.

- In general, women are more expressive, self-disclosing, and more concerned about the success of their communicative relationships.
- The perceived quality of contributions by female leaders in group discussions is diminished because they are interrupted more and there is less acceptance of their ideas. Additionally, women express less confidence in their leadership ability than men do. In field studies of men and women leaders, however, fewer or no sex differences are found in leadership behavior or performance.[4]
- Women in business and professional settings may use speech patterns similar to men in similar positions if their position of authority legitimates those patterns. Role requirements and a leader's status may significantly reduce any effect of gender on conversation.[5] This is an important finding which shall be discussed again in this chapter. In many organizations, the similarities between men and women leaders outnumber their differences because behavior is related to one's position, power, and status rather than one's gender. Indeed as men and women work together in leadership capacities they learn effective behaviors from one another, depending upon the situational contexts in which they find themselves. The study of leadership behavior, in other words, should always consider one's position in the organization, as well as one's gender.
- Those individuals exhibiting androgynous (both male and female) characteristics may emerge as organizational leaders for at least two reasons. The personal qualities associated with masculinity, such as assertiveness, self-confidence, competence, are still valued in organizational settings. However, the display of feminine characteristics, such as being compassionate, nurturing, and collaborative, are valued in the types of structures characteristic of contemporary and future organizations—"flatter," less hierarchical entities that encourage fluid communication, teamwork, and employee empowerment.

While a plethora of research studies can shed light on behavioral differences of men and women leaders observed in laboratory settings, or in groups within organizations, it is also interesting to note a couple of in-depth analyses of organizational leaders and the comparisons between them.

Over twenty years ago, Henry Mintzberg conducted diary studies of five male executives. His study became the basis of a well-known book entitled *The Nature of Managerial Work*. Mintzberg found that the men he studied:

- Worked at a rapid pace, with no breaks in activity; 60 percent of their time was taken up in formal meetings
- Considered unscheduled moments with subordinates as interruptions, causing them to perceive discontinuity and fragmentation of the work day
- Spared little time for activities unrelated to work and were isolated intellectually
- Preferred phone calls and face-to-face interaction
- Maintained a complex network of relationships with people outside their organizations; 22–38 percent of their time was spent outside the office with colleagues and/or clients
- Lacked time for reflection and/or thinking
- Identified themselves solely with their jobs
- Had difficulty sharing information—to them it was a source of power[6]

More recently, Sally Helgesen conducted in-depth studies of four women leaders. The results of her research showed that these women:

- Worked at a steady pace, but with small breaks scheduled during the day; 40–60 percent of their time was spent in formal meetings
- Did not view unscheduled tasks and encounters as interruptions; they wanted to be accessible in the office and did not use secretaries as barriers
- Made time for activities not directly related to their work (all of these women had children)
- Preferred phone calls and face-to-face interaction as means of communicating; however, they also attended to mail as a way of continuing relationships
- Maintained a network of relationships with people external to their organizations; this networking occupied about 20–40 percent of their time
- Focused on the long-term; took time to consider the "big picture"
- Saw their own identities as complex and multifaceted, not solely tied to their careers
- Scheduled time during their day to share information[7]

According to Helgesen, these findings indicate that women's ways of leading include teaching, guiding, and attending to communication and information-sharing—ways particularly suitable for the innovative, flexible organizational structures that have begun emerging in this society and that will continue to develop in the twenty-first century. Moreover, she suggests, the expectations of women leaders may be different from those of their male counterparts; they expect that "a woman's work is never done" and therefore tend to be process oriented. Satisfaction is derived from *doing* work, not just completing it, from participating in the process as well as seeing a final product.

While Mintzberg's and Helgesen's results are indeed interesting, their observations are based on in-depth studies of very few subjects. Another major contribution to the study of gender and leadership is the work of Dr. Alice Eagly of Purdue University who has reviewed numerous studies comparing men and women as leaders. At the 1991 conference of the American Psychological Association, Dr. Eagly presented several conclusions based on a review of multiple studies. Her findings include the following.

- Women proceed with more collaboration and sharing of decision making in many organizational settings than do men.
- Gender prejudice only exists under some conditions—those in which women strongly violate gender role expectations or place themselves in clear-cut role conflict. In other words, gender prejudice may exist against a female airline pilot but not against a woman who heads the airline's department of human resources. A woman appointed as one of the Joint Chiefs of Staff might face gender prejudice, but a female officer selected as head of nurses in a large military hospital probably would not.
- Women engage in fewer of the task-oriented behaviors typically identified with leadership, and exhibit more of the interpersonal-oriented behaviors that may place an individual in a supportive role. For instance, it is perceived that women engage less in the communication processes of giving directions, disciplining, and delegating and are seen more as motivators and caretakers of a workforce.
- There is no overall sex difference in employee perceptions of leadership effectiveness. However, ratings of leadership *satisfaction* favored women and ratings of leadership *ability* favored men. In others words, the respondents in a number of the studies Eagly summarized apparently would rather work for a woman but judge men to be more able leaders.
- Women fare less well in masculine organizational environments, but fare better in organizations perceived to be more feminine, such as schools or social service agencies. That is, greater opportunities for advancement exist for women in those organizations traditionally dominated by women or those built around occupations thought of as feminine, such as nursing, teaching, and counseling.
- People are particularly distrustful of women who have masculine leadership styles or who occupy highly male-dominated roles, such as sheriff, corporate chief executive, or coach of a men's sports team.[8]

When Rosabeth Moss Kanter published her 1977 case study examining men and women in a corporation, she made an interesting observation that may also have been a prediction:

The effectiveness of women leaders, then, like that of men, is a response to opportunities for power, to a favorable position in the power structure. Both men and women can exercise their authority more productively and with better response when they have power behind it. This, too, is a standard organizational cycle: power breeds effectiveness at getting results, which enhances power. But psychological "sex differences" seem to play a limited role, if any, once women are given a chance and access to power.[9]

It is important to consider that men and women leaders may indeed exhibit similar leadership behaviors if they are in positions of similar status and power. However, the number of women in positions of high status that hold great power is not at all comparable to the number of men holding such positions. Nor do members of racial minorities exist in significant numbers in the higher ranks of organizations. As one researcher has observed, women and racial minorities: (1) are numerical minorities within societal and organizational power elites; (2) share characteristics of lower status American society; and (3) are subject to negative stereotypes and attributions concerning work-related competencies and fitness for managerial responsibilities.[10]

Because of the changing demographics of organizations, and the statistics illustrating that the number of minorities in leadership positions in American organizations is disproportionately low, any study of organizational leadership should consider the effects of race and ethnicity on an individual's opportunity to emerge and perform as an organizational leader.

RACE, ETHNICITY, AND LEADERSHIP

There is a lack of research on leadership emergence and performance among racial and ethnic minorities. In great part, this is because the number of these individuals in executive positions is small compared to the number of whites in these positions. Most of the studies on gender and leadership, for instance, tend to include white women as subjects, and their findings are not necessarily generalizable to minority women. Indeed, as of 1990 the number of white women in management was greater than the number of minorities, men *and* women.[11] Although women account for 40 percent of all managerial positions, white women hold more than 97 percent of these positions. African American women comprise only three percent of the women in corporate management, with less than one percent in top executive positions.[12] Only within the last decade has there been any significant research studying attitudes and experiences of minorities as organizational *members*. A review of such studies has found that: (1) organizational experiences differ within and across minority groups; and (2) Hispanic, Asian, and African American managers are subject to negative stereotyping in organizations.[13]

Attitudes toward minorities have been shown in one study to affect individuals' commitment to their organization. In a study of 1,705 supervisory and nonsupervisory workers employed in a state agency and two Fortune 100 companies, the more minorities in a unit, the less commitment whites expressed toward their companies.[14] Whites in work units with no minorities were most attached to their organizations. Employee attachment also was affected by the numbers of women present in a work unit. The more women in such a unit, the more men expressed detachment from the organization. Conversely, the more men on their work teams, the more committed women were to their organizations. The possible explanations for these attitudes are: (1) women and minorities generally possess less power and status in organizations than men and white organizational members, and these individuals therefore equate working in a demographically diverse organization to working in a lower status environment; or (2) white men may feel they have to "curb their language and behavior in a diverse workplace."[15]

While this study did not analyze attitudes of organizational leaders, others have reported the differential experiences of women and minority managers due to race and/or gender. One study, based on interviews with Anglo, African American, and Hispanic managers in a corporate environment, found that "blacks reported more incidents of feeling excluded from the organization. Black men and women were more likely to describe situations where they believed others to be uncomfortable with them because of color and to relate feelings of their own discomfort in the work environment."[16] White men and women, however, did not report any instances of exclusion based on race, although the women interviewed did indicate they felt left out of the informal organization because they were females. This study lent credence to the observation that African American managers feel less acceptance as organizational members than do white managers, and spend an inordinate amount of time dealing personally and professionally with issues of inclusion. As a result, exhibiting leadership in the face of discrimination makes a difficult task even more challenging. Such is particularly the case for minority women.

RACE, GENDER, AND LEADERSHIP

Within recent years, several scholars have studied the combined effects of racism and sexism on leadership. The terms "double jeopardy" or "double whammy" describe the negative effects African American women face because they are both black *and* female. Ella Bell, who studies behaviors of African American career women, emphasizes that many of these individuals may feel they must step in and out of two different worlds, or two cultures, to succeed in both of them.

One culture is the organizational culture in which they work, which is a dominant white culture; the other is the minority community in which many of these individuals live. According to Bell: "Assimilation requires blacks to conform to the traditions, values, and norms of the dominant white culture. Under these circumstances, black professional women divest themselves of their culture of origin, the black community. Instead, they attempt to fit into the dominant white community, where there are few models or images of black womanhood."[17] As a result, these women not only may experience the differential treatment at work that white women may experience, including exclusion from both formal and informal organizational networks, they also are constantly attempting to maintain ties to the community in which they live, "where they assume active roles with their families, significant others, and in social groups, the church, and organizations dedicated to uplifting the black race."[18] In other words, a host of environmental and organizational influences, including those that conflict with each other such as family and organizational cultures, affect the leadership behaviors of African American women. Increased study of these influences is important to research on the interrelationships among race, gender, and leadership because leaders are products of both their personal *and* professional environments.

Dramatic demographic changes in the workforce that will affect the emergence of women and minorities in positions of leadership is only one reason why diversity in organizations should be studied. Additionally, a look at the behaviors exhibited by different kinds of leaders informs any study of leadership. Finally, the research conducted on gender, racial, and ethnic effects on leadership is increasing because the number and influence of leaders who understand more than one culture is increasing.

BEHAVIORS OF MULTICULTURAL LEADERS

One of the more interesting studies of multicultural leaders, those who are members of, or knowledgeable about, more than one racial or ethnic culture, has been conducted by Manual Ramirez III. The subjects he studied were male Latinos. Some of these individuals had extensive knowledge of, or experience in, other cultures and were judged to be multicultural individuals. Those who were only familiar with Latino culture were categorized as monocultural. Ramirez found five dimensions of group leader behavior that subjects with a greater degree of multicultural experience used more frequently than subjects with knowledge or experience of only one culture. Those behaviors included the following.

1. *Taking charge in the group.* Multicultural individuals were quicker to assume the leadership role; were assertive and active; and assessed group process.
2. *Communicating effectively.* Multicultural leaders asked for opinions, evaluations, and feelings; they clarified statements of members, as well as the issue being discussed.
3. *Attempting to reduce interpersonal conflict.* These individuals sought compromise solutions and were interested in mediation.

4. *Being socially sensitive and personable.* Multicultural leaders acknowledged contributions made by members and addressed members by name.

5. *Coping with stress.* Multicultural leaders exhibited fewer visible indicators of tension.[19]

Because of their experiences with and sensitivity to more than one culture, Ramirez concluded:

> *In general, high multicultural leaders appeared to have more behavioral and perspective repertoires or resources available to them. They also made more effort to communicate with the Anglo and the black group members; they made sure that all members in their group expressed their opinions and that they all understood each others' points of view. In contrast to this, monocultural leaders would tend to communicate more with the Latino group members, often ignoring the Anglo and black members. Monocultural leaders were also less concerned with ensuring that points of view expressed by individual members were understood by others in their group.*[20]

The reasons why individuals with knowledge of, or experience with, more than one culture exhibit these leadership behaviors are not easily discovered. Perhaps personal experience gives them an appreciation of, a sensitivity to, individual differences. Perhaps their life histories have fostered an awareness of the contributions that heterogeneous group members can make to a common goal. What is significant for consideration in this chapter is that diversity within an individual's life experiences may enrich those experiences and foster attitudes and behaviors that value diversity within, and among, others. Accordingly, it is important to consider how leaders may facilitate the workforce diversification of organizations as agents, indeed as masters, of change. Leading the processes of valuing and facilitating diversity is a critical role for organizational leaders to assume. Before looking at the strategies one may use to fulfill this role, it is important to consider what "diversity" in organizations means.

THE NOTION OF "ORGANIZATIONAL DIVERSITY"

Numerically, diversity is seen in corporate America in the numbers of men and women, and different races and ethnicities, who comprise the workforce. Data published in 1991 by the U.S. Department of Labor showed that women represented 37.2 percent of all employees in ninety-four Fortune 1000-sized companies during a three-year period. Minorities represented 15.5 percent of these employees. In all levels of management, 16.9 percent were women and 6 percent were minorities. However, at the executive level,

6.6 percent of individuals at the rank of assistant vice-president or higher were women and only 2.6 percent were minorities.[21] Additionally, a 1990 survey conducted by the UCLA Anderson Graduate School of Management and Korn/Ferry International, an executive search firm, found that minorities and women held only 5 percent of the top executive positions in the nation's 1000 largest corporations.[22] Minority women, in a 1986 study, were found to comprise between one and two percent of all corporate officers in the United States.[23]

These figures reflect what has come to be known as "the glass ceiling," an invisible barrier to the advancement of women and minorities in many American organizations. Equal employment opportunity laws and affirmative action policies have been ways used by a number of organizations to increase the numbers of women and minorities in their respective workforces, but their ascendance into leadership positions has been a slow process. In the top executive positions mentioned above, the number of minorities and women holding those positions grew from less than 3 percent in 1979 to only 5 percent in 1990.[24] Such numbers illustrate that an important function of organizational leaders, both now and in the future, is to implement programs or strategies to both value, and increase, diversity in all levels of corporate organizations.

While the term "organizational diversity" may seem a new one, different types of organizations have been diverse for many years. Workers and members of a variety of organizations are not at all homogeneous. They have different religions, educational levels, and social, cultural, and political backgrounds. They are of various ages. Some are smokers; others are nonsmokers. Some are married with children. Others are single, with and without children. All these differences represent people who have unique life experiences, expertise, opinions, values, and attitudes. In recent years, however, organizational leaders and members have become aware of the notion of organizational diversity because it has become associated with more "visible" differences than religion or education level. While some may consider diversity to be only a function of gender, race, and/or ethnicity, *all* the individuals in an organization are unique and "valuing diversity" means appreciating the uniqueness of every organizational member.

Indeed, in this book "diversity" is a term used to emphasize that all individuals, regardless of gender, ethnicity, race, religion, position, and so on, are unique and important to the functioning of their respective organizations. *Leading* diversity is a set of strategies to foster the personal and professional development of everyone in an organization. It is a means to enhance the performance of all individuals and groups, and communicates to people that they are regarded as unique persons who have something to contribute to the organization.

Research studies have demonstrated that one-shot training efforts aimed at managing and valuing diversity are generally doomed to fail, for leading diversity is not a short-term program but a long-term process. It is a process that focuses on the individual and the way in which an individual is socialized into an organization and becomes an effective and efficient member of it. Unfortunately, programs to enhance organizational diversity are considered by some executives as fads, not permanent components of an organization's culture. Such individuals turn to "experts" to create one-day workshops for organizational members with no real intention of embedding the value of diversity into their culture. Achieving "organizational diversity" as defined in this text requires planting the seeds of change and nurturing their growth through multiple messages and media, and structural as well as policy changes. Indeed, enhancing organizational diversity really means improving organizational communication because the problems generated within organizations around issues related to diversity are really communication problems. Those who study and implement programs to value and foster diversity would be well-advised to focus those programs on improving communication among organizational levels and functions, and between superiors and subordinates. In short, using individualized consideration as a leadership behavior is the most effective means of enacting a leader's commitment to organizational diversity, of celebrating the individual differences that comprise a group, or "groups of groups."

One of the barriers to valuing and leading diversity is the human tendency to use appearances as the bases for assumptions about who individuals are and what their beliefs, attitudes, and behaviors might be. When a person walks into an organization as a newcomer, organizational members are often quick to categorize that person based on his or her gender, color, dress, and initial nonverbal and verbal behaviors. In organizations, people rarely get the chance to define themselves by telling others who they are, using their own words. Instead, organizational members make assumptions about an individual's attitudes and beliefs, based often only on how one looks or behaves, not on what is known of that person as a human being. Over time, this is how we become creatures of categories or stereotypes.

If a new neighbor asks us to feed his dog while he is out of town, some of us might not hesitate to offer help because we have had positive experiences with beagles, bassets, or Chihuahuas. Others, however, might deny this request because they have only known big, mean dogs, or perhaps they were once attacked by a dog. So the meaning for "dog" is not in the word but in the mind of the listener. Meanings are not in words; they are in ourselves. Words do not carry meanings; we give meanings to words. Words are only symbols for ideas or things. They are neither inherently positive nor negative. Our sensitivities to certain words do not come from the words themselves but from our perceptions or interpretations of those words—what they mean to us personally.

How does this observation relate to organizational diversity? Diversity basically means differences, and to many people the word "differences" creates negative feelings such as fear, insecurity, and anxiety. The word "differences" is neutral; it is the meaning or value that people give to the word that makes the *subject* of diversity a sensitive and often controversial one. Differences may be seen as threatening in the workplace. Talking about differences tends to evoke stereotypes, frequently negative, and feelings of competition for scarce resources such as promotions, salary increases, bonuses, or computers.

From an organizational perspective, a working definition of diversity means differences in viewpoints, perspectives, and world views. Valuing diversity means appreciating individual differences. People generally assimilate into a group or organizational culture to foster cohesion and cooperation in the process of accomplishing tasks, but they need not do so at the expense of their uniqueness.

Leaders must understand that one of their more critical functions is *facilitating* diversity, proactively working to increase the diversity of an organization because individuals with different backgrounds, expertise, and world views enrich the processes of decision making, problem solving, and task accomplishment. However, there is often a tendency in organizations to reward normative behavior, through which people are expected to conform to a dominant culture. Conflict may be the result, particurlarly among individuals who are expected to abandon their preferred values, beliefs, companions, dress, and so on, while they are participating in organizational activities. Therefore, a leader must concurrently support individual needs as well as organizational goals by showing individualized consideration for people, thus, helping them develop as individuals, and as organizational members, to perform beyond their own expectations. While there are different operational definitions for the term "diversity," and different opinions about how to implement programs or strategies designed to foster it, issues about diversity are a significant part of an organization's reality.

FACILITATING DIVERSITY: LEADERS' USE OF STRATEGIES

As we have discussed, "valuing" and "leading" diversity are two different processes. Leading the process of workforce diversification is a proactive, not reactive, effort. Indeed, it is a change effort with all the attendant preparations and strategies involved in any attempt at transformational change.

Why is the leadership of diversity a worthwhile endeavor for an organization? Following are just a few reasons.

1. The demographics of the workforce of this society are changing dramatically and illustrate an increasingly diverse populace.

2. Organizations are making major changes in their structures, emphasizing flatter organizations where team building is valued. Fostering diversity is one way of building heterogeneous teams.
3. Greater employee involvement in decision making and problem solving is becoming an accepted, encouraged practice.
4. Maximizing human resources is particularly important in organizations that have had to downsize, or reduce, their workforce. Leading diversity is a major mechanism for utilizing the unique talents of individuals.
5. Leading diversity is a natural behavior for transformational leaders who are believers in people, who are change agents, and who see organizations not just as they are, but as they should be. For those leaders attempting to balance the well-being of people with organizational performance, leading diversity is a positive organizational practice.

The preeminent reflection of the appreciation of diversity resides within the organizational leader, by virtue of what he or she says and does in working with people who represent a variety of gender, ethnic, and other types of differences. A leader who values the uniqueness of an individual's culture does not tell jokes that are derogatory of either gender, ethnicity, race, or religion. He or she also is proactive in dealing with the work schedule of a single parent, or the access to a building for a person who is physically challenged, while insuring that the individual performs in accordance with his or her job requirements.

In addition to serving as a role model who reflects an appreciation of diversity within an organization, a leader must develop and implement strategies that create opportunities through which all individuals may meet their personal and professional goals in the organization. Three general strategies include:

1. Providing challenges—giving people the resources necessary to maximize their potential, including opportunities for networking and training to increase their knowledge
2. Giving recognition—bestowing intrinsic and extrinsic rewards to motivate individuals, such as participation in task forces, increased supervisory responsibility, and bonuses
3. Providing support—creating and maintaining an environment that recognizes the emotional, physical, and interpersonal elements of a workforce. Such an environment offers collegiality, acceptance, permission to fail, information, and feedback[25]

Specific strategies used by a variety of organizations to manage diversity generally include education and training programs to increase cultural sensitivity; career management programs that promote mentoring relationships and access to informal networks; recruitment and retention programs, including the creation of support groups; and employee benefits or services directed toward enhancing organizational diversity, such as flexible working schedules, on-site child care, and parental leave policies. Whatever the strategies created and implemented by organizational leaders, these leaders must work to insure that their organizational cultures support diversity, that is, individual differences, among organizational members. Dominant cultures, by definition, do not encourage the development of subcultures or members of nondominant groups, such as women and minorities.

Any sustained commitment to fostering organizational diversity involves embedding that commitment into an organizational culture. Leaders should use the mechanisms discussed in Chapter 4, such as paying continual attention to the effort through their words and actions; serving as role models; and emphasizing a commitment to diversity in reward structures and criteria for promotion.

Roosevelt Thomas compares organizational culture to the roots of a tree, which nurtures the growth and development of that tree.[26] One cannot institute any systemic program of change, including one devoted to facilitating organizational diversity, by grafting the program onto old roots. The underlying values and beliefs of the organizational culture must be altered to accommodate transformational change, such as downsizing, total quality management, or organizational diversity, by creating new "roots." According to Thomas, leaders may take the following steps to plant and nurture such roots.[27]

- Continually describe the "new roots," the values and beliefs supportive of diversity
- Create, and participate in, traditions and ceremonies that promote diversity, such as new employee orientations
- Create appropriate heroes and heroines, those organizational members who mentor, who empower, others
- Influence communication networks. Leaders must use informal, as well as formal, communication channels to share stories as well as implement policies that will facilitate an organizational climate supportive of change
- Recruit individuals who will act as change agents, creating and protecting new "roots"
- Build rewards for these change agents into the organization's culture—its substantive policies as well as its symbolic ceremonies

Total quality management is also a cultural change, emphasizing organizational commitment to continuous improvement, service to stakeholders, and employee empowerment. Organizations may wish to make cultural changes that facilitate total quality management and diversity simultaneously. They both represent long-term changes in an organization's way of life—changes that depend on the creation of community through communication.

Indeed, in their role as facilitators of organizational diversity, leaders must understand that the success of any strategy depends on how one communicates that strategy, because meanings are not in words but in ourselves. Verbal and nonverbal behaviors are important in exercising any leadership behavior, but are especially critical when leading diversity, where people's very identities, and pride in those identities, are at stake. They must be sure that their communication behaviors are not differential toward certain groups of individuals; that the nature of their communications with followers does not establish "in" groups and "out" groups (See Chapter 2). Accordingly, organizational leaders should emphasize the use of rich media when undertaking attempts to foster diversity, focusing on informal and formal mentoring relationships, training programs, task forces, and support groups. There is no substitute for face-to-face communication when there is a need to provide social support, show individualized consideration, or motivate one's mentees. A leader must be the reflection of an organization's commitment to valuing and fostering diversity; he or she is responsible for developing and communicating that commitment.

If current trends continue, more women and minorities will hold executive/leadership positions in American organizations during the next century than ever before. The global nature of many organizations also will foster the "internationalization" of leadership, where individuals from foreign countries may lead American organizations. Some theorists also have suggested that flatter organizational structures which emphasize fluid information flow and team building will be more suitable to women's ways of leading, and communicating leadership.

Regardless of gender, race, or ethnicity, however, power and status are great influences on the ways leaders choose to interact with followers. As this century closes and another one begins, those ways will become increasingly influenced by the technologies that are beginning to quietly change, if not transform, many of this society's organizations. In the next chapter, therefore, we consider the relationship between leadership and the use of new communication technologies in organizations.

SUMMARY

"Organizational diversity" is not a new phenomenon—diversity has existed in organizations since individuals began forming or joining groups. However, the changing demographics of this society that have focused attention on the increase in women and minorities in the workplace, also have focused press and public attention on "diversity" in organizations and the issues raised by that diversity.

For most of the last one hundred years, women and minorities have not held executive, decision-making positions in organizations—positions that may hold power within them. As an increasing number of women and minorities are appointed or promoted to such positions, they have opportunities for giving presentations, leading discussions, and making decisions in groups where they communicate with subordinates, peers, and superiors in "public" settings. These communication experiences provide the interactive contexts in which leadership may emerge.

While studies of gender and leadership have discussed differences between men and women leaders, it is quite possible that their similarities outweigh their differences. Behavior is related to one's position, power, and status, as well as gender. Consequently, the study of leadership should always consider one's position in an organization, as well as one's gender. Those individuals exhibiting androgynous characteristics may emerge as organizational leaders for two reasons. The personal qualities associated with masculinity are valued because they communicate self-confidence and competence. However, feminine characteristics, those identified as being compassionate, nurturing and collaborative, are valued in the types of structures characteristic of an increasing number of organizations—"flatter," less hierarchical entities that encourage fluid communication and teamwork.

There is a lack of research on leadership emergence and performance among racial and ethnic minorities. Research on managers in corporate environments does indicate that minority managers may feel excluded from others in the organization and spend an inordinate amount of time dealing personally and professionally with issues of inclusion. Exhibiting leadership in the face of discrimination makes a difficult task even more challenging. For example, minority women, who may experience discrimination because they are women *and* minorities, may find themselves stepping in and out of two very different cultures when they go from home to office and back each day.

Preliminary research comparing multicultural and monocultural leaders indicates that individuals understanding more than one culture may have an appreciation of individual differences and an awareness that heterogeneous members of a group or organization can make multiple contributions toward achieving a common goal. Indeed, in this chapter the term "diversity" focuses on the uniqueness of individuals within groups and organizations. Leading diversity is a set of strategies to develop everyone in an organization, personally and professionally. Using individualized consideration, a component of transformational leadership, may be the most effective means of enacting a leader's commitment to organizational diversity because it focuses on the value, and development, of each individual in the organization.

To some individuals the term "organizational diversity" is a negative one. It is equated with "differences" and differences among individuals often creates negative feelings such as fear, insecurity, and anxiety. Talking about differences tends to evoke stereotypes, frequently negative, and feelings of competition for scarce resources like promotions, salary increases, and bonuses. Consequently, facilitating organizational diversity requires the effective use of communication to create shared meanings that focus on individual differences as organizational strengths. Indeed, individuals with different backgrounds, expertise, and world views enrich the processes of decision making, problem solving, and task accomplishment. Facilitating diversity is an important leadership behavior because organizations are making major changes in their structures, emphasizing the use of team building. Fostering diversity is a way of building heterogeneous teams.

Specific strategies used by a variety of organizations to manage diversity include education and training programs; career management programs that promote mentoring relationships and networking; recruitment and retention programs, including the creation of support groups; and services or benefits such as flexible working schedules, on-site child care, and parental leave policies.

As facilitators of organizational diversity, leaders must understand that the success of any strategy depends on how one communicates that strategy. Sensitivity in the use of verbal and nonverbal behaviors is especially critical when people's very identities, and pride in those identities, are at stake. Additionally, organizational leaders should emphasize the use of rich media when undertaking attempts to foster diversity, especially using face-to-face communication when providing social support through mentoring relationships, task forces, and support groups. A leader must be the reflection of an organization's commitment to valuing and fostering diversity since he or she is responsible for developing and communicating that commitment.

QUESTIONS TO CONSIDER

1. What facts should organizational leaders know about the changing demographics of the people in this society?

2. How can the history of men and women in the workplace inform a study of gender and leadership communication?

3. What are four research findings that compare communication behaviors of women and men as organizational leaders?

4. What does the term "double jeopardy" mean in the study of the interrelationship among gender, race, and leadership?

5. What communication behaviors might one expect of a multicultural leader that may not be seen among monocultural leaders?

6. What strategies might organizational leaders utilize to foster diversity within organizations?

CASE PROBLEM

Pat Johnson is in the process of creating a long-term program to enhance organizational diversity in her 200-person state agency. The agency is responsible for promoting tourism in her state. You are in charge of creating an outline for the program which will include an ongoing training effort, a mentoring program, and other strategies you might suggest.

The agency has been in existence for over fifty years, but its functions have increased dramatically in the last twenty years as the state has created several parks around its major lakes and private developers have added family theme parks in the state's two largest metropolitan areas. The agency's workforce is 60 percent male and 40 percent female, with men holding most of the supervisory positions, and 70 percent of the employees are white.

First, create an outline of overall strategies to be used in this effort.

Second, create an outline of topics to be covered in the ongoing training sessions, for example, "definition of diversity," "differences in male and female leadership behaviors," and so on.

Use the examples of strategies discussed in this chapter, relevant information provided in this chapter, as well as other information about communication and leadership in previous chapters, to create the outline for Johnson.

ENDNOTES

1. William B. Johnston and Arnold H. Packer, *Workforce 2000* (Indianapolis: Hudson Institute, 1987).
2. Rosabeth Moss Kanter, *Men and Women of the Corporation* (New York: Basic Books, 1977).
3. S. S. Case, "Wide-Verbal-Repertoire Speech: Gender, Language, and Managerial Influence." *Women's Studies International Forum* 16 (5–6): 271–290.
4. B. Haslett, F. L. Geis, and M. R. Carter, *The Organizational Woman: Power and Paradox* (Norwood: Ablex Publishing,1992), 81–174.
5. C. Johnson, "Gender, Legitimate Authority, and Leader-Subordinate Conversations," *American Sociological Review* 59 (1): 1994, 122–135.
6. Henry Mintzberg, *The Nature of Managerial Work* (New York: Harper & Row, 1973).
7. Sally Helgesen, *The Female Advantage: Women's Ways of Leadership* (New York: Doubleday, 1990), 19–29.
8. Alice H. Eagly, "Gender and Leadership," invited address at annual meeting of the American Psychological Association, San Francisco, August, 1991, 16–18.
9. Rosabeth Moss Kanter, *Men and Women of the Corporation* (New York: Basic Books, 1977), 302.
10. Herminia Ibarra, "Personal Networks of Women and Minorities in Management: A Conceptual Framework," *Academy of Management Review* 18:1 (1993): 66.
11. Herminia Ibarra, "Personal Networks of Women and Minorities in Management: A Conceptual Framework," *Academy of Management Review* 18:1 (1993): 82. See

A. M. Morrison & M. A. VonGlinow "Women and Minorities in Management," *American Psychologist* 45(1990): 200–208.

12. D.M. Baskerville, S. H. Tucker, and D. Whittingham-Barnes, "Women of Power and Influence in Corporate America," *Black Enterprise Magazine* (August 1991): 39–58.

13. Ibid.

14. E. A. Fagenson, "Is What's Good for the Goose Also Good for the Gander? On Being White and Male in a Diverse Workforce," *Academy of Management Executive* 7 (4): 1993, 80–81.

15. Ibid., 81.

16. Mary Cianni and Beverly Romberger, "Belonging in the Corporation: Oral Histories of Male and Female White, Black, and Hispanic Managers," *Academy of Management Best Paper Proceedings* (1991).

17. Ella L. Bell, "The Bicultural Life Experience of Career-Oriented Black Women," *Journal of Organizational Behavior* 11 (1990): 462.

18. Ibid., 475.

19. Manuel Ramirez, *Psychology of the Americas* (New York: Pergamon Press, 1983).

20. Ibid., 115.

21. *A Report on the Glass Ceiling Initiative*, U.S. Department of Labor, 1991, 6.

22. Ibid.

23. Heidrick & Struggles, Inc., The Woman Corporate Officer, 1986, cited in *A Report on the Glass Ceiling Initiative*, 7.

24. *A Report on the Glass Ceiling Initiative*, U.S. Department of Labor, 1991, 6.

25. Ann Morrison, *The New Leaders* (San Francisco: Jossey-Bass Publishers, 1992), 57–80.

26. R. Roosevelt Thomas, Jr., *Beyond Race and Gender* (New York: AMACOM, 1991), 50.

27. Ibid., 56–57.

8

USING NEW COMMUNICATION TECHNOLOGIES IN ORGANIZATIONS: THE LEADER AS CHAMPION OF COMMUNICATION INNOVATIONS

Any organizational leader who reads a weekly business or news magazine will find at least one article on technology in the workplace. It may be about creating cars with robots, using cellular phones as employees travel from one destination to another, or uniting people within multinational corporations via teleconferencing. The sheer pervasiveness of the topic exhorts organizational leaders to have at least a conceptual familiarity with, and preferably a working knowledge of, today's and tomorrow's technologies.

The purpose of this chapter is to:

1. Provide an overview of the types of new information/communication technologies with which organizational leaders should be familiar
2. Discuss the uses and major effects of these technologies on organizations
3. Consider the role a leader may assume as a champion for technological innovation

The major reason for this chapter is that new communication technologies have become part of many, if not most, organizations. In an "information society" where there is an increasing demand for access to travel on "the information highway," organizations are increasingly communication intensive and rely on a constant flow of messages through multiple channels. The use of electronic mail (e-mail), facsimile transmission, videoconferencing, and group decision making via networked computers are just some of the ways that individuals comprising such organizations can engage in both task-related and social communication.

Before discussing what leaders should know about new technologies and their effects on organizations, it is beneficial to review briefly what an information, or communication, technology is and what its characteristics are.

DEFINITIONS AND TYPES OF INFORMATION/COMMUNICATION TECHNOLOGIES

A technology is the *way* work is done or *how* a task is accomplished. For example, memos can be written by pen, pencil, crayon, typewriter, or computer. All of these instruments of work are technologies. A sales report can be sent by overnight express mail, fax, or e-mail. These are also technologies.

One category of technologies of particular importance to leaders is information or communication technologies. A number of definitions for this type of technology exists. Zuboff, for instance, states that information technology is "a label that reflects the convergence of several streams of technical developments, including microelectronics, computer science, telecommunications, software engineering, and system analysis. It is a technology that dramatically increases the ability to record, store, analyze, and transmit information in ways that permit flexibility, accuracy, immediacy, geographic independence, volume, and complexity."[1] Zmud emphasizes that information technology is "the application of computer and communication technologies in the acquisition, storage, analysis, distribution, and presentation of information."[2]

The boundaries between information and communication technology have blurred with the convergence of various technical developments such that "communication technology" is sometimes used synonymously with "information technology." For purposes of discussion, a communication technology is defined here as a system with both social and technical characteristics, or "the hardware equipment, organizational structures, and social values by which individuals collect, process, and exchange information with other individuals . . ."[3]

Leaders need to know what specific technologies are available for use in their organizations and how they facilitate the accomplishment of tasks and the attainment of organizational goals. As a result, following are a few of the new communication technologies that are increasingly found in organizations.

- *Facsimile transmission (fax)*—The product is the result of merging computer and telephone technologies to send documents over telephone lines almost instantaneously. The process facilitates collaboration and decision making based on a review of documents received and/or shared rapidly. Additionally, a single document can be sent to several locations for review and response.

- *Electronic messaging or e-mail*—By sending messages via computers, individuals can communicate one-to-one, one-to-many, or many-to-many. These messages can be saved or deleted after being read. The receiver also controls when he or she wishes to read messages that are "stored" in the electronic mailbox. With networks such as the Internet, it is now possible to send and receive messages from destinations all over the world. While this communication is more impersonal that face-to-face interactions, the language used is generally conversational. (E-mail can prevent "telephone tag," however, senders must depend on the receiver to read his or her mail quickly if a response is required shortly after transmittal.)
- *Voice mail*—This voice-based electronic messaging system uses a push-button telephone. Like an answering machine, it records incoming messages and allows users to screen calls. However, it also has the capability of forwarding messages to other voice mailboxes and sending the same message to a number of individuals.
- *Audioconferencing*—Using telephone lines or satellite transmissions, individuals are able to talk to each other as they communicate over long distances. This process reduces travel time and costs; people may participate in meetings without leaving their office buildings even though they may be on different continents. Audioconferencing may save time and money, but it does not have the same advantages as face-to-face communication for complex decision-making and problem-solving sessions.
- *Videoconferencing*—Using cameras, video monitors and computers, this technology allows individuals in different locations to see each other as they interact. Common applications of videoconferencing include: intra-organizational meetings; centralized employee training; international meetings; and distance learning. This innovation is paving the way for the creation of "virtual meeting rooms," which will allow participants to see faces, documents, brochures, and a variety of printed materials as if they were actually in the same room.[4]

There are various technologies, including e-mail, that are forms of computer-mediated communication. This term refers to the ways messages can be sent and received rapidly using several types of computer-based systems. Linking computers within an organization, and creating linkages with other organizations, has established networks to greatly increase the speed with which people communicate. However, the application programs, the software, used in computers is the feature that creates multiple communication capabilities for users. "Groupware" is a category of software, and it supports collaborative interactions among groups or members of a group to accomplish organizational tasks.

These are just a few of the communication technologies increasingly used in today's organizations. In the future, one can expect multimedia e-mail systems, where voice messages, pictures, and graphics, as well as text, are exchanged. Additionally, an extension of the cellular phone phenomenon may be the personal communication network (PCN) where telephone numbers will be assigned to individuals, not to locations.[5]

CHARACTERISTICS OF NEW COMMUNICATION TECHNOLOGIES

Every technology has characteristics, both objective and perceived, that help individuals decide whether to adopt and use that technology in a particular organizational context. Leaders must recognize and review these characteristics if the technology is expected to fit with an existing organizational culture and structure. Such review is part of an important decision-making process, where leaders need to consider whether a specific technology is appropriate for a given organization. Identifying "appropriate" technologies depends on the consideration of characteristics that include the following:

1. *Relative advantage*—the degree to which the technology is perceived to be superior to that which it replaces. For instance, will a new, more complex copying machine be relatively advantageous to use compared to the old machine that was simple to run but did not perform as many functions?

2. *Compatibility*—the degree to which the new technology is perceived as being consistent with the user's (the organization's) prior experiences and values. Compatibility is as much a cultural issue as it is a technological characteristic. For example, should Avon, a renowned cosmetics firm, begin selling makeup, perfumes, toiletries, and jewelry via cable television channels to save transportation costs of its door-to-door salespersons? Perhaps not, because Avon has grown as a company through its use of these individuals who bring samples of cosmetics and catalogs into the homes of millions of women.

3. *Complexity*—the degree to which a technology is perceived as being difficult to understand and use. Macintosh computers have been introduced into countless public schools because they are user-friendly machines on which young students become computer literate, or at least computer "conscious." The use of this innovation is due in large part to the relatively simple human-computer interface—the mouse and the icons.

4. *Trialability*—the degree to which the innovation/technology can be tried. Is the technology able to be tried in several organizational workplaces at once, or is it suitable for experimentation in only one room at a time? For

instance, outfitting a script writing department with lap-top computers is easily tried because the computers are small, portable, and can be brought in on a trial basis with little effort. However, outfitting a room with facilities to make it usable for teleconferencing is not an easy or inexpensive experiment. Such rooms have certain space and electronic requirements because of the nature of the technology, and outfitting multiple rooms simultaneously to "try out" the technology is not feasible or desirable.

   5. *Communicability*—the degree to which people can find out about the innovation, or how easy it is to explain the principles behind, and the use of, the technology to potential users. For instance, telling support personnel in large organizations about the use of word processors was almost impossible if they had only used typewriters during their work life. Such individuals had to be shown how to use the keyboard and the technology's other features for successful instructions to take place. On the other hand, the communicability of lap-top computers is excellent because most potential users are already computer literate, having learned about the technology and how to use it in work stations at their offices or at home on personal computers.[6]

THE USES AND EFFECTS OF NEW TECHNOLOGIES: WHAT LEADERS SHOULD KNOW

The influence of new communication technologies can be "measured" by the number of people using them and the degree to which they affect the nature of work in organizations. One group of researchers analyzing the implementation and adoption of new technologies in organizations cites a statistic that more than two-thirds of the technical, managerial, and administrative workforce in this country use computers.[7] Just as importantly, studies of the effects of technology on people and their work find that:

> . . . *computerization can change the nature of work in many jobs, influence people's morale, affect relations with co-workers and supervisors, and improve (or worsen) levels of accomplishment. It can change the processes of analysis, forecasting, problem solving, and communication in companies and can also affect work schedules, staffing levels, and the location and structure of work units and departments. On a broader basis, technology can have a bearing on the shape and layers of hierarchy in companies, on the centralization versus decentralization of responsibilities, and on the strategies and competitiveness of an enterprise.[8]*

   Any organizational leader should understand the general concept of what a technology is and how it relates to an organization's task, structure, and culture. For instance, the telegraph, and later the facsimile and computerized databases, revolutionized law enforcement—greatly enhancing criminal investigations by making information available quickly to peace officers throughout the country. The structure and roles within police departments changed dramatically, as did their cultures, which began to rely less on informants and more on forensic evidence. The sophistication of technologies gradually affected job requirements of law enforcement officials and the creation of investigative teams according to function (e.g., homicide, robbery, sexual assault, fraud, gang control, etc.). Such teams might include investigators, psychologists, social workers, and prosecutors.

This is just one example of how technologies changed the tasks, structures, and culture within one type of organization, and leaders must understand the relationship of technology to these organizational components. One underlying principle they also must recognize is that information/communication technologies are more than machines—*they are extensions of those who use them.*

Technologies as Tools

Thirty years ago, media sociologist Marshall McLuhan suggested that mass media are the extensions of human senses. Television, for instance, allows us to see and hear beyond what our eyes and ears can pick up from our immediate environment. Moreover, McLuhan observed, "all technologies are extensions of our physical and nervous systems to increase power and speed."[9] The typewriter, telegraph, and telephone are examples of such technologies. While a paintbrush is an example of a technology, which is the extension of an artist's hand, a computer and the interconnected system of which it is a part is an extension of hands, voice, eyes, and ears. It allows one to create, send, receive, and alter messages. Moreover, the computer gives speed and power to people because it uses language—formal or informal, colloquial or statistical, comprised of words or numbers—and it can do so interactively with more than one participant in a communication network.

Leaders need to understand the notion of technologies as tools to help interpret their role in accomplishing an organization's task, and to observe and react to technology's effects on an organization, specifically on human communication. Computers and other technologies also can be extensions of a leader as a communicator. Just as leaders take care to develop appropriate messages to inform and persuade in interpersonal and public communication settings, so may new technologies be used strategically to empower, inspire, and intellectually stimulate followers to enhance the process and/or the product of leadership.

Besides understanding the types and characteristics of new communication technologies available for use, and regarding them as tools through which an organization's work gets done, leaders need to recognize that adopting one or more of these technologies is an innovation and may represent an incremental organizational change at the very least, or a radical, transformative innovation.

Technological Innovation as a Form of Organizational Change

The adoption and use of new technologies in an organization is a form of organizational change. Leaders need to understand that introducing technological innovation requires many of the same leadership behaviors as those exhibited when guiding other types of change efforts. (See Chapter 6.) Of course not all technologies will have as dramatic an effect on an organization. Replacing a company's first copying machine with one that sorts and staples will not revolutionize how business is done or how organizational members will communicate. The new machine would be an incremental innovation, a technology that is very similar to the old machine "and that requires little change in the processes of the organization to be used effectively."[10] However, substituting networked computers for typewriters in a television newsroom so that reporters have access to databases, each other's stories, and the technological ability to turn a lead into a story within hours instead of days, dramatically changes the way the newsroom works and the speed with which it does so. The adoption of such a technology is a radical innovation if it "requires significant changes in processes" and mandates "personnel to adjust their behavior and to acquire new skills to a degree far beyond that of incremental innovation."[11]

How can leaders facilitate the diffusion of these incremental or radical innovations? How can they spread the use of a technology throughout an organization using the multiple communication channels that exist within its social system? Just as one might facilitate a change effort within an organization, a leader should:

1. Involve organizational members in the adoption and diffusion process
2. Provide opportunities for continuous learning for those who will use the new technology
3. Encourage individuals' experimentation with the technology
4. Provide opportunities for communication about the technology, its advantages and its problems, among individuals in the same and different functional units and hierarchical levels[12]

However, the leader's responsibility for the adoption of a technology precedes his or her efforts to diffuse the innovation throughout an organization. There are several considerations these individuals should review when determining the need for, and the type of, a new technology of potential use in an organization. Such considerations include the following:

1. How the technology can be successfully included in the context of the entire organizational system (including its structure, strategy, procedures, and policies)
2. The potential impact of the adoption and use of the technology on the organization's task as well as on social relationships and individual concerns or anxieties
3. The social costs and benefits of the proposed technology
4. The involvement of followers in the change process
5. The potential need for retraining
6. The need for flexibility and adaptability when using the technology
7. The use of face-to-face communication as often as possible to illustrate that the new technology will not replace human communication
8. The need for the alignment of the technology with other organizational components, such as mission, structure, culture, and climate, so that all these components are moving together in the same direction (i.e., toward the attainment of organizational goals)
9. The need, on an ongoing basis, to attend to the impact of the technology on various communication patterns in the organization[13]

Understanding that technological innovation is a form of organizational change, leaders must also realize that the introduction of new technologies into organizations creates anxiety and uncertainty among organizational members, and therefore resistance, unless efforts are made to involve them in the change effort. Such is particularly the case if the change is transformational, causing major effects on organizational processes and structures, and/or monumental effects on social relationships and networks. For instance, the introduction of automation into university admission offices not only provided for faster processing of admission applications, but the system itself generated data on the academic characteristics of those applying to, accepted in, or denied access to universities. These data ultimately have had the potential to effect changes in admission procedures, and even initiate discussions about raising admission requirements at some overpopulated universities. Additionally, at some universities students register each semester using a computerized telephone system. This process is user-friendly and saves time and frustration, but it further impersonalizes the student's relationship to his or her university.

A more dramatic example is that offered by Shoshana Zuboff who describes how the introduction of computer technology created anonymity among clerks in one organization. Where once these individuals had been able to see and talk with one another over their typewriters, the introduction of computers into the organization resulted in the installation of designed work stations that prevented them from seeing, much less conversing with, each other. As Zuboff observes: "Automation meant that jobs which had once allowed them to use their bodily presence in the service of interpersonal exchange and collaboration now required their bodily presence in the service of routine interaction with a machine. Jobs that had once required their voices now insisted they be mute."[14] In private sessions with clerks affected by the technological innovation, Zuboff found that many drew disturbing self-portraits as they described how the new technology affected them. These individuals "portrayed themselves as chained to desks, surrounded by bottles of aspirin, dressed in prison stripes, outfitted with blinders closely observed by their supervisors, surrounded by walls, enclosed without sunlight or food, bleary-eyed with fatigue, solitary, frowning, and blank—without a face."[15] Clearly the introduction of computers into this organization created more than anxiety. Workers were intensely upset by the effects of the technology on their interactions with others, and their perceived "places" in the organization.

Because a variety of outcomes may occur with the introduction of a new technology, the leader as change agent must consider several processes through which a relationship may be established between a technology and organizational members. These processes include:[16]

1. *Socialization*—introducing individuals to the technology and how it is used by involving them in processes through which they acquire knowledge and skills related to the adoption of the technology
2. *Commitment*—involving organizational members in decisions affecting the adoption and use of the technology to foster their commitment to its entrance into the organization
3. *Reward allocation*—distributing different types of rewards related to individuals' use of the technology
4. *Sensing and redesign*—gathering data on the performance of the technology as it is used by organizational members and redesigning the technology to improve its performance and the ease with which it can be used. (For example, telephone systems and computer sizes and capabilities are constantly changing to accommodate suggestions and criticisms offered by those who use them in organizations.)
5. *Diffusion*—extending the technology to various parts of the organization so that more individuals have access to it

Through these processes, leaders can decrease the anxiety, uncertainty, and even animosity that may exist when an "intruding" technology makes its way into the daily lives of organizational members.

Stories such as that told by Zuboff should make leaders sensitive to the notion that the adoption and use of new technologies in organizations are a form of organizational change, and that many of the attendant concerns about change, and its potential and real effects, are important to organizational members when technologies are introduced into their midst. What Zuboff's story also illustrates is that technologies become part of, affect, and are affected by organizational culture. That is another consideration about the relationship between organizations and new communication technologies that leaders must understand.

Technology as a Component of Organizational Culture

In Chapter 4 we discussed the important function leaders assume as creators and protectors of organizational culture, such as the values, beliefs, language, rituals, and structure that comprise the "heart" of an organization. The technologies in use within an organization also are part of its culture. Just like other cultural components, they possess physical realities and help enact social ones. As we saw in the example offered by Zuboff, technologies have a physical presence in the organization that affect the social dynamics and the communicative relationships among individuals. An organizational culture is changed as the use of computers becomes part of one's daily activities, such as retrieving data from one's own machine rather than receiving information in hard copy form from others, or sharing data via computer with people in other locales rather than meeting with them face-to-face. New skills are needed by organizational members—not just typing skills but intellectual competencies to make judgments about what type of information is needed in order to make a particular decision, how much information is needed, and how it can optimally be used. As a result, learning becomes a critical competency within the organization. Additionally, as organizational members engage in self-management activities, organizational structures, an important component of culture, may very well change to become flexible and less hierarchical.

There are other ways that technologies affect organizational culture. According to a number of executives, their experiences in end-user computing revealed the following perceptions about technology's influences on organizational communication.

1. Information flows directly to those who need to have it, rather than along the prescribed organizational chart.
2. Communication is more frequent at all organizational levels.
3. Written communications are more succinct and less formal.
4. Employees have access to external databases that give them information about external influences on the organization.
5. As executive use of computers increases, end-user computing, the process through which people with little technical training can access, review, and disseminate information, is adopted more quickly throughout the organization.

6. E-mail cuts through organizational boundaries as well as organizational layers, thereby increasing the free flow of information and communication throughout an organization.
7. End-user computing improves the accuracy, clarity, timeliness, and relevance of information accessed and shared.[17]

More directly related to organizational leadership, some researchers have noted that leader–member relations and the power inherent in a given position may be influenced by characteristics of technologies. As was the case with technologies that first engaged in the nineteenth century, such as the telegraph and telephone, these new ways of communicating increase the speed of information acquisition and message transmission, as well as the power of those who have access to and control of information and the media through which it is disseminated. If information is power, then understanding and controlling the ways it can be acquired and disseminated is an empowering process for potentially any organizational member, regardless of one's job title or place on an organizational chart.

Hulin and Roznowski have found that group cohesiveness, the number of face-to-face interactions, and the expert power attributed to a leader are "very likely" related to a technology in use.[18] Their studies also suggest that technologies in organizations have less effect on tasks than on the structure of work activities, organizational climate, communication networks, and leader–follower interactions—all components of organizational culture.

Organizational cultures both affect, and are affected by, the adoption and use of technologies. Organizational leaders need to understand that culture affects attitudes about a new technology and the acceptance of it by organizational members. A culture that values worker equality will not support a technology that gives only some individuals computers and the resultant access to information. Leaders must understand that in such cultures, the introduction of new technologies must not create in-groups and out-groups through which people are treated differentially and unequally.

Organizational culture not only affects attitudes about technology, it may facilitate the implementation of it. If a culture values speed, innovation, and the results that technology may bring to the organization, such as increased information flow among all organizational levels, that culture will value the introduction and use of the new technology.

New technologies may pose the following threats to organizational members: isolation, boredom, loss of social interaction, reduction in the workforce (including the elimination of middle managers who may have been information mediaries in times past), and de-skilling, or turning individuals' tasks into menial work, such as merely inputting data while the computer becomes responsible for analyzing, formatting, and presenting information.

The responsibility for making technology an accepted, nonthreatening component of organizational culture resides with its leader. The technologies of use to an organization should be part of its vision and its goals. In other words, the technologies appropriate for an organization's use should be embedded, or reinforced, as part of its culture. If a technology is to be implemented in an existing culture, organizational leaders should:

- Anticipate opposition to it and devise plans to deal with the opposition (just as might be done in an organizational change process)
- Inform top management about the technology so they can understand it and explain it to others
- Introduce organizational members to the technology early, through a variety of communication channels, including meetings as well as written communications[19]

To illustrate the effects of a technology on an organizational culture, consider the use of groupware in organizations that value teams to accomplish tasks. Groupware is a type of software used in computer systems to facilitate group work electronically. In order to be considered groupware, this software must: (1) allow people to communicate electronically; (2) facilitate the management of information used in common; and (3) incorporate within its features the understanding that it will be used by a group, not individuals.[20] Two major purposes of groupware are to increase information sharing and to avoid redundancy. Groupware allows people to work together on a document, either in the same location or different locations. It provides communal work space and can facilitate the management of face-to-face meetings. Groupware may also support asynchronous communication, or communication that occurs at different times. Its potential advantages lie in its ability to increase the speed of decision making and reduce face-to-face meeting frequency, meeting length, missed communications due to telephone tag, and time lost to interruptions.[21]

Designed to facilitate group interaction, groupware's effect on organizations may be to "change their structures and transform their operations. Instead of being highly layered, they will become horizontally ordered into ever-shifting communities of knowledge workers and specialists."[22] Later in this chapter we will consider the effects organizational communication technologies have on leaders. In the case of groupware, leadership is shared as a task evolves, or as different members assume this role as a group evolves.

Technology's Place in Existing Communicative Relationships

A story is told that when Henry David Thoreau was informed that a new invention, the telephone, would enable someone in Maine to talk to someone in Texas he responded, "That's nice—but what will they talk about?" This is an example of an honest inquiry about the relationship of technology to social reality. What Thoreau did not consider as he spent time writing, sometimes in seclusion, was that the world was "growing smaller." New channels of communication, including mass media, were creating opportunities to learn about places and people distant from one's own abode. People in Maine and Texas might indeed have common interests, even familial or friendship bonds that would give them plenty to talk about. Thoreau needed to understand, as do leaders, that technology is introduced in organizations (or societies) within existing webs of communicative relationships. Technologies must be woven through, or embedded in, existing webs of communicative relationships and networks when they are introduced and used in organizations. Such relationships may facilitate the adoption of a technology or, conversely, may be enhanced through its use.

Several notable scholars have suggested that the use of technology in an organization is affected by the social context in which it exists. If you are part of a network of relationships where organizational members use computers to accomplish tasks and engage in computer-mediated communication, such as e-mail, you are likely to use the technology because you are *socially influenced* to do so. How does such influence manifest itself? The most direct way, according to results of research conducted in organizations, is by overt statements organizational members make about the characteristics of the technology or its use to accomplish tasks. Individuals in the same communication network weave these statements into their own evaluations of it.[23] Specifically, one study of perceptions of e-mail found that an individual's perceptions were significantly related to his or her supervisor's attitudes and those of the five persons with whom each had the most communication in the organization, that is, with whom they were united in a communication network. Another study found that people with more e-mail experience and training rated e-mail as a richer medium than people without such training and experience.[24] In short, the type of medium one chooses to use in an organization is affected by the communicative relationships in which one is involved.

The effects of prominent communicators in an organization or in a network within an organization on the diffusion and use of new media also has considerable research support, as does the range of contacts one has in the organization or network. As Contractor and Eisenberg write: "Individuals who communicate with a diverse set of people bring new information, alternative perspectives, and often a greater degree of influence to the media perceptions of others in the group."[25]

Communication is important as the process used to teach about a technology and how to use it. Collaborative communication among employees from different units and different hierarchical levels helps people discover ways of integrating technology into the organization. People give each other new perspectives and novel ideas about a technology's use. Therefore, learning is not a passive process but an active one in which organizational members share information to adjust to new ways of performing work. As Michael J. Papa found in his research:

> *Adapting to new technology on the job often involves a trial-and-error process in which employees make mistakes and require assistance to solve problems. An employee is more likely to receive needed information if he or she has a large and diverse circle of contacts. Employees who interact with only a few co-workers in their own department are less likely to find the information they need than employees who have contacts in different departments and hierarchical levels of the organization.*[26]

New technologies, such as networked computers, support collaborative work in organizations—-work that depends on intensive communication. Such tools operate in real time, are highly interactive, readily accept new data, and are adaptable to surroundings. They provide shared space where organizational members can work on tasks as groups via their computers. Just as people around a conference table can create an advertising campaign by brainstorming, drawing their thoughts on an easel with differently colored pens, and erasing and changing each other's ideas, so can groups work collaboratively using certain computer programs.

The implications of collaborative technological activity for leaders are many. New technologies will enhance task-related leadership in groups and also will allow leaders more hands-on involvement with collaborative activities. As Michael Schrage has written in *Shared Minds,* individuals' abilities to lead others "will be as much a function of their competence with these tools as any particular personal charms. Collaborative leaders will have a repertoire of techniques that can guide a group to a successful solution to a problem, draw out the latent talents of team members, and project an otherwise inaccessible vision onto the shared space."[27] Additionally, "both executives and middle managers will spend a greater portion of their time collaborating on documents deemed important to their organizations. Budgets, training procedures, strategic plans, quarterly reports, and other documents will increasingly be produced collaboratively in real time, not processed in long cycles of draft and revision."[28] In other words, collaborative work using computers currently exists, but will become increasingly infused into the culture of organizations.

Leaders must understand that cultures can facilitate or impede the diffusion of new technologies throughout organizations; and these technologies (i.e., e-mail, voice mail, audioconferencing, facsimile transmission, groupware, etc.) will have individual and collective impacts on organizational culture. Leaders would do well to remember that networks of communication relationships may be dramatically affected by a new communication technology, and they must guide this form of organizational change carefully lest it cause individual and group resistance sufficiently strong to damage the process of technological diffusion. In the guidance process, leaders should assume the role of technological champion, facilitating the adoption and use of new communication technologies through their words and actions. Before analyzing this organizational role, it is worthwhile to review what research studies tell us about leaders' current use of new technologies and their effects on leader behavior.

Leaders as Users of Communication Technologies

A variety of studies analyzing the communication behaviors of executives have found that such individuals prefer face-to-face communication over other forms of interaction, including the use of technological innovations. Surveys of top and middle managers in Fortune 500 companies found that:

- Top executives rarely or never used computer-mediated communication.
- Executives and middle managers most frequently used personal contact as a source of information.
- Younger managers used computers more than middle-aged managers, and older managers used computers less than middle-aged managers.
- The most frequent use of personal computers was for e-mail.
- Voice mail and fax machines were also used, but face-to-face communication or use of the telephone was still preferred to computer-mediated communication.
- Use of e-mail does not necessarily lead to greater use of personal computers for other purposes—managers continue to feel that personal contacts are more effective in the conduct of business.[29]

The researchers summarizing these findings observed: "The patterns of use we observed support a conclusion that information systems and personal computers have been put in place because technology has allowed them to be, rather than because of needs or consideration of the value of technology to enhance connections or relationships. As a result, not all managers have embraced the new technology and learned to use it effectively."[30]

Other researchers, in analyzing several studies of managerial use of computer-mediated communication, found that such use did not lead to a decrease in the use of other media or personal contact. Indeed, subjects preferred personal contact and telephone, followed by writing and e-mail.[31] The scholars also found, as have other researchers, that new communication technologies used in organizations supplement, rather than replace, face-to-face communication. Further, they facilitate an increase in new contacts, laterally or downward in the organization.

The "computer revolution" has not occurred among top executives. Computers may sit for show on credenzas or work tables in executive offices, but many are not used, or are used minimally. However, the executives of tomorrow, that is, those of the twenty-first century, will be individuals raised on computer games at home, computer courses in schools, and computerized word processing in universities. Their computer usage habits may, therefore, be very different.

Of course the studies mentioned in these pages focused on executives and managers, individuals who may or may not be *leaders* as we have defined the term. Later in this chapter we will discuss the proactive and visionary roles that leaders must assume in introducing and facilitating the use of communication technologies in organizations. Before focusing on these roles, however, it is beneficial to review what effects technologies have on organizational leaders and their communication behaviors.

Effects of Communication Technologies on Leaders

In the process of creating, articulating, and implementing visions, leaders may use new communication technologies to generate and analyze data, create documents of persuasion and motivation using this data, and communicate directly to organizational members. E-mail affords opportunities to inform, persuade, motivate, and receive feedback. Teleconferencing is used to make decisions while saving money and travel time. Networked computers offer decision support systems to provide executives data about the organization specifically for the purpose of making decisions and solving problems. Some of the effects these technologies have on leaders include the following:

- Saving time, which can be used for thinking, visioning, and communicating with organizational members or external constituencies of the organizations
- Providing accessibility to individuals at various organizational levels, in different functions, and in different locales, in order to obtain data as well as feedback
- Providing communication choices to leaders, so they may have opportunities to use mediated and face-to-face communication when appropriate
- Providing tools so that leaders may exhibit instrumental and symbolic leadership behaviors; new communication technologies give organizational leaders the opportunity to accomplish more of their own work, at their own desks, while still using both mediated and face-to-face communication to motivate and intellectually stimulate organizational members

Leaders are not just beneficiaries of the blessings of technologies—they must facilitate the careful introduction of these tools into their organizations. Consequently, it is important to consider the role a leader plays as a technological champion, an informed change agent, who encourages technological innovation within his or her own culture.

The Leader as Technological Champion

Not all leaders utilize new technologies in their own day-to-day work. Nevertheless, *any* leader is important to the adoption and use of these "tools" if he or she acts as an advocate on their behalf. Because leaders are by definition influential in an organization, they are leaders of opinion and instigators of actions to introduce and utilize new technologies. As champions, leaders make decisions about which technologies to acquire, what resources to invest in them, and to what degree they will be implemented throughout the organization.[32] A technological champion need not be a leader at the "top" of an organization. The characteristics that this person should possess include expertise, credibility, and the ability to persuade— someone who is either quite knowledgeable about the technology in question and/or who understands the organization's need for the technology in order to facilitate the achievement of its goals. Leaders, as technological champions, must have the political and communication skills to deal with organizational members who possess varying levels of commitment to technological change. Indeed, researchers who conducted a study of middle managers as leaders during a process of technological change suggest that such leaders should have problem-solving and other implementation skills that translate top management's vision into technological change.[33]

Leaders as technological champions need to understand that technological change is a type of organizational change and therefore requires attention to culture, structure, strategy, climate, and the interrelationships among them. Such change requires the same skills and behaviors exhibited by leaders as change agents, and more specifically, those ascribed to transformational leaders. Because such leaders are follower focused and change oriented, they may be more effective in overcoming barriers or resistance to change. (See Chapter 6.)

A study of over 150 chief executive officers in Canadian firms who oversaw the implementation of a technological innovation found that champions "rely on highly communicative types of influence strategies, such as coalition formation and reasoning, to create support for their innovations."[34] The study also found that these individuals, because they were executives, had more opportunities for building networks through which to share information and create support for new ideas. The basic communication behaviors of these leaders as technological champions are described by the researchers as "the articulation of a compelling vision of the innovation's potential for the organization, the expression of confidence in others to participate effectively in the initiative, the display of unconventional, innovative actions to achieve goals, the belief in one's capacities to initiate change, and the assessment of environmental resources and constraints for bringing about change."[35]

While understanding that the purpose, functions, and advantages of various communication technologies is necessary for any leader acting as a technological champion, it is not sufficient for facilitating technological innovations. The value of a communication technology is not the hardware from which it is made, but the management of that technology within the system of task and social relationships that comprise an organization. Accordingly, leaders as technological champions should be attendant to:

1. Using new technologies, as appropriate, to serve as role models for the adoption and use of those innovations (e.g., e-mail, teleconferencing)
2. Establishing mechanisms to elicit feedback from all organizational levels about their experiences with the technology, including face-to-face communications
3. Appointing senior level people to serve as chief information officers and/or chief technology officers, to integrate technological considerations into other organizational decisions, and to communicate the importance of information management and technological management[36]

Now, and in the future, an increasing number of leaders must recognize the importance of appointing individuals with expertise in information management and technology management to assume critical roles in the planning and implementation of organizational goals and the conduct of organizational activities on a day-to-day basis. A chief information officer can assume several roles to assist leadership efforts within an organization, including the following:

1. Aiding the organization in understanding its information requirements
2. Identifying sources of information to satisfy these requirements
3. Promoting organizational knowledge about, and understanding of, available information resources[37]

A chief technology officer is particularly appropriate for those organizations needing multiple technologies for optimum operation, such as messaging systems, computer-assisted communications, and collaborative tools for group decision making and problem solving. This individual serves as an adviser to the organizational leader(s) on hardware and software needs; appropriate technologies required considering organizational size, task, structure, culture, and goals; and the information/communication functions potential technologies must perform.

As important as these individuals may be to an organization, organizational leaders in the 1990s and the beginning of the twenty-first century must not delegate all responsibilities for technological innovation and management to technical experts. They must consider technological innovations in the process of creating an organizational vision, integrate technological functions into the work of the organization, and continually be aware of technological trends that affect the hardware and software components of each innovation. Most importantly, leaders must regard new technologies as integral parts of a continuously learning, adaptive organization—not just as tools for accomplishing specific tasks.

LEADERS' USE OF NEW TECHNOLOGIES— IMPLICATIONS FOR THE FUTURE

Although a variety of research studies shows that executives at the pinnacle of organizational hierarchies are not using new communication technologies to the extent that other organizational members use them, such usage is increasing and will continue to do so. Nevertheless, such technologies are not expected to replace face-to-face interaction as the preferred medium of communication by leaders. They understand the importance of seeing and hearing one's competitors or colleagues to validate the perceptions one accumulates, including those about individuals' expertise, knowledge, personal loyalty, or level of organizational commitment.

However, new communication/information technologies are making information available to leaders more quickly than ever before. Those who control access to information, and the media from which it comes, also control the process of organizational decision making. Because new technologies can put leaders in touch with geographically dispersed organizational units at literally any time of the day, leaders potentially wield great influence in the conduct of organizational life. Also, because new technologies facilitate social as well as task-related communication, control over various types of communication relationships is a potential and potent power for organizational leaders. However, it is possible that leaders in the future will have *less* control over such relationships than in the past because new technologies are changing the structure and cultures of organizations. Flatter, more flexible entities, with decentralized, self-managing units, now require a leader to be more coordinator than commander.

These are some of the observations of those who study the adoption and use of technology in organizations, and the relationship of that use to leadership. However, questions remain that leaders must continue to ask as they create, or renew, organizations in the future. Such questions include the following:

- What are the implications for organizational leadership if new technologies allow work to be conducted at home, or at multiple decentralized sites?

- While new technologies potentially provide leaders with virtually unlimited information, what mechanisms of control, if any, should leaders consider adopting to avoid overload and to allow themselves sufficient time for visioning and motivating?
- Assuming the proliferation of new technologies in organizations, how will they change the communicative relationships among organizational members that facilitate task accomplishment and social interaction?
- In what ways can leaders integrate the use of new technologies into forms of human communication of importance to organizational members?
- How will new communication/information technologies affect leadership behaviors?

Finally:

- What implications do the use of new technologies have for the definition of "organization" and "organizational leadership"?

This is a critical question for our consideration as we move to the final chapter and its discussion of leadership and followership in the twenty-first century.

SUMMARY

A technology is the way work is done or the means through which a task is accomplished. Pens, crayons, typewriters, and computers are all technologies. Leaders need to know what specific technologies are available for use in their organizations and how they facilitate the attainment of goals. Examples of technologies that facilitate communication within or among organizations include facsimile transmission (fax), electronic messaging (e-mail), audioconferencing, and videoconferencing.

To determine whether a specific technology is appropriate for his or her organization, a leader needs to recognize and review that technology's characteristics, including its compatibility, complexity, trialability, and communicability.

Technologies may affect tasks, structures, and cultures, and leaders must understand the relationship of technology to organizations and their members. Serving as a champion of innovation requires that a leader involve organizational members in the process of introducing and diffusing the innovation throughout the organization, encouraging experimentation with the technology and teaching people how to use the technology. Before taking on the mantle of technological champion, however, a leader must review a variety of considerations about a technology that may be introduced into an organization. Such considerations include the potential impact of the adoption and use of the technology, its social costs and benefits, the involvement of followers in the innovation process, and the need for the technology to be "aligned" with other organizational components, such as mission, structure, and culture.

Leader–member relations may be influenced by the characteristics of new communication technologies. Computer-based technologies have increased the speed of information acquisition and message transmission, and potentially have increased the power of those who have ready access to those messages. As a result, leaders must understand that organizational cultures affect, and are affected by, the use of technologies. Culture affects attitudes about a new technology, and values and beliefs affect the adoption of a new tool for a task. Conversely, technologies affect cultures—an e-mail system should not create in-groups and out-groups through which people are treated differently and unequally. It is the leader's responsibility to insure the smooth introduction of a new technology into an organizational culture, and to recognize that the culture can facilitate or impede the diffusion of new technologies through that culture.

Part of a leader's orientation toward a new technology is determined by his or her use of technologies in general. A variety of studies indicates that many executives prefer face-to-face communication over other forms of interaction and that computer-mediated communication is rarely used. However, younger managers are more apt to use computers because they have "grown up" in a society where computers for office use, as well as entertainment, have proliferated. Nevertheless, new communication technologies supplement, rather than replace, face-to-face communication.

Aside from the influences that leaders exert over computer usage, technologies also have effects on leaders. Such effects include: saving time, providing accessibility to individuals and information one otherwise would not have, and giving communication choices to leaders so they have more than one "tool" with which to communicate to individuals throughout the organization.

Technological champions need not be leaders at the "tops" of organizations. However, such an individual should possess expertise, credibility, the ability to persuade, and be someone who understands the organization's need for a specific technology.

Leaders as technological champions need to understand that technological change is a type of organizational change; it requires attention to culture, structure, strategy, climate, and the interrelationships among them. They must consider technological innovation as an ongoing process, not a series of computerized products. As champions of change, leaders must ask how new communication technologies will affect where and how work will be accomplished in the future, how it will be controlled and rewarded, and how such technologies will affect human communication as individuals go about the business of working and socializing. Another critical question from the perspective of this book is: What implications do the use of new technologies have for the notion of "organizational leadership"?

QUESTIONS TO CONSIDER

1. What is a technology? What are examples of communication technologies?

2. Explain the following sentences:

   Technological innovation is a form of organizational change.

   Organizational cultures affect, and are affected by, the adoption of new communication technologies.

   Leaders should be technological champions.

   People are socially influenced to use communication technologies in organizations.

3. What questions should a leader ask when determining the need for a new technology in his or her organization?

4. Name five influences that computer technologies have on human communication in organizations.

5. Describe the types of communication technologies leaders use and the purposes for which they use them.

6. What effects do new communication technologies have on leaders in organizations?

CASE PROBLEM

Clare Berry, Vice President of Sales at One Life National Insurance Company, has been given the authority to purchase computers for all her salespersons and connect them with the Internet system. This is a welcome change for several of the newer, younger salespeople. However, it is a bit anxiety producing for older individuals who are not computer literate. The new system will provide the use of e-mail, access to on-line services via the Internet, a computer calendar for the program, and other programs for instructional use so that continuing education courses, or parts of courses, can be taken "on-line."

   You are Berry's technology consultant with a background in speech communication. She has asked you to advise her on how to introduce, and encourage the use of, the computer system. Specifically, she has asked you to prepare a written document that contains the following:

1. Suggested communication strategies for introducing the system to all salespersons

2. An outline describing the purposes of computer technologies in organizations like yours, and how they can be used to facilitate, not detract from, human communication in the organization

3. Ways you can "champion" this innovation among organizational members
4. Strategies for involving a number of salespeople in the adoption and diffusion of the new system throughout the program

(Note: You may wish to work with other students in class to develop this document for "Ms. Berry.")

ENDNOTES

1. Shoshana Zuboff, *In the Age of the Smart Machine* (New York: Basic Books, 1984), 415.
2. Robert W. Zmud, "Opportunities for Strategic Information Manipulation Through New Information Technology," in *Organizations and Communication Technology*, eds. Janet Fulk and Charles Steinfeld (Newbury Park: Sage Publications, 1990), 95.
3. Everett M. Rogers, *Communication Technology: The New Media in Society* (New York: The Free Press, 1986), 2.
4. Chelse Benham and Marcus Shaffer, "Videoconferencing," in *Communication Technology Update,* 3d ed., ed. August E. Grant (Boston: Butterworth-Heinemann, 1994).
5. August E. Grant and Liching Sung, eds., *1992 Communication Technology Update* (Austin, TX: Technology Futures, Inc.).
6. E. M. Rogers, *Diffusion of Innovations,* 3d ed. (New York: The Free Press, 1983); Ronald E. Rice and Bonnie McDaniel Johnson, *Managing Organizational Innovation* (New York: Columbia University Press, 1987).
7. Philip H. Mirvis, Amy L. Sales, and Edward J. Hackett, "The Implementation and Adoption of New Technology in Organizations: The Impact on Work, People, and Culture," *Human Resource Management* 30:1 (Spring 1991): 113.
8. Ibid.,113–114.
9. Marshall McLuhan, *Understanding Media: The Extensions of Man* (New York: McGraw-Hill, 1964), 90.
10. Urs E. Gattiker, *Technology Management in Organizations* (Newbury Park: Sage Publications, 1990), 24.
11. Ibid., 24.
12. Ibid., adapted from pp. 146–153.
13. E. A. More and R. K. Laird, *Organizations in the Communications Age* (New York: Sydney: Pergamon Press, 1985), adapted from pp. 168–170.
14. Zuboff, *In the Age of the Smart Machine,* 141.
15. Ibid., 141–142.
16. Paul S. Goodman, Terri L. Griffith, and Deborah B. Fenner, "Understanding Technology and the Individual in an Organizational Context," in *Technology and Organizations,* eds. Paul S. Goodman, Lee S. Sproull, and Associates (San Francisco: Jossey-Bass Publishers, 1990): 56–64.
17. N. Dean Meyer and Mary E. Boone, *The Information Edge,* 2d ed. (Homewood, IL: Dow Jones-Irwin, 1989), 247–248, 251.

18. Charles L. Hulin and Mary Roznowski, "Organizational Technologies: Effects on Organizations' Characteristics and Individuals' Responses," *Research in Organizational Behavior,* 7 (JAI Press, 1985), 68.

19. H. Noori, *Managing the Dynamics of New Technologies* (Englewood Cliffs, NJ: Prentice-Hall, 1990), adapted from Exhibit 9.11.

20. Susanna Opper and Henry Fersko-Weiss, *Technology for Teams* (New York: Van Nostrand Reinhold, 1992), 25.

21. Ibid., adapted from pp. 44–47.

22. Ibid., 17–18.

23. Janet Fulk, Joseph Schmitz, and Charles W. Steinfeld, "A Social Influence Model of Technology Use," in *Organizations and Communication Technology,* eds. Janet Fulk and Charles Steinfeld (Newbury Park: Sage Publications, 1990), 121.

24. Ibid. , 129–130.

25. Noshir S. Contractor and Eric M. Eisenberg, "Communication Networks and New Media in Organizations," in *Organizations and Communication Technology,* eds. Janet Fulk and Charles Steinfeld (Newbury Park: Sage Publications, 1990), p. 155.

26. Michael J. Papa, "Communication Network Patterns and Employee Performance with New Technology," *Communication Research* 17:3 (1990): 363–364.

27. Michael Schrage, *Shared Minds* (New York: Random House, 1990), 189.

28. Ibid. 192.

29. Sharon M. McKinnon and William J. Bruns, Jr., *The Information Mosaic* (Boston: Harvard Business School Press, 1992).

30. McKinnon and Bruns, *The Information Mosaic,* 190.

31. More and Laird, *Organizations in the Communications Age* (New York: Pergamon Press, 1985), 133.

32. James G. March and Lee S. Sproull, "Technology, Management, and Competitive Advantage," in *Technology and Organizations,* eds. Paul S. Goodman, Lee S. Sproull, and Associates (San Francisco: Jossey-Bass Publishers, 1990).

33. Carol A. Beatty and Gloria L. Lee, "Leadership among Middle Managers—An Exploration in the Context of Technological Change," *Human Relations* 45:9 (1992): 986–987.

34. Jane M. Howell and Christopher A. Higgins, "Leadership Behaviors, Influence Tactics, and Career Experiences of Champions of Technological Innovation," *Leadership Quarterly* 1:4 (1990).

35. Ibid., 260.

36. Paul A. Strassman, *The Business Value of Computers* (New Canaan, CT: The Information Economics Press, 1990), 511.

37. G. Michael Ashmore, "A New Approach for Managing Information Technology," *Journal of Business Strategy* (January-February 1989), adapted from p. 58.

9

COMMUNICATING LEADERSHIP: SUMMARY OBSERVATIONS AND SUGGESTIONS FOR THE FUTURE

Throughout the chapters of this book we have looked at leadership characteristics, behaviors, and styles. We have also studied leaders as creators and sustainers of organizational culture, decision makers, change agents, facilitators of diversity, and champions of new communication technologies. In the Preface we observed that leadership is sometimes praised more than it is practiced. However, that is not due to an inherent weakness in the human character. Leadership is difficult, tiring, time-consuming, and sometimes a thankless endeavor. It requires constant efforts to balance organizational and individual goals, and task and social relationships. It demands conscientious attention to communication, an understanding of what messages and media are appropriate in a given situational context for a specific audience and whether that audience is one person in an organization, a small group, or a functional unit of 2000.

In much of the academic literature on leadership, the communicative relationship between leaders and followers is described as interaction between supervisors and subordinates. In this text research findings are reported on superior–subordinate communication because studies on how people interact in this relationship are those that comprise the majority of research literature on leader–follower communication. These studies have been conducted largely in hierarchical, multilevel organizations where face-to-face and written media are the predominant channels in use. But supervisors are not necessarily leaders, and subordinates are not always followers. Consequently, those who study leadership must begin to differentiate it from managing or supervising as they conduct research because the behaviors and roles of leaders may be very different from those exhibited by managers/ supervisors. Moreover, as has been stressed throughout these pages, the structure of organizations is changing. The technologies used to work and communicate are changing. Finally, the relationship between those who have traditionally given and traditionally received commands and instructions is changing.

LEADERSHIP COMMUNICATION: DIFFERENT PERSPECTIVES

Studies of superior–subordinate communication generally have found that these individuals spend much of their time interacting with each other.[1] Good supervisors historically have been seen as people who like to communicate, are good listeners, make requests rather than give orders, and are open in communicative settings.[2] Similarly, studies analyzing the relationship between leadership and communication style have found that perceptions of a leader as warm, open, attentive, and relaxed (positive style constructs) correlated positively with subordinate satisfaction of supervision.[3]

In the early 1980s one of the few books devoted specifically to a study of leadership communication focused on the difference between a person-oriented leadership communication style and a task-oriented leadership communication style. (Much of what is discussed in Chapter 3 draws similar conclusions, but is more detailed in its analyses.) The author, Ernest Stech, suggested that a person-oriented leader (one who is follower-focused) uses a communication style where he or she:[4]

- Communicates frequently and enjoys it
- Prefers oral communication in face-to-face settings
- Exhibits attending and responding behaviors when listening to others
- Makes requests, not demands, and communicates agreement and praise
- Includes feelings and morale as important content in his or her communication
- Concentrates on communication via informal networks

Conversely, Stech observed, a task-oriented leader exhibits a communication style through which he or she:

- Communicates less than a person-oriented leader and regards communication as an interruption during a day's work
- Prefers writing to oral, face-to-face interactions
- Dominates conversations
- Commands, orders, and often communicates criticism

- Focuses his or her interaction on disseminating information and discussing tasks and procedures
- Concentrates on the use of formal channels

As we observed in Chapter 3, however, being person oriented as opposed to task oriented is not always an either/or proposition. Leaders may exhibit behaviors associated with both styles, depending on the situational contexts in which they find themselves. Future studies of leadership communication style must consider the changes currently underway in the contemporary design of organizational structures, the diffusion of new communication technologies in organizations, and the increasingly interdependent leader–follower relationship that we will discuss later in this chapter. How one communicates is affected by the opportunities and constraints that are inherent in certain structures, specific technologies, and relationships that comprise an organizational culture.

Analyzing leader–follower relationships by focusing on communication style, however, is an incomplete approach to the study of leadership communication in organizations. An additional approach is that of reviewing communicative *roles* leaders assume. In *The Nature of Managerial Work*, Henry Mintzberg introduced three sets of managerial behavior roles that leaders perform: interpersonal, informational, and decisional. Interpersonal roles are sets of behaviors related to status and authority and involve the development of interpersonal relationships. Through informational roles leaders receive and send information necessary for an organization's operations. Finally, decisional roles are those a leader assumes that have an impact on organizational decisions, such as conflict manager, negotiator, and allocator of resources.[5] In the process of everyday interaction, according to Nick Trujillo, leaders "perform" these roles in a variety of situational contexts that help construct organizational reality for leaders and organizational members.[6] The performance of interpersonal roles creates a sense of *sociability* in organizations. Enacting information roles reduces uncertainty and provides data for sense-making among organizational members, thereby creating a sense of *knowledgeability* about organizational life. Finally, the performance of *decisional* roles creates a sense of organizational rationality for organizational members. Leaders perform these roles in a series of communication episodes, such as a face-to-face employee evaluation, a meeting to organize the work week, or a chat about after-work social plans. Any episode may illustrate one or more of these performances. Leader–follower communication can also be discussed in terms of the roles leaders assume that are discussed in the various chapters of this text. The leader as creator of culture, decision maker, or change agent performs all the roles discussed by Mintzberg and Trujillo.

As organizations adopt new structures to adapt to the changing environments around them, and as new technologies afford leaders a variety of choices through which to interact with organizational members, the communicative relationships between leaders and followers will change. Present-day organizational members are better educated than previous generations of Americans. Consequently, they may have greater aspirations and expectations. They possess a number of ways with which to communicate as they are increasingly required to interact with more than one "boss" in the information chain. They work in groups, using new communication technologies to narrow the geographic and psychosocial distance that traditionally separated leaders and organizational members. They are educated as "professionals" to identify, access, and use information in the processes of decision making and problem solving. Consequently, "leaders" and "followers" often work in tandem as partners. Indeed, the leader–follower relationship in organizations may begin to resemble that relationship as it supposedly exists in a democratic society where leaders derive their power from those they govern.

LEADERS AND FOLLOWERS: THE NOTION OF INTERDEPENDENCY

James McGregor Burns, a political scientist, energized the study of leadership in his 1978 book where he coined the term "transformational" leadership. In that volume he emphasized the symbiotic relationship between leaders and followers: "Leadership, unlike naked power-wielding, is thus inseparable from followers' needs and goals. The essence of the leader–follower relation is the interaction of persons with different levels of motivations and of power potential . . . in pursuit of a common or at least joint purpose."[7] Similarly, John Gardner, a student of leadership in governmental settings, observed in 1990 that leadership is essentially conferred by followers, that the difference between executives and leaders is that *"executives are given subordinates; they have to earn followers."*[8] As Heller and Van Til suggest in a listing of propositions about the leader–follower relationship: "Leaders and followers, in any context, share a common fate of responsibility for their family, group, organization, or nation. From their joint participation emerges the success or failure of their enterprise."[9]

As we discussed in the last chapter, leaders wield influence in organizations, which enables them to initiate programmatic change, serve as champions for the adoption of new communication technologies, and infuse values into a newly born organizational culture. The *process* of leadership, however, depends on mutual influence between leaders and followers. This mutuality creates a relationship that is multidirectional, in which influence flows in all directions, not just top down. It is also noncoercive, based on the use of persuasion rather than unilateral or dictatorial action.[10]

Part of the problem in conceptualizing the interdependency of leaders and followers is the use of the term "followers." As Joseph Rost observes, in the industrial era within American society, followers were "(1) part of the sweaty masses and therefore separated from the elites, (2) not able to act intelligently without the guidance and control of other(s), (3) willing to let other people (elites) take control of their lives, and (4) unproductive unless directed by others."[11] As a result, the concept of "followers" became associated with subordinates in management research literature—passive beings told what to do by active individuals identified as leaders. Leaders and managers mistakenly became identified synonymously as well. (See Chapter 1.)

Even though the hierarchical superior–subordinate relationship is still seen in organizations and referred to by scholars, a more contemporary notion of followers includes the following five points of identification offered by Rost.[12]

1. Followers are active participants in the leadership process.
2. Followers can be active in varying degrees, at various times.
3. Followers can become leaders and leaders can become followers in the leadership relationship. Leadership can be a process through which influence is directed upward and horizontally as well as downward.
4. People can be leaders in one organization or group and followers in another group. (A person can be a leader at work and a follower at church or vice versa.)
5. Followers are in a leadership relationship. They are not in the process of followership. They have different roles in the relationship, may do different things in the relationship, but they are in that relationship with leaders.

The extent, the depth, and the length of a leader–follower relationship varies. In part the characteristics of that relationship in organizations vary depending on whether leadership is direct or indirect.

Direct Leadership

Direct leadership describes the process through which leaders communicate with followers by direct interaction. Its characteristics include the following:[13]

1. Communication ordinarily can be two-way.
2. Leaders and followers know one another personally.
3. The number of followers per leader must be highly limited.
4. Interactions can be spontaneous, reactive, adaptive, and do not necessarily require long-term commitments.

Consequently, direct leadership takes place when a leader interacts with his or her immediate subordinates in a group, such as at a staff meeting. It also occurs when a leader interacts on a one-to-one basis with each follower, as in performance evaluations. However, in organizations the potential exists for leaders to influence individuals who do not report directly to them. Such is the process of indirect leadership.

Indirect Leadership

There are at least two processes that result in indirect leadership: cascading and bypassing.[14] Cascading is the process of influencing individuals throughout an organization who do not report directly to a given leader. Through observation, informal interaction, or believing stories one hears about a person, an individual is witness to a leader's behavior and models it. Cascading has a ripple effect through organizational levels which is started by the leadership behaviors of one person.

Indirect leadership is also conducted by bypassing, through which one influences individuals at organizational levels beyond one's own direct subordinates. Mentoring someone else's subordinate, or championing the idea of someone who does not report to you, are examples of bypassing.

Direct and indirect leadership are not just reflections of top-down leadership. Individuals can be influenced through communication directed upward in an organization. The use of feedback, as well as articulation of one's expectations, may influence leaders. Offering an idea in a committee meeting on which individuals with greater influence sit, illustrates how a person can "lead" others through the articulation of a suggestion that ultimately is accepted. Providing feedback on a new policy or program also informs, and may persuade, "leaders" in an organization about the worth of that policy or program and may determine whether it is continued.

Reverse cascading and bypassing can also be used by people at lower levels of an organization to affect decisions made at higher levels. For instance, a middle manager may be on a committee with a company executive and offer an idea that influences one of the executive's decisions. Or, a staff member may write a memo shared among an organization's executive level, and someone who is not her immediate supervisor may use that information in a problem-solving process. Additionally, indirect leadership may take place horizontally when peers, co-workers, and colleagues influence each other in daily meetings or special task forces.

Finally, indirect leadership is exhibited through special efforts, particularly when the goal is organizational transformation (i.e. pervasive and large-scale change). A leader may influence the attitudes and values of many people throughout an organization using stories, symbols, and other components of an organization's culture. When a football coach changes the main philosophy that guides play calling, and concurrently emphasizes the team's previous winning tradition, he is attempting to engage the support of alumni as well as athletes. Leaders may influence both internal and external constituencies of an organization by utilizing language and actions to manage meaning. Such is the case when a candidate presents his or her campaign values and goals to the party faithful at a national convention, but the speech is simultaneously heard by voters throughout the country. Finally, a leader may use the process of empowerment, delegating power throughout the organization to create other leaders within it.

Whether leadership is direct or indirect, the leader–follower relationship is interdependent. Influence is exerted downward, upward, and laterally, and depends on the process of communication. As Woodrow Wilson once wrote: "The ear of the leader must ring with the voices of the people."[15]

That ear must also be sensitive to the sounds and trends that will affect the leader–follower relationship in the future. Some of those are mentioned in Chapter 2. Others include the following, as suggested by Guy Benveniste in his thoughts about the twenty-first century organization.[16]

1. World-wide competition for new ideas will affect organizations of the future. We will learn from other countries and cultures about novel processes and practices, particularly in the field of commerce, because our society is increasingly a global or international one.
2. The increased education of the work force will help raise the aspirations and expectations of employees.
3. The feminization of organizational culture will occur, not only because more women will be in the workplace, but more women will hold positions of influence and authority. Their increased participation in the life of organizations will prompt a reconceptualization of the boundaries of family and one's life at work.
4. New communication and information technologies will not change organizations in and of themselves, but decisions about them and their use may dramatically foster organizational change.
5. The institutionalization of rapid change, caused by factors such as foreign competition and technological developments, will make organizational change a continuing phenomenon as opposed to a unique occurrence.

These trends, and those discussed other places in this text, may call for the reconceptualization of an "organization." Changes in the demographics of the work force, in communication technologies, and in organizational structures may affect the notion of what an organization is and what its superordinate goals should be.

RECONCEPTUALIZING THE NOTION OF "ORGANIZATION"

While we have emphasized that an organization is not a place but the purposeful interaction of individuals working together on a task, environmental trends and their effects on organizational components (e.g., climate, culture, task, structure) require a new look at what the term "organization" may mean in the future. An organization is not a place, as Karl Weick has stated, but it does involve the occupation of space by at least two individuals engaged in purposeful communication, even if they are thousands of miles apart. As structures become less hierarchical, and as new technologies are used by leaders and organizational members to work collaboratively, the notion of organization may be defined as a minimum of two people communicating face-to-face or through mediating technologies.

The concept of a "networked organization" is a new one, and little research has focused on its communicative properties. Indeed, the term itself has at least two meanings. Those who view a networked organization from a technology perspective consider it as an entity in which computers are connected for the purpose of transmitting information. From a human perspective it is "one in which people are connected to one another in diverse forums to exchange ideas and other resources" and this exchange depends on a technical infrastructure.[17] In an environment where offices of a multinational corporation are geographically dispersed, a networked organization may keep people in touch with one another through teleconferencing and e-mail, to name just two technologies. Such contact prevents units of organizations from psychologically drifting apart, from feeling separate and differentially treated by those in power, or even in conflict with each other. A number of years ago, General Electric faced this problem when it opened plants in different parts of the United States. At that time, no computer-mediated technology was available to create unity among the organization's various plants. To remind GE employees that they were all in the same family, regardless of function, location, or hierarchical level, a spokesman was hired to visit these sites and give pep talks to employees. Sometimes he would speak at five or six locations in one day. This job, perhaps more than his acting career, gave Ronald Reagan the practice he needed to prepare for campaign speaking and presidential press conferences when he ran for, and became, a governor and later a two-term president. Today videoconferencing might be used by GE to foster communication among its distant and disparate units.

Whether networking is accomplished through the creation of temporary teams, a person with a computer and a phone jack sending and receiving information from a make-shift workstation, or several individuals in different European countries designing a car via groupware, there is a *link* that exists between them. That link is the connective tissue between human beings that makes technology worth the time, training, and money it costs to use it.

The concept of the networked organization is an evolving one. Nevertheless, one can already surmise that such structures, which combine human and technological elements, have implications for the future study of organizational cultures as well as social architectures. A networked organization may be comprised of multiple subcultures, all under the roof of a multi-functional, multihierarchical entity. It may be a hundred individuals communicating to their offices from permanent workstations at home, perhaps hundreds of miles from headquarters. If "organization" in the future means a composite of small groups, such as quality circles, project teams, and task groups, or a number of individuals connected via technology, what are the implications for the organizational culture—the values, beliefs, and rituals of that entity? How does a seemingly fragmented culture, or a compilation of subcultures, affect organizational climate? Will task-related groups that come together for a particular purpose and then dissipate when their work is done experience an organizational culture and climate differently than individuals in more formal, hierarchical structures? What effects do the adaptive, flexible structures have on interpersonal and organizational communication, and on the communicative relationships between leaders and other organizational members? Perhaps most importantly from our perspective, what constitutes "leadership" in organizations undergoing structural, cultural, and technological change?

RECONCEPTUALIZING THE NOTION OF ORGANIZATIONAL LEADERSHIP

The concept of the networked organization underscores the need for a leader to remember that an organization is a community of individuals created by communication, whether face-to-face or mediated. In the preceding pages we have offered a variety of observations about organizational leadership from a communication perspective. Some of the insights that should come to mind include the following:

- Through the creation and dissemination of messages, using verbal and nonverbal behaviors, leaders manage meaning. They serve as interpreters, educators, and advocates in the process of helping organizational members make sense out of situational contexts.
- While this text discusses leadership with a focus on organizational communication, leaders can learn much from theories of rhetoric and interpersonal communication. Indeed, much of the communication in which a leader is engaged is one-to-one or in small groups. In any communication setting, understanding one's audience, situational context, and the appeals one can use to construct appropriate messages are critical contributions from rhetorical theory. In short, a leader must understand the wisdom of using poetry to communicate power.

- Organizations are not places, they are people with common goals who share meaning by participating in communicative relationships.
- Leaders use the process of communication to embed, maintain, and change organizational cultures—systems of relationships with shared values, beliefs, language, and rituals. A culture is a web of relationships created through interaction that gives an organization its identity and uniqueness. As the reflection of an organization's culture, a leader is its creative voice and its symbol to both internal and external constituencies.
- An organizational leader guides decision development and implementation through the use of a variety of media and the creation of multiple messages. Communication is used to search for information, identify alternatives, choose a decision, and implement that choice. The quality of the process affects the quality of the product.
- In contemporary society, perhaps an organizational leader's most important role is that of change agent. Initiating change depends on the ability of the leader to create and communicate a vision, a preferred picture of the organization in the future. It also requires him or her to develop and implement strategies that will accomplish change, including the motivation of organizational members to accept and participate in the change effort.
- As facilitators of organizational diversity, leaders understand that communication allows one to express the value of each organizational member by supporting, rewarding, and challenging individuals in their attempts to develop personally and professionally. Communication is a process used to offer social support through individualized consideration, to celebrate the unique contribution of each individual who comprises the organization.
- New communication technologies allow organizational leaders the opportunity to weave many, far-reaching communicative relationships within and between organizations. A leader has the potential, through the advent of these technologies, to "reach out and touch" organizational members across the seas or down the hall, and to do so quickly to many individuals simultaneously. While there is no substitute for the richness of face-to-face communication as a means of communication, new technologies give leaders tools to fulfill their responsibilities as sustainers of culture, decision makers, change agents, facilitators of diversity, and champions of innovation.

Considering the changes we have discussed that are affecting and will continue to affect organizations and their members, what observations can be made about the nature of organizational leadership in the future?

- Leadership will continue to be diffused throughout organizations—exhibited by individuals in teams, or groups, and/or within multiple organizational levels as power is distributed throughout organizations by appointed or elected leaders. Even at the top level of an organization, leadership may be exercised by teams of executives with decision-making responsibilities assigned in accordance with individual expertise.

- Leadership may increasingly be mediated through the use of advanced communication technologies—but leaders will continue to understand the need to establish and maintain working relationships through face-to-face communication.

- There are scholars who suggest that the increase of women in decision-making positions within organizations will result in the "feminization" of leadership, characterized by a variety of nurturing behaviors. However, women, like men, will exhibit behaviors appropriate for given situations, selected from a continuum of choices—task oriented as well as follower focused. The nature of leadership, in general, whether exhibited by men or women, may change as individuals learn to use behaviors that are effective in given situational contexts and that have long-term positive effects, including improved organizational effectiveness, increased employee morale, enhanced innovations in products or processes.

- Leadership will become increasingly distinguishable from management as behaviors such as risk taking and creative decision making are used to guide organizations through times of both incremental and transformational change.

- The ability to understand one's audience and create appropriate messages in interpersonal and mediated contexts, and to realize that both words and actions create meanings for organizational members, will increasingly be a valued skill among those emerging as leaders in organizations. As we have seen throughout this text, communication is the process central to accomplishing the goals and fulfilling the roles integral to the development and survival of an organization.

This text began with a word to the reader—a personal comment from the author. That is also how it ends. The following thoughts are reflections about the process of leadership and its relationship to communication—thoughts the author would like remembered beyond the last day of class.

Traits, behaviors, styles, and roles—leadership is all these things and more. Charisma, knowledge, and experience—we see it work, or fail, better than we can define it. Perhaps we should remember that, like things that are of most consequence in life, the best qualities of leadership are invisible to the eye.

Leaders must be purposeful and passionate. They must understand that the roles of change agent, decision maker, and technological champion are interrelated, and even integrated, into what a leader should be. They should be concerned about the quality of each day for followers but always dedicated to better tomorrows.

Leaders must have visions that are reflections of high-minded ideals but conceived with feet firmly planted on stable ground. A central theme in any vision should be to change, to challenge, and to invest time and attention in those who conduct the day-to-day work of the organization—to reward and support—to champion novel ideas as well as new technologies.

Leadership is the commitment one makes and undertakes to focus on plans and possibilities to see potential in problems. Just like rivers run through a countryside creating their own paths, a leader's vision, energy, and commitment to an organization avoids and indeed rejects the notion of boundaries.

Leadership exists only through communication. It is an interactive journey that humans share as they enact a communal vision and pursue individual dreams.

Finally, those who aspire to leadership must understand the importance of community—interrelated webs of life created through human interaction. Leadership requires the establishment and nurturance of such webs, constructed by communication and perpetuated through the ongoing connections people make with each other in the conduct of organizational life.

SUMMARY

Exhibiting leadership is often thought of as solely a top-down process. Such a perspective originates from research studies of and experience in formal, hierarchical organizations. However, the use of work teams and the adoption of new communication technologies have helped create new perspectives about organizational leadership and attendant communication behaviors. Working in tandem, leaders and followers may create interdependent relationships. Additionally, in changing situational contexts the leadership role may be assumed by more than one person. At times, leader–follower roles may be reversed.

The process of leadership depends on mutual influence between leaders and followers; this mutuality creates a relationship that may be multidirectional. Additionally, contemporary notions of leadership emphasize that followers are active participants in the process of leadership, be it direct or indirect. Direct leadership is the process through which individuals influence their immediate subordinates. Indirect leadership is the process of influencing those organizational members beyond one's direct supervision, such as when the priorities of a university president influence her institution's alumni as they pledge financial support.

Organizations undergoing structural, cultural, and technological change are reconceptualizing the notion of "leadership." Communicating leadership means understanding one's audiences in face-to-face and mediated contexts and creating appropriate messages to help organizational members make sense out of the environment that surrounds them. Leaders are increasingly important as creators of culture, decision makers, and change agents. These roles require the use of communication to develop shared meanings, search and use information effectively, and create and communicate visions to enhance an organization's future and guide it through eras of change.

QUESTIONS TO CONSIDER

1. Discuss why the leader–follower relationship is an interdependent one.

2. Compare and contrast "direct" leadership and "indirect" leadership.

3. What is a "networked" organization and what effects might it have on communicative relationships between leaders and other organizational members?

4. What are four ways in which individuals communicate leadership?

5. What are four observations that might be made about the nature of organizational leadership in the future, and its resultant effects on communication between leaders and followers?

CASE PROBLEM

You are on a committee that is searching for a new president of your university. The former president is retiring soon, having been in office for ten years. The institution, a public university, faces decreased funding from your state legislature and alumni financial support is also declining. In general, the university has a very good reputation, although some departments have declined dramatically in quality and one task of the new president will be to reallocate resources and possibly close two or more departments. He or she will also have to deal with declining faculty morale because of a lack of salary raises for the last four years. Additionally, a significant segment of the student body is upset because the university has raised tuition by 25 percent over the last four years.

Three candidates, all from other major public universities, are coming to interview for the position.

1. Based on information given in this case problem, what characteristics should this person possess?
2. What leadership behaviors will be of particular importance in the new presidency?
3. What questions about leadership and communication style should you ask during the interviews?
4. What questions about the individual's perspectives on decision making, organizational culture, and the initiation of a change effort should you ask each candidate?

5. What questions should you ask about facilitating organizational diversity and championing technological innovations?

6. What questions should you ask each candidate about how he or she prefers to communicate leadership in organizations?

ENDNOTES

1. Fredric Jablin, "Superior-Subordinate Communication: The State of the Art," *Psychological Bulletin*,86 (1979): 1208.
2. W. Charles Redding, *Communication within the Organization: An Interpretive Review of Theory and Research* (New York: Industrial Communication Council, 1972).
3. An example of one such study was that conducted by Douglas D. Backer and Daniel C. Ganster, "Leader-Communication Style: A Test of Average versus Veretical Dyad Linkage Models," *Group and Organization Studies* 10:3 (September 1985), 255.
4. Ernest Stech, *Leadership Communication*, (Chicago: Nelson-Hall, 1983).
5. Nick Trujillo, "Performing 'Mintzberg's Roles,'" in *Communication and Organizations, an Interpretive Approach*, eds. Linda L. Putnam and Michael E. Pacanowsky (Beverly Hills: Sage Publications, 1983).
6. Ibid.
7. James McGregor Burns, *Leadership* (New York: Harper & Row, 1978), 19.
8. John W. Gardner, *On Leadership* (New York: The Free Press, 1990), 24.
9. Trudy Heller and Jon Van Til, "Leadership and Followership: Some Summary Propositions," *Journal of Applied Behavorial Science* 18:3 (1982): 406.
10. Joseph C. Rost, *Leadership for the Twenty-First Century* (New York: Praeger, 1991).
11. Ibid., 107.
12. Ibid., adapted from 108–109.
13. Francis J. Yammarino, "Indirect Leadership," in *Improving Organizational Effectiveness through Transformational Leadership*, eds. Bernard M. Bass and Bruce J. Avolio (Thousand Oaks, CA: Sage Publications, 1993), adapted from p. 29.
14. Ibid., pp. 35–38.
15. Woodrow Wilson, *Leaders of Men* (Princeton, NJ: Princeton University Press, 1952), 43.
16. Guy Benveniste, *The Twenty-First Century Organization* (San Francisco: Jossey-Bass Publishers, 1994).
17. Lee Sproull and Sara Kiesler, *Connections* (Cambridge, MA: MIT Press, 1991), 12.

INDEX

animated communication style, 65
Anthony, W. P., 56
attentive communication style, 65, 68
audioconferencing, 171, 184
authority-obedience leadership, 54
autocratic leaders, 53
Avolio, B. J., 61

Baker, D. D., 68
Bandler, R., 137
Barge, J. K., 53
Bass, B. M., 3, 4, 12, 18, 56, 62, 115, 120
Beckhard, R., 129
behavioral approach to decision making, 101
behavioral theory of leadership, 16–17
Bell, E. L., 156
Bennis, W., 13
Benveniste, G., 199
Bergquist, W., 43, 44
Beyer, J. M., 88, 92
Bibeault, D. B., 138–139
Blake, R., 54, 55
Blanchard, 57
Brzezinski, Z., 66
Burns, J. M., 18, 60, 196
bypassing, 198

cascading, 198
"categories of phenomena", 76

change agents, 61, 62, 63, 134
    leadership for, 141–142
"change masters", 139
change strategies, 134
charisma, 62
charismatic leadership, 136
classical theories of organization, 26–27
"cognitive lenses", 133
cognitive resources theory of leadership, 16
communication strategies, 137–138
communication style, 50, 64–69
communication technologies, 33–34, 202, 203
    characteristics of, 172–173
    definition and types of, 170–172
    future use of, by leaders, 187–188
    uses and effects of, 173–187
conflict management as leadership behavior, 10
Conner, D. R., 127
consideration, 54, 62
    individualized, 62
    as leadership behavior, 10
contentious communication style, 65
contingency theories of leadership, 16
Contractor, N. S., 181
country club leadership style, 54
criticism as leadership behavior, 10
Cronin, T., 4

Daft, R. L., 108
decision makers, 107
decision making
  analytical approach to, 101, 119
  charismatic approach to, 119
  consultative approach to, 119
  decentralization of, 33
  influences affecting, 110–113
  models of, "garbage can", 104–105
  models of, 101–105
    limited rational, 102–103
    political, 103–104
    rational, 101–102
  processes of, 113–118
  searching for and using information in,
    105–110
  styles of, 118–121
decision participation as leadership
  behavior, 10
decision takers, 107
decision taking, 103
delegation as leadership behavior, 10, 107
democratic leaders, 53
democratic leadership styles, 56
Denison, D. R., 82
descriptive approach to decision making,
  101
Devanna, M. A., 63
direct leadership, 197–198
directive leaders, 55
discipline as leadership behavior, 10
displacement activity, 139
Doelger, J. A., 103
dominant communication style, 65, 68
dramatic communication style, 65
DuBrin, A. J., 58
Dukerich, J. M., 6

Eagly, Dr. A. H., 154
echoing, 86
Ehrlich, S. B., 6
Eisenberg, E. M., 181
Eisenhardt, K., 118
electronic messaging (e-mail), 171, 184
"empowerment" in organizational change,
  139–141
enabling, process of, 136
enactment, process of, 25
energizing, process of, 136
environmental influences
  affecting decision making, 110–111
  affecting leaders, 40–42
envisioning, process of, 136

equity theory of organizations, 28
ethnicity and leadership, 155–156
Evered, R., 87
exchange theory of leadership, 17–19

facilitating diversity, strategies for, 161–164
facsimile (fax) transmission, 170–171
Fann, G. L., 109
fantasy dialogue, 86
feeling approach to decision making, 118
Fiedler, F. E., 16, 52
first-order change, 128
"flatter" organizations, 31–32, 93, 187
follower-focused leaders, 62
follower-focused leadership styles, 56
followers and leaders, interdependency of,
  196–199
Fram, E. H., 58
"framing", 59–60, 137, 138
friendly communication style, 65
functional blindness, 138

Ganster, D. C., 68
"garbage can" model of decision making,
  104–105
Garcia, J. E., 16
Gardner, J. W., 2, 3, 196
gender and leadership, 149–155, 156–157
Gibbons, T. C., 61
"glass ceiling", 159
great man theory of leadership, 11–12
Grinder, J., 137
group influences affecting decision
  making, 112–113
groupware, 172, 180

Harris, H., 129
Hawes, L. C., 108
headship, 2–3
Helgesen, S., 153
Heraclitus, 126
Hersey, P., 57
Heskett, J. L., 81
historical model of decision making, 105
Hulin, C. L., 179
human relations model of organizations, 28
human resources model of organizations, 28
humanistic theories of leadership, 15–16
humanistic theories of organization, 27–28

impoverished leadership styles, 54
impression-leaving communication style,
  65

incremental change, 128
indirect leadership, 198–199
information dissemination as leadership
   behavior, 10
information technology. *See*
   communication technologies.
initiating structure, 54
innovative leadership, 92
institutionalization theory of
   organizations, 29
instrumental leadership, 131, 136
integrative theory of organization, 28–30
interaction facilitation as leadership
   behavior, 10
interpretive-symbolic perspective on
   organizational communication, 30
intuitive person, 118
issue characteristics affecting decision
   making, 113

Jacobs, T. O., 18
Jacques, E., 18
Jaffe, D. T., 140
Janis, I. L., 115
Jung, C., 118

Kanter, R. M., 129, 134, 139, 150, 151, 154
Kelley, R. E., 8
Kimberly, J. R., 130
Kotter, J. P, 81
Kubler-Ross, E., 127

laissez-faire leaders, 53
leader/member exchange theory of
   leadership, 17
leader(s)
   as advocate, 8
   autocratic, 53
   and communication technologies,
      173–187
      future implications for, 187–188
   democratic, 53
   directive, 55
   as educator, 7–8
   environmental influences affecting,
      40–42
   follower-focused, 62
   and followers, 196–199
   as interpreter, 7
   laissez-faire, 53
   multicultural, behaviors of, 157–158
   participative, 55
   relations-oriented, 54

task-oriented, 54
   use of strategies in facilitating diversity
      by, 161–164
leadership
   behavior, 9–11, 58
   for change agents, 141–142
   communication, 194–196
   concepts of, 3–5
   cultural approach to, 74–75
   differences between headship,
      management, and, 2–3
   and ethnicity, 155–156
   "feminization" of, 203
   and gender, 149–155, 156–157
   organizational
      concepts of, 5–9
      reconceptualizing, 201–204
   in organizational change
      1960–2000, 31–35
      communication of, 133–139
      conditions affecting, 131–132
   organizational components affecting,
      35–39
   in organizational culture, 89–95
   organizational theory and, 45–46
   and race, 155–157
   romanticization of, 6
   style(s), 50–52, 136
      traditional perspectives of,
         52–59
      types of, 92, 107, 131, 132, 196,
         197–199
   theories, 11–19
      behavioral, 16–17
      exchange, 17–19
      great man, 11–12
      humanistic, 15–16
      personal/situational, 14–15
      situational, 14
      trait, 12–14
      transactional, 60
      transformational, 59–64
leading diversity, 159
Lengel, R. H., 108
Lewin, K., 52, 53, 129
Likert, R., 15
limited rational model of decision making,
   102–103

Maccoby, M., 13
maintenance leadership, 59, 92
management, 2–3
"managerial grid", 54

Mayo, E., 28, 32, 51
McGregor, D., 15, 28
McPhee, R. D., 39
meaning, management of, 6–8
mechanistic perspective on organizational
    communication, 30
Meindl, J. R., 6
Mintzberg, H., 152–153, 195
Misumi, J., 59
mixed scanning, 116
modern organizations, 43
Mouton, J., 54, 55
multicultural leaders, behaviors of,
    157–158

Nadler, D. A., 136
Nanus, B., 13, 44–45
narrow outlooks, 139
The Nature of Managerial Work, 152, 195
Norton, R., 64, 65
nova model of decision making, 105
Nutt, P. C., 105, 119

off-the-shelf model of decision making,
    105
open communication style, 65
organizational change
    affecting leadership, 1960–2000, 31–35
    leadership in
        communication of, 136–139
        conditions affecting, 131–132
    nature of, 127–129
    process of
        "empowerment" in, 139–141, 129–132
        leadership behaviors in, 133–136
    technological innovation in, 175–178
organizational climate, 38–39
organizational communication, 30–31
organizational culture, 37–38
    communication in
        as creating/recreating process, 84–86
        language, 86–87
        myths, 87
        rites, 87–89
    concepts of, 75–82
    functions, 77–82
    sources, 77
    creation and change of, 89–93
    leadership in, 93–95
    technological components of, 178–180
organizational diversity, 158–161
organizational influences affecting
    decision making, 111–112

organizational leadership
    concepts of, 5–9
    reconceptualizing, 201–204
organizational linkages affecting leaders,
    41–42
organizational models, 28, 29
organizational resources, 36–37
    human and material, 36
    power, 36
    technologies, 37
organizational structure, 35–36
organizational subcultures, 82–84
organizational tasks, 35
organizational theories, 26–30
    classical, 26–27
    humanistic, 27–28
    integrating leadership and, 45–46
    integrative/systems, 28–30
organizational traits, 24
"organization man" leadership styles, 55
organizations
    bureaucratization in, 27
    definitions of, 23–26
    future characteristics of, 44–45
    postmodern, 42–44
    reconceptualizing, 200–201
organizing, process of, 25

Papa, M. J., 182
participative leaders, 55
participative leadership styles, 55–56
"path goal" theory of leadership, 16–17
Pelton, W. J., 119
performance leadership, 59
personal/situational theory of leadership,
    14–15
Peters, T. J., 13
Pfeffer, J., 5
planned change, 128
political influences affecting leaders, 40
political model of decision making,
    103–104
Poole, M. S., 39, 103
The Postmodern Organization, 43
postmodern organizations, 42–44
praise-recognition as leadership behavior,
    10
premodern organizations, 43
prescriptive approach to decision making,
    101
problem-solving as leadership behavior, 10
psychological perspective on
    organizational communication, 30

Quinn, R. E., 130

race and leadership, 155–157
Ramirez, M., 157–158
rational model of decision making, 101–102
Redding, W. C., 39, 67
"reframing", 137
refreezing, 129
relational behavior, 57
relations-oriented leader, 54
relations-oriented leadership styles, 56
relaxed communication style, 65
representation as leadership behavior, 10
resource dependence theory of
    organizations, 29
rhetorical environment, 39
"rich" information media, 108–110, 138
role clarification as leadership behavior, 10
"roots", 163
Rost, J. C., 197
Roznowski, M., 179

satisficing, 116
Schein, E.A., 75, 76, 88, 89, 90, 91, 93, 129
Schrage, M., 182
scientific management, 26
Scott, C. D., 140
search model of decision making, 105
second-order change, 128
seeking leadership, 107
Senge, P., 141
sensing person, 118
Shared Minds, 182
Simon, H. A, 100
situational leadership style, 56, 57–58
situational theory of leadership, 14
Skinner, B. F., 16
Smeltzer, L. R., 109
The Social Psychology of Organizing, 24
socioeconomic influences affecting leaders,
    40
sociotechnical model of organizations, 29
Sorensen, T., 114
speculative approach to decision making,
    119
sporadic processes of decision making, 114
Stech, E., 194–195
Stodgill, R. M., 3, 4, 12, 13–14, 54, 62
substantive leadership, 131
symbolic leadership, 132
systems-interactive perspective on
    organizational communication, 30
systems theory of organizations, 28–30

task behavior, 57
task-focused leadership styles, 56
task groups, creation and use of, 32–33
task-oriented leader, 54
Taylor, F. W., 26–27
team management leadership styles, 55
technology. *See* communication
    technologies.
teleconferencing. *See* audioconferencing.
thinking approach to decision making,
    118
Thomas, R. R., 163
Tichy, N., 61, 63
time span orientation (TSO), 58–59
trait theory of leadership, 12–14
traits, organizational, 24
transactional leadership, 18, 60
transformational change, 128, 132
transformational leadership, 18, 59–64,
    196
Trice, H. M., 88, 92
Trujillo, N., 195
Tushman, M., 136

unfreezing, 129
unplanned change, 128

vertical-dyad linkage theory of leadership,
    17
videoconferencing, 171
vigilant information processing, 115
vigilant problem solving, 116
Visionary Leadership, 44–45
voice mail, 171
Vroom, V., 55

Waterman, R. T., 13
"ways-of-thinking", 133
Weber, M., 27
Weick, K., 7, 24, 25, 44, 200
Wilson, W., 199
work facilitation as leadership behavior, 10
work teams, creation and use of, 32–33
Workforce 2000, 148–149

Yetton, P., 55
Yukl, G. A., 9–10

Zmud, R. W., 170
Zuboff, S., 170, 176, 177, 178